Your certification story= A chance to win a FREE Microsoft Press ebook

W9-ARN-328

Microsoft® CERTIFIED
20 Years | 20 Ways

Celebrate our first 20 years of Microsoft Certification with 20 Years|20 Ways, a year-long effort that lets you grow your career and seed opportunity for the next generation. By working together, we can help IT pros, developers, and students around the world have a better career and a better life.

Aspiring IT pros, developers and students around the world want to hear from you.

- What has certification meant for you and your career?

- What are your future plans for certification?

- What are the biggest opportunities for the next generation and how does certification fit in?

Each week, the top 3 storytellers will get a free Microsoft Press ebook.

Share your story for a chance to win at aka.ms/2020story!

verso verse
vestido dress
vestir(se) (i) (de) to dress (as)
vez, la time
   de vez en cuando from time to
   time
   tal vez perhaps
viento wind
vientre, el womb
villano, -a common person
visera visor
vivo, -a keen, intense
vizcaíno, -a Biscayan
volar (ue) to fly
voluntad, la will
voto vow

voz, la voice
   en voz alta in a loud voice
vuelta return
vuestro, -a your

Y

ya now, already
yegua mare
yelmo helmet
yerba grass
yerro error, mistake

Z

zanca long-legged

NTC SPANISH CULTURAL AND LITERARY TEXTS AND MATERIAL

Contemporary Life and Culture
"En directo" desde España
Cartas de España
Voces de Puerto Rico
The Andean Region

Contemporary Culture—in English
Spain: Its People and Culture
Welcome to Spain
Life in a Spanish Town
Life in a Mexican Town
Spanish Sign Language
Looking at Spain Series

Cross-Cultural Awareness
Encuentros culturales
The Hispanic Way
The Spanish-Speaking World

Legends and History
Leyendas latinoamericanas
Leyendas de Puerto Rico
Leyendas de España
Leyendas mexicanas
Dos aventureros: De Soto y Coronado
Muchas facetas de México
Una mirada a España

Literary Adaptations
Don Quijote de la Mancha
El Cid
La Gitanilla
Tres novelas españolas
Dos novelas picarescas
Tres novelas latinoamericanas
Joyas de lectura
Cuentos de hoy
Lazarillo de Tormes
La Celestina
El Conde Lucanor
El burlador de Sevilla
Fuenteovejuna
Aventuras del ingenioso hidalgo
    Don Quijote de la Mancha

Civilization and Culture
Perspectivas culturales de España
Perspectivas culturales de Hispanoamérica

 For further information or a current catalog, write:
National Textbook Company
a division of *NTC Publishing Group*
4255 West Touhy Avenue
Lincolnwood, Illinois 60646-1975 U.S.A.

Microsoft®

Introducing
Windows Server® 2012

Mitch Tulloch with the
Windows Server Team

PUBLISHED BY
Microsoft Press
A Division of Microsoft Corporation
One Microsoft Way
Redmond, Washington 98052-6399

Copyright © 2012 by Microsoft Corporation

All rights reserved. No part of the contents of this book may be reproduced or transmitted in any form or by any means without the written permission of the publisher.

Library of Congress Control Number: 2012938436
ISBN: 978-0-7356-7397-7

Printed and bound in the United States of America.

First Printing

Microsoft Press books are available through booksellers and distributors worldwide. If you need support related to this book, email Microsoft Press Book Support at mspinput@microsoft.com. Please tell us what you think of this book at *http://www.microsoft.com/learning/booksurvey*.

Microsoft and the trademarks listed at *http://www.microsoft.com/about/legal/en/us/ IntellectualProperty/Trademarks/EN-US.aspx* are trademarks of the Microsoft group of companies. All other marks are property of their respective owners.

The example companies, organizations, products, domain names, email addresses, logos, people, places, and events depicted herein are fictitious. No association with any real company, organization, product, domain name, email address, logo, person, place, or event is intended or should be inferred.

This book expresses the author's views and opinions. The information contained in this book is provided without any express, statutory, or implied warranties. Neither the authors, Microsoft Corporation, nor its resellers, or distributors will be held liable for any damages caused or alleged to be caused either directly or indirectly by this book.

Acquisitions Editor: Anne Hamilton
Developmental Editor: Valerie Woolley
Project Editor: Valerie Woolley
Editorial Production: Diane Kohnen, S4Carlisle Publishing Services
Copyeditor: Susan McClung
Indexer: Jean Skipp
Cover: Twist Creative . Seattle

Contents at a Glance

Contents

What do you think of this book? We want to hear from you!

Microsoft is interested in hearing your feedback so we can continually improve our
books and learning resources for you. To participate in a brief online survey, please visit:

microsoft.com/learning/booksurvey

What do you think of this book? We want to hear from you!

Microsoft is interested in hearing your feedback so we can continually improve our
books and learning resources for you. To participate in a brief online survey, please visit:

microsoft.com/learning/booksurvey

Foreword

Windows Server 2012 introduces a plethora of new features to address the evolved needs of a modern IT infrastructure and workforce. The core of this experience is the need to scale out, virtualize, and move workloads, applications, and services to the cloud. Windows Server 2012 incorporates our experience of building, managing, and operating both private and public clouds, all based on Windows Server. We used that experience to create an operating system that provides organizations a scalable, dynamic, and multi-tenant-aware platform that connects datacenters and resources globally and securely. Clouds, whether deployed as public or private, rely on the same technology and provide consistency for applications, services, management, and experiences when they are deployed in a hosted environment, in a single-server, small office, or in your corporate datacenter. They are all the same, and the platform should scale consistently and be managed easily from the small business office to the infinitely large public cloud.

The Windows Server team employed a customer-focused design approach to design in-the-box solutions that address customers' real-world business problems. We realized that we needed to cloud-optimize environments by providing an updated, flexible platform. We also knew that it was incumbent upon us to enable IT professionals to implement the next generation of technologies needed for future applications and services. We focused on end-to-end solutions that are complete and work out of the box with the critical capabilities for the deployments needed for the mobile and always-connected users, workforce, and devices.

To achieve these goals, we carefully planned a complete virtualization platform with flexible polices and agile options that would enable not only a high-density and scalable infrastructure for all workloads and applications, but also enable simple and efficient infrastructure management. Once in place, with maximized uptime and minimized failures and downtimes, the value proposition of an open and scalable web platform that is aligned to and uses the lowest-cost commodity storage and networking provides a comprehensive solution better than any other platform.

In addition, Windows Server 2012 provides next-generation data security and compliance solutions based on strong identity and authorization capabilities that are paramount in this evolving cloud-optimized environment. The mobile, work-everywhere culture demands not only compliance, but also protection against the latest threats and risks.

And, last but not least, Windows Server 2012 comes with the needed reliability, power efficiency, and interoperability to integrate into environments without requiring numerous and complex add-ons, installations, and additional software to have a working solution.

As one of the senior engineering leaders in the Server and Cloud Division of Microsoft, we have an opportunity to change the world and build the Windows Server 2012 platform to host public and private clouds all over the world. We took our experience and learning from Hotmail, Messenger, Office 365, Bing, Windows Azure, and Xbox Live . . . all of which run on Windows Server to design and create Windows Server 2012 so that others are capable of building their own private clouds, hosting the latest applications, or deploying the next set of cloud services with world-class results.

This book is compiled from the expertise we have gained from the public clouds that we have run for years, as well as the experience from many experts on how to use the Hyper-V and Windows Server technologies optimally. We wanted to provide this book as a preview of the engineering team's inside knowledge and the best practices from the early adopter deployments of Windows Server during the beta. It provides a unique introduction and preview on how to cloud-optimize your environment with Windows Server 2012!

David B. Cross

Director of Program Management

Microsoft Corporation

Introduction

Windows Server 2012 is probably the most significant release of the Windows Server platform ever. With an innovative new user interface, powerful new management tools, enhanced Windows PowerShell support, and hundreds of new features in the areas of networking, storage, and virtualization, Windows Server 2012 can help IT deliver more while reducing costs. Windows Server 2012 also was designed for the cloud from the ground up and provides a foundation for building both public and private cloud solutions to enable businesses to take advantage of the many benefits of cloud computing.

This book represents a "first look" based on the public beta release of Windows Server 2012 and is intended to help IT professionals familiarize themselves with the capabilities of the new platform. Although certain features may change between now and RTM, much of the basic functionality likely will remain as described here, meaning that most of what you learn from reading this book will continue to benefit you as you begin to evaluate and deploy Windows Server 2012 in your own environment.

Direct from the source

A major feature of this book is the inclusion of sidebars written by members of the Windows Server team, Microsoft Support engineers, Microsoft Consulting Services staff, and others who work at Microsoft. These sidebars provide an insider's perspective, "direct from the source," that include both "under-the-hood" information concerning how certain features work, as well as strategies, tips, and best practices from experts who have been working with the platform during its early stages. Sidebars are highlighted in the text and include the contributor's name and title at the bottom.

Acknowledgments

The author would like to express his special thanks to the numerous people working at Microsoft who took time out from their busy schedules to write sidebars for this book and/or peer-review its content to ensure technical accuracy. In recognition of their contribution towards making this book a more valuable resource, we'd like to thank the following people who work at Microsoft (unless otherwise indicated) for contributing their time and expertise to this project:

Joshua Adams, Manjnath Ajjampur, Jeff Alexander, Ted Archer, Vinod Atal, Jonathan Beckham, Jeevan Bisht, David Branscome, Kevin Broas, Brent Caskey, Patrick Catuncan, Al Collins, Bob Combs, Wilbour Craddock, David Cross, Kevin daCosta, Robb Dilallo (Oakwood Systems Group), Laz Diaz, Yuri Diogenes, Sean Eagan, Yigal Edery, Michael Foti, Stu Fox, Keith Hill, Jeff Hughes, Corey Hynes (HynesITe Inc.), Mohammed Ismail, Ron Jacob, Tomica Kaniski, Alex A. Kibkalo, Praveen Kumar, Brett Larison, Alex Lee, Ian Lindsay, Carl Luberti, Michel Luescher, John Marlin, John McCabe, Robert McMurray, Harsh Mittal, Michael Niehaus, Symon Perriman, Tony Petito, Mark Piggott, Jason Pope, Artem Pronichkin, Satya Ramachandran, Ramlinga Reddy, Colin Robinson, John Roller, Luis Salazar, Stephen Sandifer (Xtreme Consulting Group Inc), Chad Schultz, Tom Shinder, Ramnish Singh, Don Stanwyck, Mike Stephens, Mike Sterling, Allen Stewart, Jeff Stokes, Chuck Swanson, Daniel Taylor, Harold Tonkin, Sen Veluswami, Matthew Walker, Andrew Willows, Yingwei Yang, John Yokim, Won Yoo, David Ziembicki, and Josef Zilak.

If we've missed anyone, we're sorry!

The author also would like to thank Valerie Woolley at Microsoft Learning; Diane Kohnen at S4Carlisle Publishing Services; and Susan McClung, the copyeditor.

Errata & book support

We've made every effort to ensure the accuracy of this book and its companion content. Any errors that have been reported since this book was published are listed on our Microsoft Press site at oreilly.com:

http://go.microsoft.com/FWLink/?Linkid=251569

If you find an error that is not already listed, you can report it to us through the same page.

If you need additional support, email Microsoft Press Book Support at mspinput@microsoft.com.

Please note that product support for Microsoft software is not offered through the addresses above.

We want to hear from you

At Microsoft Press, your satisfaction is our top priority, and your feedback our most valuable asset. Please tell us what you think of this book at:

http://www.microsoft.com/learning/booksurvey

The survey is short, and we read every one of your comments and ideas. Thanks in advance for your input!

Stay in touch

Let's keep the conversation going! We're on Twitter: *http://twitter.com/MicrosoftPress*.

CHAPTER 1

The business need for Windows Server 2012

This chapter briefly sets the stage for introducing Windows Server 2012 by reviewing what cloud computing is all about and why cloud computing is becoming an increasingly popular solution for business IT needs. The chapter then describes how Windows Server 2012 can provide the ideal foundation for building your organization's private cloud.

The rationale behind cloud computing

Cloud computing is transforming business by offering new options for businesses to increase efficiencies while reducing costs. What is driving organizations to embrace the cloud paradigm are the problems often associated with traditional IT systems. These problems include:

- High operational costs, typically associated with implementing and managing desktop and server infrastructures
- Low system utilization, often associated with non-virtualized server workloads in enterprise environments
- Inconsistent availability due to the high cost of providing hardware redundancy
- Poor agility, which makes it difficult for businesses to meet evolving market demands

Although virtualization has helped enterprises address some of these issues by virtualizing server workloads, desktops, and applications, some challenges still remain. For example, mere virtualization of server workloads can lead to virtual machine (VM) sprawl, solving one problem while creating another.

Cloud computing helps address these challenges by providing businesses with new ways of improving agility while reducing costs. For example, by providing tools for rapid deployment of IT services with self-service capabilities, businesses can achieve

1

a faster time-to-market rate and become more competitive. Cloud-based solutions also can help businesses respond more easily to spikes in demand. And the standardized architecture and service-oriented approach to solution development used in cloud environments helps shorten the solution development life cycle, reducing the time between envisioning and deployment.

Cloud computing also helps businesses keep IT costs under control in several ways. For example, the standardized architecture of cloud solutions provides greater transparency and predictability for the budgeting process. Adding automation and elastic capacity management to this helps keep operational costs lower. Reuse and re-provisioning of cloud applications and services can help lower development costs across your organization, making your development cycle more cost effective. And a pay-as-you-go approach to consuming cloud services can help your business achieve greater flexibility and become more innovative, making entry into new markets possible.

Cloud computing also can help businesses increase customer satisfaction by enabling solutions that have greater responsiveness to customer needs. Decoupling applications from physical infrastructure improves availability and makes it easier to ensure business continuity when a disaster happens. And risk can be managed more systematically and effectively to meet regulatory requirements.

Making the transition

Making the transition from a traditional IT infrastructure to the cloud paradigm begins with rethinking and re-envisioning what IT is all about. The traditional approach to IT infrastructure is a *server-centric* vision, where IT is responsible for procuring, designing, deploying, managing, maintaining, and troubleshooting servers hosted on the company's premises or located at the organization's central datacenter. Virtualization can increase the efficiency of this approach by allowing consolidation of server workloads to increase system utilization and reduce cost, but even a virtualized datacenter still has a server-centric infrastructure that requires a high degree of management overhead.

Common characteristics of traditional IT infrastructures, whether virtualized or not, can include the following:

- Limited capacity due to the physical limitations of host hardware in the datacenter (virtualization helps maximize capacity but doesn't remove these limitations)
- Availability level that is limited by budget because of the high cost of redundant host hardware, network connectivity, and storage resources
- Poor agility because it takes time to deploy and configure new workloads (virtualization helps speed up this process)
- Poor efficiency because applications are deployed in silos, which means that development efforts can't be used easily across the organization
- Potentially high cost due to the cost of host hardware, software licensing, and the in-house IT expertise needed to manage the infrastructure

By contrast to the traditional server-centric infrastructure, cloud computing represents a *service-centric* approach to IT. From the business customer's point of view, cloud services can be perceived as IT services with unlimited capacity, continuous availability, improved agility, greater efficiency, and lower and more predictable costs than a traditional server-centric IT infrastructure. The results of the service-centric model of computing can be increased productivity with less overhead because users can work from anywhere, using any capable device, without having to worry about deploying the applications they need to do their job.

The bottom line here is that businesses considering making the transition to the cloud need to rethink their understanding of IT from two perspectives: the type of sourcing and the kinds of services being consumed.

Cloud sourcing models

Cloud sourcing models define the party that has control over how the cloud services are architected, controlled, and provisioned. The three kinds of sourcing models for cloud computing are:

- **Public cloud**   Business customers consume the services they need from a pool of cloud services delivered over the Internet. A public cloud is a shared cloud where the pool of services is used by multiple customers, with each customer's environment isolated from those of others. The public cloud approach provides the benefits of predictable costs and pay-as-you-go flexibility for adding or removing processing, storage, and network capacity depending on the customer's needs.

    For example, Microsoft Windows Azure and Microsoft SQL Azure are public cloud offerings that allow you to develop, deploy, and run your business applications over the Internet instead of hosting them locally on your own datacenter. By adopting this approach, you can gain increased flexibility, easier scalability, and greater agility for your business. And if your users only need Microsoft Office or Microsoft Dynamics CRM to perform their jobs, you can purchase subscriptions to Office 365 or Microsoft Dynamics CRM Online from Microsoft's public cloud offerings in this area as well. For more information on Microsoft's public cloud offerings, see *http://www.microsoft.com/en-us/server-cloud/public-cloud/.*

- **Private cloud**   The customer controls the cloud, either by self-hosting a private cloud in the customer's datacenter or by having a partner host it. A private cloud can be implemented in two ways: by combining different software platforms and applications, or by procuring a dedicated cloud environment in the form of an appliance from a vendor.

    For example, customers have already been using the Hyper-V virtualization capabilities successfully in the current Microsoft Windows Server 2008 R2 platform, with the Microsoft System Center family of products, to design, deploy, and manage their own private clouds. And for a more packaged approach to deploying private clouds, Microsoft's Private Cloud Fast Track program provides customers with a standard reference architecture for building private clouds that combines Microsoft software, consolidated guidance, value-added software components, and validated compute, network, and storage configurations from original equipment manufacturer (OEM) partners to create a turnkey approach for deploying scalable, preconfigured, validated infrastructure platforms for deploying your own on private cloud. For more information on the Private Cloud Fast Track and to see a list of Fast Track Partners, see *http://www.microsoft.com/en-us/server-cloud/private-cloud/hyperv-cloud-fast-track.aspx*.

The private cloud approach allows you the peace of mind of knowing you have complete control over your IT infrastructure, but it has higher up-front costs and a steeper implementation curve than the public cloud approach. For more information on Microsoft's private cloud offerings, see *http://www.microsoft.com/en-us/server-cloud/private-cloud/*. As you will soon see, however, the next generation of Hyper-V in the Windows Server 2012 platform delivers even more powerful capabilities that enable customers to deploy and manage private clouds.

- **Hybrid cloud**   The customer uses a combination of private and public clouds to meet the specific needs of their business. In this approach, some of your organization's IT services run on-premises while other services are hosted in the cloud to save costs, simplify scalability, and increase agility. Organizations that want to make the transition from traditional IT to cloud computing often begin by embracing the hybrid cloud approach because it allows them to get their feet wet while remaining grounded in the comfort of their existing server-centric infrastructure.

  One difficulty with the hybrid cloud approach, however, is the management overhead associated with needing duplicate sets of IT controls, one set for traditional infrastructure and others for each kind of cloud service consumed. Regardless of this, many organizations that transition to the cloud choose to adopt the hybrid approach for various reasons, including deployment restrictions, compliance issues, or the availability of cloud services that can meet the organization's needs.

Cloud service models

Cloud computing also can be considered from the perspective of which kinds of services are being consumed. The three standard service models for cloud computing are as follows:

- **Software as a service (SaaS)**   This approach involves using the cloud to deliver a single application to multiple users, regardless of their location or the kind of device they are using. SaaS contrasts with the more traditional approach of deploying separate instances of applications to each user's computing device. The advantages of the SaaS model is that application activities can be managed from a single central location to reduce cost and management overhead. SaaS typically is used to deliver cloud-based applications that have minimal support for customization, such as email, Customer Relationship Management (CRM), and productivity software. Office 365 is an example of a SaaS offering from Microsoft that provides users with secure anywhere access to their email, shared calendars, instant messaging (IM), video conferencing, and tools for document collaboration.

- **Platform as a service (PaaS)**   This approach involves using the cloud to deliver application execution services such as application run time, storage, and integration for applications that have been designed for a prespecified cloud-based architectural framework. By using PaaS, you can develop custom cloud-based applications for your business and then host them in the cloud so that users can access them anywhere over the Internet. PaaS also can be used to create multi-tenant applications that multiple users can access simultaneously. And with its high degree of support for application-level customization, PaaS can enable integration with your older applications and interoperability with your current on-premises systems, though some applications may need to be recoded to work in the new environment. SQL Azure is an example of a PaaS offering from Microsoft that allows businesses to provision and deploy SQL databases to the cloud without the need of implementing and maintaining an in-house Microsoft SQL Server infrastructure.

- **Infrastructure as a service (IaaS)**   This approach involves creating pools of compute, storage, and network connectivity resources that then can be delivered to business customers as cloud-based services that are billed on a per-usage basis. IaaS forms the foundation for SaaS and PaaS by providing a standardized, flexible virtualized environment that typically presents itself to the customer as virtualized server workloads. In the IaaS model, the customer can self-provision these virtualized workloads and can customize them fully with the processing, storage, and network resources needed and with the operating system and applications the business requires. By using the IaaS approach, the customer is relieved of the need to purchase and install hardware and can spin up new workloads to meet changing demand quickly. The Hyper-V technology of the Windows Server platform, together with the System Center family of products, represents Microsoft's offering in the IaaS space.

Microsoft cloud facts

Did you know the following facts about Microsoft's public cloud offerings?

- Every day, 9.9 billion messages are transmitted via Windows Live Messenger.
- There are 600 million unique users every month on Windows Live and MSN.
- There are 500 million active Windows Live IDs.
- There are 40 million paid MS online services (BPOS, CRM Online, etc.) in 36 countries.
- A total of 5 petabytes of content is served by Xbox Live each week during the holiday season.
- A total of 1 petabyte+ of updates is served every month by Windows Update to millions of servers and hundreds of millions of PCs worldwide.
- There are tens of thousands of Windows Azure customers.

- There are 5 million LiveMeeting conference minutes per year.
- Forefront for Exchange filters 1 billion emails per month.

Technical requirements for successful cloud computing

If you're considering moving your business to the cloud, it's important to be aware of the ingredients of a successful cloud platform. Figure 1-1 illustrates the three standard service models for implementing private and public cloud solutions.

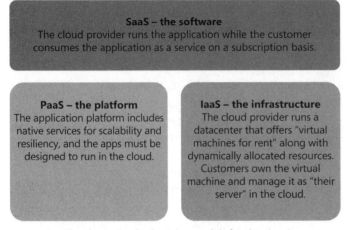

SaaS – the software
The cloud provider runs the application while the customer consumes the application as a service on a subscription basis.

PaaS – the platform
The application platform includes native services for scalability and resiliency, and the apps must be designed to run in the cloud.

IaaS – the infrastructure
The cloud provider runs a datacenter that offers "virtual machines for rent" along with dynamically allocated resources. Customers own the virtual machine and manage it as "their server" in the cloud.

FIGURE 1-1 The three standard service models for the cloud.

The hierarchy of this diagram illustrates that both IaaS and PaaS can be used as the foundation for building SaaS. In the IaaS approach, you build the entire architecture yourself, for example with load-balanced web servers for the front end and clustered servers for your business and data tiers on the back end. In fact, the only difference between IaaS and a traditional datacenter is that the apps are running on servers that are virtual instead of physical.

By contrast, PaaS is a completely different architecture. In a PaaS solution, like Windows Azure, you allow Azure to handle the "physical" aspect for you when you take your app and move it to the cloud. Then, when you have spikes in demand (think the holiday season for a retail website), the system automatically scales up to meet the demand and then scales back down again when demand tapers off. This means that with PaaS, you don't need to build a system that handles the maximum load at all times, even when it doesn't have to; instead, you pay only for what you use.

But the IaaS model is much closer to what customers currently use today, so let's focus more closely on the IaaS service model, which often is described as "virtual machines for rent." The two key components of IaaS are a hypervisor-based server operating system and a cloud and datacenter management solution. These two components, therefore, form the foundation of any type of cloud solution—public, private, or hybrid.

Let's examine the first component: namely, a hypervisor-based server operating system. What attributes must such a platform have to be suitable for building cloud solutions? The necessary technical requirements must include the following:

- Support for the latest server hardware and scaling features, including high-performance networking capabilities and reduced power consumption for green computing

- A reliable, highly scalable hypervisor that eliminates downtime when VMs are moved between hosts

- Fault-tolerant, high-availability solutions that ensure that cloud-based services can be delivered without interruption

- Powerful automation capabilities that can simplify and speed the provisioning and management of infrastructure resources to make your business more agile

- Support for enterprise-level storage for running the largest workloads that businesses may need

- The ability to host a broad range of virtualized operating systems and applications to provide customers with choices that can best meet their business needs

- An extensible platform with public application programming interfaces (APIs) that businesses can use to develop custom tools and enhancements that they need to round out their solutions

- The ability to pool resources, such as processing, network connectivity, and storage, to provide elasticity so that you can provision and scale resources dynamically in response to changing needs

- Self-service capabilities, so that pooled resources can be provisioned quickly according to service-level agreements for increased agility

- A built-in system for monitoring resource usage, so that those consuming resources can be billed on a pay-for-only-what-you-use basis

- Infrastructure transparency, so that customers can concentrate on deploying the applications and services that they need without having to worry about the underlying infrastructure

Microsoft's current hypervisor-based server operating system, Windows Server 2008 R2, already meets many of these requirements to a high degree, and Microsoft and other enterprises have been using it extensively as a foundation for building both private and public clouds. As we will soon see, however, Windows Server 2012 brings even more to the table for building highly scalable and elastic cloud solutions, making it the first truly cloud-optimized server operating system.

The second component for building a cloud is the management part, and here, System Center 2012 provides the most comprehensive cloud and datacenter management solution available in the marketplace. System Center 2012 spans physical, virtual, and cloud environments using common management experiences throughout and enables end-to-end management of your infrastructure and applications.

Support for Windows Server 2012 in System Center 2012 will be added in the form of a service pack, so soon you will be able to take advantage of using Windows Server 2012 as the foundation for building the type of cloud solution that is best for your business. You can find out more about the Community Technology Preview (CTP) of System Center 2012 Service Pack 1 on the System Center Virtual Machine Manager Blog on TechNet at *http://blogs.technet.com/b/scvmm/archive/2012/03/09/system-center-2012-ctp-for-windows-server-8-beta-support-now-available.aspx.*

The business need for Windows Server 2012

Cloud computing in general, and private clouds in particular, have emerged as a response to the high cost and lack of agility of traditional approaches to IT. The needs of IT users and the rate of technological change have increased significantly. At the same time, the need to improve IT efficiency and reduce costs are high-priority objectives in most businesses today.

Server consolidation through virtualization has been a key driver of cost savings over the past several years. Windows Server 2012 and Hyper-V provide significant improvements in scalability and availability, which enables much higher consolidation ratios. Combined with the flexibility of unlimited VM licensing in some Windows SKUs, high-density virtualization can reduce costs significantly. With Windows Server 2012 and Hyper-V supporting clusters up to 64 nodes running up to 4,000 VMs, a relatively small amount of physical hardware can support a large amount of IT capability.

Further improving the consolidation story is the ability to run significantly larger VMs, resulting in a higher percentage of physical servers being candidates for virtualization. Individual Windows Server 2012 VMs are able to support 32 virtual processors and 1 terabyte (TB) of random access memory (RAM), providing the ability to virtualize the vast majority of physical servers deployed today. Examples include large database servers or other high-scale workloads that previously could not be virtualized.

In addition to scale, a substantial number of new capabilities in the Windows Server 2012 and Hyper-V platform enable cloud computing scenarios. Definitions of cloud computing vary; however, one of the most commonly utilized definitions is from the U.S. National Institutes for Standards and Technology (NIST), which defines five "essential" characteristics of cloud computing solutions, including on-demand self-service, broad network access, resource pooling, rapid elasticity, and measured service. These attributes enable the agility and cost savings expected from cloud solutions.

Virtualization alone provides significant benefits, but it does not provide all the cloud attributes defined by NIST. A key tenet of Windows Server 2012 is to go beyond virtualization. What this means is providing the foundational technologies and features that enable cloud attributes such as elasticity, resource pooling, and measured service, while providing significant advancements in the virtualization platform.

- For the on-demand self-service cloud attribute, Windows Server 2012 provides foundational technology that enables a variety of user interfaces, including self-service portals by providing hundreds of Windows PowerShell cmdlets related to VM provisioning and management, that enable management solutions such as System Center to provide self-service user interfaces.

- For the broad network access cloud attribute, Windows Server 2012 and Hyper-V provides new network virtualization technology that enables a variety of VM mobility, multi-tenancy, and hosting scenarios that remove many of today's network limitations. Other technologies, such as DirectAccess, enable secure remote connectivity to internal resources without the need for virtual private networks (VPNs).

- For the resource pooling cloud attribute, the combination of the operating system, Network, and Storage virtualization technologies in Windows Server 2012 enable each component of the physical infrastructure to be virtualized and shared as a single large resource pool. Improvements to Live Migration enable VMs and their associated storage to be moved to any Hyper-V host in the datacenter with a network connection. Combined, these technologies allow standardization across the physical and virtual infrastructure with the ability of VMs to be distributed optimally and dynamically across the datacenter.

- For the rapid elasticity cloud attribute, Windows Server 2012 provides the ability to provision VMs rapidly using technologies such as offloaded data transfer (ODX), which can use capabilities in storage systems to clone or create VMs very rapidly to enable workload elasticity. Thin provisioning and data de-duplication enable elasticity without immediate consumption of physical resources.

- For the measured service cloud attribute, Windows Server 2012 provides a variety of new resource metering capabilities that enable granular reporting on resource utilization by individual VMs. Resource metering enables scenarios such as chargeback reporting based on central processing unit (CPU) utilization, memory utilization, or other utilization-based metrics.

In addition to advanced server consolidation and cloud attributes that help drive down IT cost and increase agility, Windows Server 2012 provides the capability to reduce ongoing operational expenses (OpEx) by providing a high degree of automation and the ability to manage many servers as one. A key cost metric in

IT is the number of servers that an individual administrator can manage. In many datacenters, this number is small, typically in the double digits. In highly automated datacenters such as Microsoft's, an individual administrator can manage thousands of servers through the use of automation.

Windows Server 2012 delivers this automation capability through the Server Manager user interface's ability to manage user-defined groups of servers as one, plus the ability of PowerShell to automate activities against a nearly unlimited number of servers. This reduces the amount of administrator effort required, enabling administrators to focus on higher-value activities.

Taken together, the capabilities provided by Windows Server 2012 deliver the essential cloud attributes and the foundation for significant improvements in both IT cost and agility.
David Ziembicki
Senior Architect, U.S. Public Sector, Microsoft Services

Four ways Windows Server 2012 delivers value for cloud computing

Let's now briefly look at four different ways that Windows Server 2012 can deliver value for building your cloud solution beyond what the current platform that Windows Server 2008 R2 is capable of delivering. The remaining chapters of this book will explore the powerful new features and capabilities of this cloud-optimized operating system in more detail, along with hands-on insights from insiders at Microsoft who have developed, tested, and deployed Windows Server 2012 and for select customers during the beta testing stage of product development.

Foundation for building your private cloud

Although previous versions of Windows Server have included many capabilities needed for implementing different cloud computing scenarios, Windows Server 2012 takes this a step further by providing a foundation for building dynamic, multi-tenant cloud environments that can scale to meet the highest business needs while helping to reduce your infrastructure costs. Hyper-V in Windows Server 2008 R2 has already helped many businesses reduce their operational costs through server consolidation. The next version of Hyper-V, together with other key features of Windows Server 2012, goes even further by enabling you to secure virtualized services by isolating them effectively, migrate running VMs with no downtime even outside of clusters, create replicas of virtualized workloads for offsite recovery, and much more. The result is to provide a platform that is ideal as a foundation for building private clouds for even the largest enterprises.

Windows Server 2012 provides your business with a complete virtualization platform that includes multi-tenant security and isolation capabilities to enforce network isolation between workloads belonging to different business units, departments, or customers on a shared infrastructure. Network Virtualization, a new feature of Hyper-V, lets you isolate network traffic from different business units without the complexity of needing to implement and manage virtual local area networks (VLANs). Network Virtualization also makes it easier to integrate your existing private networks into a new infrastructure by enabling you to migrate VMs while preserving their existing virtual network settings. And network quality of service (QoS) has been enhanced in Windows Server 2012 to enable you to guarantee a minimum amount of bandwidth to VMs and virtual services so that service level agreements can be achieved more effectively and network performance can have greater predictability. Being able to manage and secure network connectivity resources effectively are an important factor when designing cloud solutions, and these capabilities of Windows Server 2012 make this possible.

Windows Server 2012 also helps you scale your environment better, achieve greater performance levels, and use your existing investments in enterprise storage solutions. With greatly expanded support for host processors and memory, your virtualization infrastructure now can support very large VMs that need the highest levels of performance and workloads that require the ability to increase significantly in scale. Businesses that have already invested in Fibre Channel storage arrays for their existing infrastructures can benefit from Virtual Fibre Channel, a new feature of Hyper-V that lets you directly connect to your storage area network (SAN) from within the guest operating system of your VMs. You also can use Virtual Fibre Channel to virtualize any server workloads that directly access your SAN, enabling new ways of reducing costs through workload virtualization. You also can cluster guest operating systems over Fibre Channel, which provides new infrastructure options you can explore. And the built-in ODX support ensures that your VMs can read and write to SAN storage at performance levels matching that of physical hardware, while freeing up the resources on the system that received the transfer. With storage a key resource for any cloud solution, these improvements make Windows Server 2012 an effective platform for building clouds.

Windows Server 2012 also provides a common identity and management framework that supports federation, enables cross-premises connectivity, and facilitates data protection. Active Directory Federation Services (AD FS) is now built into the product and provides a foundation for extending Active Directory identities to the cloud, allowing for single sign-on (SSO) to resources both on-premises and in the cloud. Site-to-site VPNs can be established to provide cross-premises connectivity between your on-premises infrastructure and hosting providers you purchase cloud services from. You even can connect directly to private subnets within a hosted cloud network, using your existing networking equipment that uses industry-standard IKEv2-IPsec protocols. And you can enhance business continuity and simplify disaster recovery by using the new Hyper-V Replica feature that provides asynchronous replication of virtual machines over IP-based networks to remote sites. All these features help provide the foundation that you need to build your private cloud.

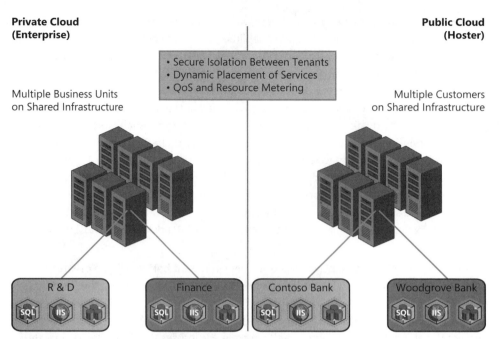

Private Cloud (Enterprise)

Public Cloud (Hoster)

- Secure Isolation Between Tenants
- Dynamic Placement of Services
- QoS and Resource Metering

Multiple Business Units on Shared Infrastructure

Multiple Customers on Shared Infrastructure

R & D

Finance

Contoso Bank

Woodgrove Bank

FIGURE 1-2 Windows Server 2012 provides a foundation for multi-tenant clouds.

Highly available, easy-to-manage multi-server platform

Cost is the bottom line for most businesses, and even though virtualization has allowed many organizations to tap into efficiencies that have helped them do more with less with their datacenters, maintaining these efficiencies and preventing interruptions due to failures, downtimes, and management problems remain a key priority. Windows Server 2012 helps you address these issues by providing enhanced availability features, more flexible storage options, and powerful new management capabilities.

Windows Server 2012 enhances availability by extending the Live Migration capabilities of Hyper-V in previous Windows Server versions with a new feature called Live Storage Migration, which lets you move virtual hard disks while they are attached to running VMs with no downtime. Live Storage Migration simplifies the task of migrating or upgrading storage when you need to perform maintenance on your SAN or file-based storage array, or when you need to redistribute the load. Built-in NIC teaming gives you fault-tolerant networking without the need to use third-party solutions, and it also helps ensure availability by preventing connectivity from being lost when a network adapter fails. And availability can be further enhanced through transparent failover, which lets you move file shares between cluster nodes with no interruption to applications accessing data on these shares. These improvements can provide benefits for both virtualized datacenters and for the cloud.

Windows Server 2012 also provides numerous efficiencies that can help you reduce costs. These efficiencies cover a wide range of areas, including power consumption, networking, and storage, but for now, let's just consider storage. The new file server features of Windows Server 2012 allow you to store application data on server message block (SMB) file shares in a way that provides much of the same kind of availability, reliability, and performance that you've come to expect from more expensive SAN solutions. The new Storage Spaces feature provides built-in storage virtualization capabilities that enable flexible, scalable, and cost-effective solutions to meet your storage needs. And Windows Server 2012 integrates with storage solutions that support thin provisioning with just-in-time (JIT) allocations of storage and the ability to reclaim storage that's no longer needed. Reducing cost is key for enterprises, whether they still have traditional IT infrastructures or have deployed private clouds.

Windows Server 2012 also includes features that make management and automation more efficient. The new Server Manager takes the pain out of deploying and managing large numbers of servers by simplifying the task of remotely deploying roles and features on both physical and virtual servers. Server Manager also can be used to perform scenario-based deployments of the Remote Desktop Services role, for example to set up a session virtualization infrastructure or a virtual desktop infrastructure (VDI) environment quickly. PowerShell 3.0 has powerful new features that simplify the job of automating numerous aspects of a datacenter, including the operating system, storage, and networking resources. PowerShell workflows let you perform complex management tasks that require machines to be rebooted. Scheduled jobs can run regularly or in response to a specific event. Delegated credentials can be used so that junior administrators can perform mission-critical tasks. All these improvements can bring you closer to running your datacenter or private cloud as a truly lights-out automated environment.

Deploy web applications on-premises and in the cloud

The web platform is key to building a cloud solution. That's because cloud-based services are delivered and consumed over the Internet. Windows Server 2012 includes web platform enhancements that provide the kind of flexibility, scalability, and elasticity that your business needs to host web applications for provisioning cloud-based applications to business units or customers. Windows Server 2012 is also an open web platform that embraces a broad range of industry standards and supports many third-party platforms and tools so that you can choose whatever best suits the development needs for your business.

Because most organizations are expected to follow the hybrid cloud approach that combines together both on-premises infrastructure and cloud services, efficiencies can be gained by using development symmetry that lets you build applications that you can deploy both on-premises and in the cloud. Windows Server 2012 provides such development symmetry through a common programming language supporting both Windows Server and the Windows Azure platform; through a rich collection of applications that can be deployed and used across web application and data tiers; through the rich Microsoft Visual Studio–based developer experience, which lets you develop code that can run both on-premises and in the cloud; and through other technologies like the Windows Azure Connect, which lets you configure Internet Protocol Security (IPsec)–protected connections between your on-premises physical/virtual servers and roles running in the Windows Azure cloud.

Building on the proven application platform of earlier Windows Server versions, Windows Server 2012 adds new features and enhancements to enable service providers to host large numbers of websites while guaranteeing customers predictable service levels. These improvements make Windows Server 2012 the ideal platform for building and managing hosting environments and public clouds. To enable the highest level of scalability, especially in shared hosting environments, Microsoft Internet Information Services (IIS) 8.0 in Windows Server 2012 introduced multicore scaling on Non-Uniform Memory Access (NUMA), which enables servers that can scale effectively beyond 32 processors and across NUMA nodes. This capability enables your web applications to scale up quickly to meet sudden spikes in demand. And when demand falls again, IIS CPU throttling enables your applications to scale down to minimize costs. You also can use IIS CPU throttling to ensure that applications always get their fair share of processor time by specifying a maximum CPU usage for each application pool. And to manage the proliferation of Secure Sockets Layer (SSL) certificates for your hosting environment, or to be able to add web servers to a web farm quickly without the need to configure SSL manually on them, the new Centralized SSL Certificate Support feature of Windows Server 2012 takes the headache out of managing SSL-based hosting environments.

IIS 8.0 in Windows Server 2012 also provides businesses with great flexibility in the kinds of web applications that they can develop and deploy. ASP.NET 4.5 now supports the latest HTML 5 standards. PHP and MySQL also are supported through the built-in IIS extensions for these development platforms. And support for the industry-standard WebSocket protocol enables encrypted data transfer over real-time bidirectional channels to support AJAX client applications running in the browser. All these features and enhancements provide flexibility for building highly scalable web applications, hosted either on-premises or in the cloud.

Enabling the modern work style

The consumerization of IT through the trend towards BYOD or "bring your own device" environments is something that businesses everywhere are facing and IT is only beginning to get a handle on. The days of IT having full control over all user devices in their infrastructure are probably over, with the exception of certain high-security environments in the government, military, and finance sectors. Accepting these changes requires not just new thinking but new technology, and Windows Server 2012 brings features that can help IT address this issue by enabling IT to deliver on-premises and cloud-based services to users while maintaining control over sensitive corporate data.

Remote Access has been enhanced in Windows Server 2012 to make it much easier to deploy DirectAccess so that users can always have the experience of being seamlessly connected to the corporate network whenever they have Internet access. Setting up traditional VPN connections is also simpler in Windows Server 2012 for organizations that need to maintain compatibility with existing systems or policies. BranchCache has been enhanced in Windows Server 2012 to make it scale greater, perform better, and be managed more easily. Deploying BranchCache is now much simpler and enables users to run applications remotely and access data more efficiently and securely than before. And as previously mentioned in this chapter, Server Manager now lets you perform scenario-based deployments of the Remote Desktop Services role to implement session virtualization or VDI in your environment more easily.

To remain productive as they roam between locations and use different devices, users need to be able to access their data using the full Windows experience. New features and improvements in Windows Server 2012 now make this possible from any location on almost any device. RemoteFX for WAN enables a rich user experience even over slow WAN connections. Universal serial bus (USB) is now supported for session virtualization, allowing users to use their USB flash drives, smartcards, webcams, and other devices when connecting to session hosts. And VDI now includes user virtual hard disks (VHDs) for storing user personalization settings and cached application data so that the user experience can be maintained across logons.

Windows Server 2012 also gives you greater control over your sensitive corporate data to help you safeguard your business and meet the needs of compliance. Central access policies can be used to define who is allowed to access information within your organization. Central audit policies have been enhanced to facilitate compliance reporting and forensic analysis. The Windows authorization and audit engine has been re-architected to allow the use of conditional expressions and central policies. Kerberos authentication now supports both user and device claims. And Rights Management Services (RMS) has been made extensible so partners can provide solutions for encrypting non-Office files. All these improvements enable users to connect securely to on-premises or cloud-based infrastructure so that they can be more productive in ways that meet the challenges of today's work style while maintaining strict control over your corporate data.

Up next

The chapters that follow will dig deeper into these different ways that Windows Server 2012 can deliver value by examining in more detail the new features and capabilities of this cloud-optimized platform. Each chapter also includes sidebars written by insiders on the Windows Server team at Microsoft, by Microsoft Consulting Services experts in the field, and by Microsoft Support engineers who have been working with the platform from Day 1. To begin with, let's look more closely at how Windows Server 2012 can provide the perfect foundation for building your organization's private cloud.

CHAPTER 2

Foundation for building your private cloud

- A complete virtualization platform **19**
- Increase scalability and performance **49**
- Business continuity for virtualized workloads **69**
- Up next **79**

This chapter describes some of the new features of Windows Server 2012 that make it the ideal platform for building a private cloud for your organization. With enhancements to Hyper-V virtualization, improvements in scalability and performance, and business continuity support for virtualized workloads, Windows Server 2012 provides a solid foundation for building dynamic, highly scalable multi-tenant cloud environments.

Windows Server 2012: The foundation for building your private cloud

Delivering a solid foundation for a private cloud requires a robust virtualization platform, scalability with great performance, and the ability to span datacenters and integrate with other clouds. Windows Server 2012 was designed to address key private cloud needs through advances in computer, storage, and network virtualization.

Compute virtualization, provided by Hyper-V in Windows Server 2012, has been improved to support significantly larger host servers and guest virtual machines (VMs). This increases the range of workloads that can be virtualized. A new feature called *Guest NUMA* enables large virtual machines with many virtual CPUs (vCPUs) to achieve high performance by optimizing a VM's vCPU mappings to the underlying physical server's Non-Uniform Memory Access (NUMA) configuration. Large increases in Hyper-V scalability and Dynamic Memory provide for much higher density of VMs per server with larger clusters. VM mobility through Live Migration and live storage migration, regardless of whether the VM is hosted on a cluster, enable a number of new scenarios for optimization of resources in private cloud scenarios.

Windows Server 2012 delivers new network virtualization capability as well as private virtual local area networks (VLANs), opening a number of new networking scenarios, including multi-tenant options required for hosting and private cloud scenarios. These technologies enable a tenant to utilize their own IP addressing schemes, even if it overlaps with other tenants, while maintaining separation and security. Windows Server 2012 also introduces a new extensible virtual switch. The extensible switch delivers new capabilities such as port profiles and is a platform that third parties can use to build switch extensions for tasks like traffic monitoring, intrusion detection, and network policy enforcement. In both private cloud scenarios and hosting scenarios, secure multi-tenancy is often a requirement. Examples could include separating the finance department's resources from the engineering department's resources or separating one company's resource you are hosting from another's. Windows Server 2012 networking technologies provide for shared infrastructure and resource pooling while enabling secure multi-tenancy.

Storage virtualization is a major investment area in Windows Server 2012. Storage Spaces, SMB 3, Cluster Shared Volumes (CSV2), and several other new storage features provide a high-performance, low-cost storage platform. This storage platform allows Hyper-V VMs to be run from Windows Server 2012 continuously available file shares on Windows storage spaces. Such shares can be accessed using the new SMB 3 protocol, which when combined with appropriate network hardware, provides high-speed, low-latency, multichannel-capable storage access. These technologies provide a robust storage platform at a cost point much lower than was previously possible. For environments with significant existing investments in storage area network (SAN) technology, Windows Server 2012 now enables Fibre Channel host bus adapters (HBAs) to be virtualized, allowing VMs direct access to Fibre Channel–based SAN storage.

Another critical component of a private cloud infrastructure is disaster recovery capability. Windows Server 2012 introduces the Hyper-V Replica feature, which allows VMs to be replicated to disaster recovery sites, which reduces the time required to restore service should a primary datacenter suffer a disaster.

With the large number of new features and improvements, automation becomes a critical requirement, both for consistency of deployment and for efficiency in operations. Windows Server 2012 includes about 2,400 new Windows PowerShell cmdlets for managing the various roles and features in the platform. PowerShell can be used either directly or through Microsoft and third-party management systems to automate deployment, configuration, and operations tasks. The new Server Manager in Windows Server 2012 allows multiple servers to be grouped and managed as one. The objective of these improvements is to increase administrator efficiency by increasing the number of servers each administrator can manage.

The range of technology delivered in Windows Server 2012 can be used in a variety of ways to enable private cloud scenarios. For a large, centralized enterprise, large-scale file and Hyper-V clusters can deliver a platform able to run thousands or tens of thousands of highly available VMs. For cases where secure multi-tenancy is required, network virtualization and private VLANs can be used to deliver secure and isolated networks for each tenant's VMs. With continuously available file shares for storing VMs combined with Live Migration and Live Storage Migration, VMs can be moved anywhere in the datacenter with no downtime.

The compute, network, and storage virtualization provided by Windows Server 2012 deliver resource pooling, elasticity, and measured service cloud attributes. These capabilities are further improved by disaster recovery and automation technologies. With these and other features, Windows Server 2012 delivers the foundation for the private cloud.
David Ziembicki
Senior Architect, U.S. Public Sector, Microsoft Services

A complete virtualization platform

Virtualization can bring many benefits for businesses, including increased agility, greater flexibility, and improved cost efficiency. Combining virtualization with the infrastructure and tools needed to provision cloud applications and services brings even greater benefits for organizations that need to adapt and scale their infrastructure to meet the changing demands of today's business environment. With its numerous improvements, Hyper-V in Windows Server 2012 provide the foundation for building private clouds that can use the benefits of cloud computing across the business units and geographical locations that typically make up today's enterprises. By using Windows Server 2012, you can begin transitioning your organization's datacenter environment toward an infrastructure as a service (IaaS) private cloud that can provide your business units with the "server instances on demand" capability that they need to be able to grow and respond to changing market conditions.

Hosting providers also can use Windows Server 2012 to build multi-tenant cloud infrastructures (both public and shared private clouds) that they can use to deliver cloud-based applications and services to customers. Features and tools included in Windows Server 2012 enable hosting providers to fully isolate customer networks from one another, deliver support for service level agreements (SLAs), and enable chargebacks for implementing usage-based customer billing.

Let's dig into these features and capabilities in more detail. We'll also get some insider perspective from experts working at Microsoft who have developed, tested, deployed, and supported Windows Server 2012 during the early stages of the product release cycle.

Scenario-focused design in Windows Server 2012

One of the best things about Windows Server 2012 is that it was designed from the ground up, with a great focus on actual customer scenarios. Windows Server is the result of a large engineering effort, and in past releases, each organization delivered its own technology innovations and roadmap in its respectively relevant area. The networking team would build great networking features; the storage team would innovate on file and storage systems; the manageability team would introduce PowerShell to enable a standard way to manage servers, and so on.

Windows Server 2012 is different. Instead of having vertical technology-focused roadmaps and designs, it was built around specific customer scenarios for the server. I was the scenario leader for the "hosted cloud" scenario, which was all about building the most cloud-optimized operating system ever built and aligning multiple feature crews on enabling enterprises and hosting providers to build clouds that are better than ever.

Scenario-focused design starts by understanding the business need and the real customer pain points and requirements. During the planning phase, we talked to a very long list of customers and did not limit ourselves to any specific technology. Instead, we have framed the discussion around the need to build and run clouds and discovered pain points, such as the need to offer secure multi-tenancy and isolation to your cloud tenants, so that hosting providers can be more efficient in utilizing their infrastructure and lowering their cost. There's also a need to be able to automate manual processes end to end because manual processes just don't cut it anymore, and the need to lower the cost of storage because customers were clearly overpaying for very expensive storage even when they don't really need it. We then translated that understanding into investments that cross technology boundaries that will solve those business problems and satisfy the customer requirements.

For example, to enable multi-tenancy, we didn't just add some access control lists (ACLs) on the Hyper-V switch. Instead, we've built a much better Hyper-V switch with isolation policy support and added network virtualization to decouple the physical cloud infrastructure from the VM networks. Then we added quality of service (QoS) policies to help hosting providers ensure proper SLAs for different tenants and resource meters to enable them to measure and charge for activities, and we also ensured that everything will be fully automatable (via PowerShell, of course), in a consistent way.

Here's another example: we didn't just add support for a new network interface card (NIC) technology called *Remote Direct Memory Access* (RDMA). Instead, we've designed it to work well with file servers and provide SMB Direct support to enable the use of file servers in a cloud infrastructure over standard Ethernet fabric, and used storage spaces for low-cost disks. This way, competitive performance compared to SANs is made available at a fraction of the cost.

Finally, scenario-focused design doesn't actually end at the design phase. It's a way of thinking that starts at planning but continues all the way through execution, internal validation, external validation with our TAP program, partner relations, documentation, blogging, and, of course, bringing the product to market. Basically, at every stage of the Windows Server 2012 execution cycle, the focus was on making the scenario work, rather than on making specific features work.

This kind of a scenario-focused requires an amazingly huge collaborative effort across technology teams. This is exactly where Windows Server 2012 shines and is the reason you're seeing all of these great innovations coming together in one massive release that will change the way clouds are built.
Yigal Edery
Principal Program Manager, Windows Server

Hyper-V extensible switch

The new Hyper-V extensible switch in Windows Server 2012 is key to enabling the creation of secure cloud environments that support the isolation of multiple tenants. The Hyper-V extensible switch in Windows Server 2012 introduces a number of new and enhanced capabilities for tenant isolation, traffic shaping, protection against malicious virtual machines, and hassle-free troubleshooting. The extensible switch allows third parties to develop plug-in extensions to emulate the full capabilities of hardware-based switches and support more complex virtual environments and solutions.

Previous versions of Hyper-V allowed you to implement complex virtual network environments by creating virtual network switches that worked like physical layer-2 Ethernet switches. You could create external virtual networks to provide VMs with connectivity with externally located servers and clients, internal networks to allow VMs on the same host to communicate with each other as well as the host, or private virtual networks (PVLANs) that you can use to completely isolate all VMs on the same host from each other and allow them to communicate only via external networks.

The Hyper-V extensible switch facilitates the creation of virtual networks that can be implemented in various ways to provide great flexibility in how you can design your virtualized infrastructure. For example, you can configure a guest operating system within a VM to have a single virtual network adapter associated with a specific extensible switch or multiple virtual network adapters (each associated with a different switch), but you can't connect the same switch to multiple network adapters.

What's new however is that the Hyper-V virtual switch is now extensible in a couple of different ways. First, you can now install custom Network Driver Interface Specification (NDIS) filter drivers (called *extensions*) into the driver stack of the virtual switch. For example, you could create an extension that captures, filters, or forwards packets to extensible switch ports. Specifically, the extensible switch allows for using the following kinds of extensions:

- Capturing extensions, which can capture packets to monitor network traffic but cannot modify or drop packets
- Filtering extensions, which are like capturing extensions but also can inspect and drop packets
- Forwarding extensions, which allow you to modify packet routing and enable integration with your physical network infrastructure

Second, you can use the capabilities of the Windows Filtering Platform (WFP) by using the built-in Wfplwfs.sys filtering extension to intercept packets as they travel along the data path of the extensible switch. You might use this approach, for example, to perform packet inspection within your virtualized environment.

These different extensibility capabilities of the Hyper-V extensible switch are intended primarily for Microsoft partners and independent software vendors (ISVs) so they can update their existing network monitoring, management, and security software products so they can work not just with physical hosts, but also with VMs deployed within any kind of virtual networking environment that you might possibly create using Hyper-V in Windows Server 2012. In addition, being able to extend the functionality of the Hyper-V networking by adding extensions makes it easier to add new networking functionality to Hyper-V without needing to replace or upgrade the switch. You'll also be able to use the same tools for managing these extensions that you use for managing other aspects of Hyper-V networking, namely the Hyper-V Manager console, PowerShell, and Windows Management Instrumentation (WMI). And because these extensions integrate into the existing framework of Hyper-V networking, they automatically work with other capabilities, like Live Migration.

Table 2-1 summarizes some of the benefits of the Hyper-V extensible switch from both the IT professional and ISV perspective.

TABLE 2-1 Benefits of the Hyper-V extensible switch

Key Tenets	Benefit to ISVS	Benefit to IT Professionals
Open platform w/public API	Write only the functionalities desired	Minimal footprint for errors
First-class citizen of system	Free system services (e.g., Live Migration)	Extensions from various ISVs work together
Existing API model	Faster development	Larger pool of extension implementers
Logo certification and rich framework	Higher customer satisfaction	Higher extension quality
Unified Tracing thru virtual switch	Lower support costs	Shorter downtimes

Configuring virtual switches

Figure 2-1 shows the Windows Filtering Platform (WPF) extension selected in the Virtual Switch Manager of the Hyper-V Console in the beta version of Windows Server 2012. Note that once extensions are installed on the host, they can be enabled or disabled and also have their order rearranged by moving them up or down in the list of switch extensions.

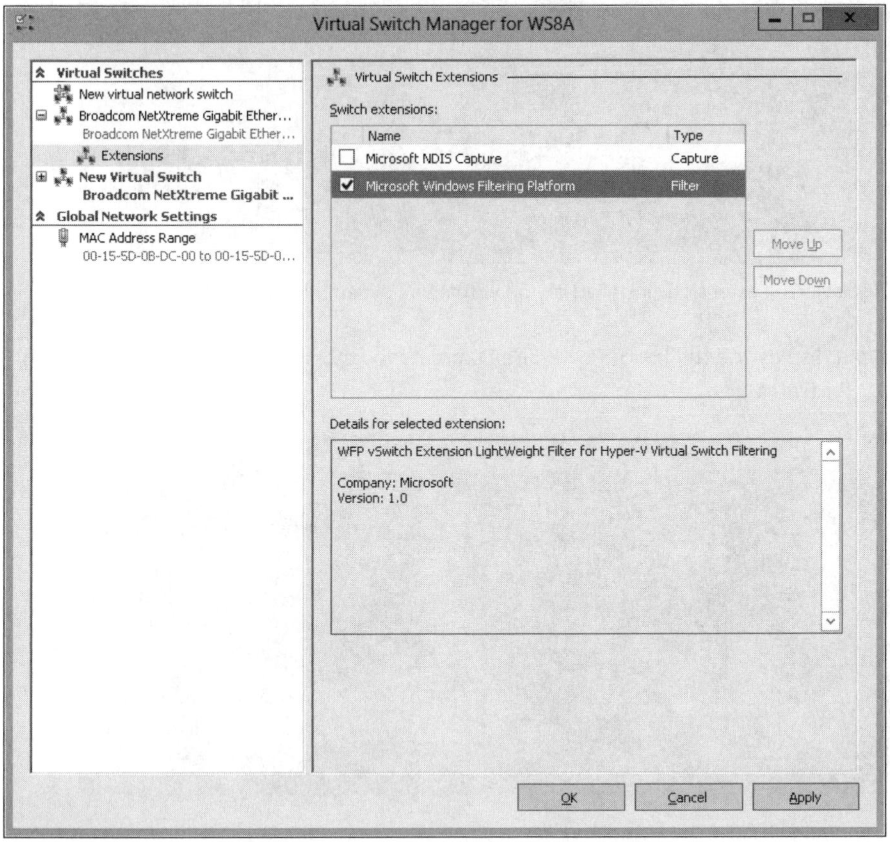

FIGURE 2-1 Virtual switch extensions for the Hyper-V extensible switch.

You can also use PowerShell to create, delete, and configure extensible switches on Hyper-V hosts. For example, Figure 2-2 shows how to use the *Get-VMSwitchExtension* cmdlet to display details concerning the extensions installed on a specific switch.

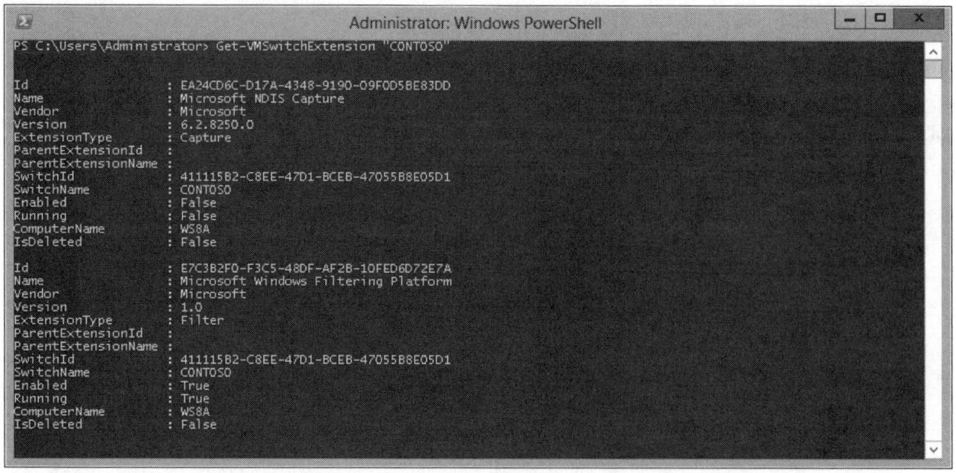

```
Administrator: Windows PowerShell
PS C:\Users\Administrator> Get-VMSwitchExtension "CONTOSO"

Id                    : EA24CD6C-D17A-4348-9190-09F0D5BE83DD
Name                  : Microsoft NDIS Capture
Vendor                : Microsoft
Version               : 6.2.8250.0
ExtensionType         : Capture
ParentExtensionId     :
ParentExtensionName   :
SwitchId              : 411115B2-C8EE-47D1-BCEB-47055B8E05D1
SwitchName            : CONTOSO
Enabled               : False
Running               : False
ComputerName          : WS8A
IsDeleted             : False

Id                    : E7C3B2F0-F3C5-48DF-AF2B-10FED6D72E7A
Name                  : Microsoft Windows Filtering Platform
Vendor                : Microsoft
Version               : 1.0
ExtensionType         : Filter
ParentExtensionId     :
ParentExtensionName   :
SwitchId              : 411115B2-C8EE-47D1-BCEB-47055B8E05D1
SwitchName            : CONTOSO
Enabled               : True
Running               : True
ComputerName          : WS8A
IsDeleted             : False
```

FIGURE 2-2 Displaying all extensions installed on the virtual switch named CONTOSO.

You also can display the full list of PowerShell cmdlets for managing the extensible switch, as Figure 2-3 illustrates.

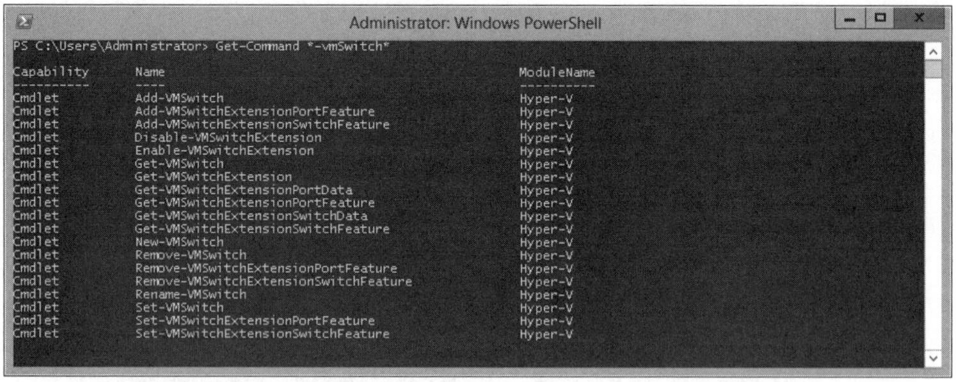

```
Administrator: Windows PowerShell
PS C:\Users\Administrator> Get-Command *-vmSwitch*

Capability      Name                                         ModuleName
----------      ----                                         ----------
Cmdlet          Add-VMSwitch                                 Hyper-V
Cmdlet          Add-VMSwitchExtensionPortFeature             Hyper-V
Cmdlet          Add-VMSwitchExtensionSwitchFeature           Hyper-V
Cmdlet          Disable-VMSwitchExtension                    Hyper-V
Cmdlet          Enable-VMSwitchExtension                     Hyper-V
Cmdlet          Get-VMSwitch                                 Hyper-V
Cmdlet          Get-VMSwitchExtension                        Hyper-V
Cmdlet          Get-VMSwitchExtensionPortData                Hyper-V
Cmdlet          Get-VMSwitchExtensionPortFeature             Hyper-V
Cmdlet          Get-VMSwitchExtensionSwitchData              Hyper-V
Cmdlet          Get-VMSwitchExtensionSwitchFeature           Hyper-V
Cmdlet          New-VMSwitch                                 Hyper-V
Cmdlet          Remove-VMSwitch                              Hyper-V
Cmdlet          Remove-VMSwitchExtensionPortFeature          Hyper-V
Cmdlet          Remove-VMSwitchExtensionSwitchFeature        Hyper-V
Cmdlet          Rename-VMSwitch                              Hyper-V
Cmdlet          Set-VMSwitch                                 Hyper-V
Cmdlet          Set-VMSwitchExtensionPortFeature             Hyper-V
Cmdlet          Set-VMSwitchExtensionSwitchFeature           Hyper-V
```

FIGURE 2-3 Displaying all PowerShell cmdlets for managing virtual switches.

Troubleshooting virtual switches

Microsoft also has extended Unified Tracing through the Hyper-V extensible switch, which makes it easier for you to diagnose problems that may occur. For example, if you are experiencing issues that you think might be connected with the extensible switch, you could attempt to troubleshoot the problem by turning on tracing using the Netsh command like this:

```
netsh trace start provider=Microsoft-Windows-Hyper-V-VmSwitch capture=yes
capturetype=vmswitch
```

Then you would try and reproduce the issue while tracing is turned on. Once a repro has occurred, you could disable tracing with netsh trace stop and then review the generated Event Trace Log (ETL) file using Event Viewer or Network Monitor. You also could review the System event log for any relevant events.

Performance monitoring improvements

Windows Server 2012 exposes more Event Tracing for Windows (ETW) data providers and performance items than Windows Server 2008 R2. With this exposure comes the vital need for the IT professional to know which datasets are relevant to their specific monitoring situation. It's not feasible nor appropriate to just gather everything, for system monitoring has in it a touch of physics . . . a modified Heisenberg uncertainty principle is afoot; One cannot monitor a system without impacting it to some degree. To how much of a degree is at question. Finely tuned data collector sets by Performance Analysis of Logs (PAL; see http://pal.codeplex.com) can be used by the IT professional to ensure they are only gathering the data necessary to their problem set, so as to not negatively impact system performance too heavily while monitoring or baselining systems.

One advantage to using ETW data providers rather than performance counter object items is that ETW providers come from the kernel itself typically, rather than coming from user mode measurements. What this means is that the data from ETW data providers is more accurate and more reliable and also puts a lower load on the system. ETW logging is unlikely to suffer from missing data sets due to high system load as well. Look for guidance on which items to collect though before diving in; ETL tracing can grow log files quickly.

Jeff Stokes
Platforms PFE

Additional capabilities

A number of other advanced capabilities also have been integrated by Microsoft into the Hyper-V extensible switch to help enhance security, monitoring, and troubleshooting functionality. These additional capabilities include the following:

- **DHCP guard**   Helps safeguard against Dynamic Host Configuration Protocol (DHCP) man-in-the-middle attacks by dropping DHCP server messages from unauthorized VMs pretending to be DHCP servers
- **MAC address spoofing**   Helps safeguard against attempts to use ARP spoofing to steal IP addresses from VMs by allowing VMs to change the source MAC address in outgoing packets to an address that is not assigned to them

- **Router guard** Helps safeguard against unauthorized routers by dropping router advertisement and redirection messages from unauthorized VMs pretending to be routers

- **Port mirroring** Enables monitoring of a VM's network traffic by forwarding copies of destination or source packets to another VM being used for monitoring purposes

- **Port ACLs** Helps enforce virtual network isolation by allowing traffic filtering based on media access control (MAC) or IP address ranges

- **Isolated VLANs** Allows segregation of traffic on multiple VLANs to facilitate isolation of tenant networks through the creation of private VLANs (PVLANs)

- **Trunk mode** Allows directing traffic from a group of VLANs to a specific VM

- **Bandwidth management** Allows guaranteeing a minimum amount of bandwidth and/or enforcing a maximum amount of bandwidth for each VM

- **Enhanced diagnostics** Allows packet monitoring and event tracing through the extensible switch using ETL and Unified Tracing

Most of these additional capabilities can be configured from the graphical user interface (GUI) by opening the VM's settings. For example, by selecting the network adapter under Hardware, you can specify bandwidth management settings for the VM. Figure 2-4 shows these settings configured in such a way that the VM always has at least 50 MBps of network bandwidth available, but never more than 100 MBps. If your hosts reside in a shared cloud being used to provision applications and services to business units or customers, these new bandwidth management capabilities can provide the benefit of helping you meet your SLAs with these business units or customers.

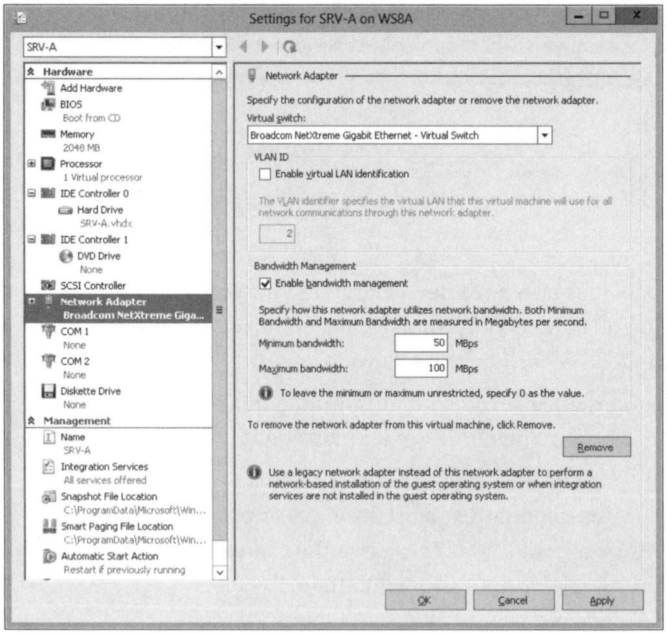

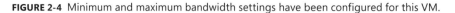

FIGURE 2-4 Minimum and maximum bandwidth settings have been configured for this VM.

Clicking the + sign beside Network Adapter in these settings exposes two new pages of network settings: Hardware Acceleration and Advanced Features. We'll examine the Hardware Acceleration settings later in this chapter, but for now, here are the Advanced Features settings which lets you configure MAC address spoofing, DHCP guard, router guard, and port mirroring for the selected network adapter of the VM, as shown in Figure 2-5.

As the sidebar demonstrates, you also can use PowerShell to configure and manage the various advanced capabilities of the Hyper-V extensible switch.

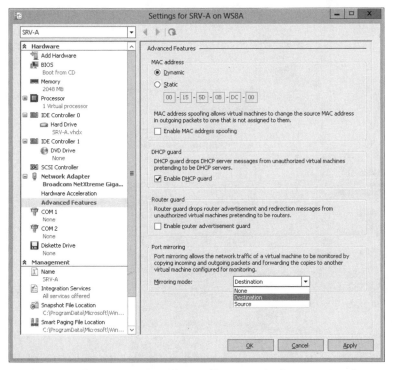

FIGURE 2-5 Configuring advanced features for network adapter settings for a VM.

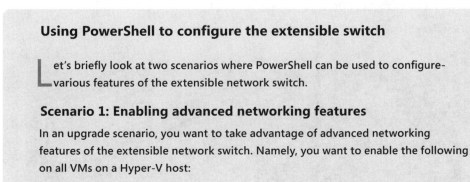

Using PowerShell to configure the extensible switch

Let's briefly look at two scenarios where PowerShell can be used to configure various features of the extensible network switch.

Scenario 1: Enabling advanced networking features

In an upgrade scenario, you want to take advantage of advanced networking features of the extensible network switch. Namely, you want to enable the following on all VMs on a Hyper-V host:

- DHCP Guard

- Enable router advertisement guard

- Enable Virtual Machine Queue (VMQ)

Here's what a VM looks like without any of the advanced networking features enabled:

Now let's do this on a Hyper-V host on every single VM on the Hyper-V host.

First, let's list all the VMs by issuing the *Get-VM* cmdlet:

We have four VMs on this host. Let's activate DHCP Guard, router advertisement guard, and VMQ in a single line:

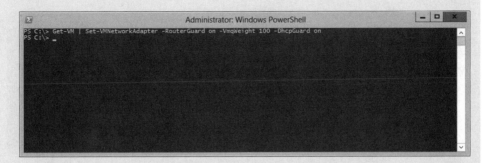

```
PS C:\> Get-VM | Set-VMNetworkAdapter -RouterGuard on -VmqWeight 100 -DhcpGuard on
PS C:\> _
```

Once the PowerShell prompt has returned, we can view the settings on any VM on this host:

Note: to do this in a Hyper-V cluster, simply prepend the previous statement with Get-ClusterGroup:

```
PS C:\> Get-ClusterGroup

Name                               OwnerNode          State
----                               ---------          -----
Available Storage                  hv01               Offline
Cluster Group                      hv02               Online
dc02                               hv02               Offline
Demo - iSCSI - vm07-win8server     hv02               Online
Demo - LIVE Storage Migration - vm02...  hv01         Offline
Demo - NIC Teaming - vm06-win8server  hv01            Offline
rep                                hv01               Online
vm01                               hv02               Online
vm03-win2008r2sp1                  hv01               Offline
vm04-win2008r2sp1                  hv02               Online
vm05-win8client                    hv02               Online
wds02                              hv01               Offline

PS C:\> _
```

Scenario 2: Configure ACLs on a VM

Most organizations have a management network segment and will typically associate a physical NIC on the management network segment. Suppose you want to limit the network segment associated with the virtual NIC connected to the management network. Here's how you'd create an ACL to accomplish this:

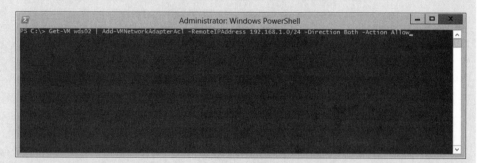

```
PS C:\> Get-VM wds02 | Add-VMNetworkAdapterAcl -RemoteIPAddress 192.168.1.0/24 -Direction Both -Action Allow_
```

This cmdlet allows both inbound and outbound traffic to the VM named wds02 from the 192.168.1.0/24 segment. To view the settings:

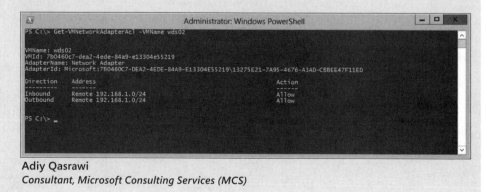

```
PS C:\> Get-VMNetworkAdapterAcl -VMName wds02

VMName: wds02
VMId: 7b0460c7-dea2-4ede-84a9-e13304e55219
AdapterName: Network Adapter
AdapterId: Microsoft:7B0460C7-DEA2-4EDE-84A9-E13304E55219\13275E21-7A95-4676-A3AD-CBBEE47F11ED

Direction    Address                          Action
---------    -------                          ------
Inbound      Remote 192.168.1.0/24            Allow
Outbound     Remote 192.168.1.0/24            Allow

PS C:\> _
```

Adiy Qasrawi
Consultant, Microsoft Consulting Services (MCS)

Learn more

IT pros can expect Microsoft partners and ISVs to take advantage of the extensible switch capabilities of Hyper-V in Windows Server 2012 as new versions of their network monitoring, management, and security products begin to appear. For example:

- Cisco Systems has announced that its Cisco Nexus 1000V distributed virtual switch will enable full VM-level visibility and security controls in Hyper-V environments; see *http://newsroom.cisco.com/press-release-content?type=webcontent&articleId=473289.*

- inMon Corp. has announced that their sFlow traffic monitoring software will deliver comprehensive visibility into network and system resources in Hyper-V virtual environments; see *http://www.inmon.com/news/20111003.php.*

- 5nine Software has announced that version 3.0 of 5nine Security Manager will be the first completely host-based Virtual Firewall with Anti-Virus (AV) for Windows 8; see *http://www.5nine.com/News/news-firewall3-preview.aspx.*

For an overview of the requirements, implementation, and manageability of the Hyper-V extensible switch, see the topic "Hyper-V Virtual Switch Technical Preview" in the TechNet Library at *http://technet.microsoft.com/en-us/library/hh831452.aspx.* For additional overviews of the Hyper-V extensible switch, see the topic "Hyper-V Virtual Switch Overview," at *http://technet.microsoft.com/en-us/library/hh831823.aspx* and the topic "Introducing Hyper-V Extensible Switch," at *http://blogs.technet.com/b/server-cloud/archive/2011/11/08/windows-server-8-introducing-hyper-v-extensible-switch.aspx.*

For a detailed overview of how the Hyper-V extensible switch operates and how to write extensions for the switch, see the topic "Hyper-V Extensible Switch" in the Windows Hardware Development section of MSDN at *http://msdn.microsoft.com/en-us/library/windows/hardware/hh598161(v=vs.85).aspx.*

For a sample base library that can be used to implement a filter driver for the Hyper-V extensible switch, see the topic "Hyper-V Extensible Virtual Switch extension filter driver" in the Samples section of Dev Center—Hardware on MSDN at *http://code.msdn.microsoft.com/windowshardware/Hyper-V-Extensible-Virtual-e4b31fbb.*

For more information on PowerShell cmdlets like *Get-VMSwitch, Get-VMSwitchExtension, Set-VMSwitchExtensionSwitchFeature,* and other cmdlets for configuring and managing the Hyper-V extensible switch, see "Hyper-V Cmdlets in Windows PowerShell" in the TechNet Library at *http://technet.microsoft.com/library/hh848559.aspx.*

Network virtualization

As discussed in Chapter 1, "The business need for Windows Server 2012," in the IaaS cloud computing model, the cloud provider runs a datacenter that offers "VMs for rent" along with dynamically allocated resources. The customer owns the VM and manages it as "its server" in the cloud. The meaning of the terms *cloud provider* and *customer* can differ, of course, depending on whether you're talking about a shared private cloud or a shared public cloud. Specifically, the following points apply:

- In the shared private cloud scenario, the cloud provider is the organization itself, which owns and operates its own datacenter, whereas the customers might be different business units, departments, or offices in different locations.

- In the shared public cloud scenario, the cloud provider is the hosting company, whereas the customers might be large enterprises, mid-sized companies, or even small businesses. The hosting company owns and manages the datacenter and may "rent out" servers to customers, offer colocation of customer-owned servers, or both.

In both scenarios, the cloud provider can provide the numerous benefits of cloud computing to its customers, but typically not without problems using today's technologies. For example, VLANs are typically used by cloud providers to isolate the servers belonging to one customer from those belonging to other customers and provisioned from the same cloud. VLANs accomplish this by adding tags to Ethernet frames. Then Ethernet switches can be configured to enforce isolation by allowing nodes that have the same tag to communicate with each other, but not with nodes having a different tag. But VLANs have several limitations:

- They have limited scalability because typical Ethernet switches support no more than 1,000 VLAN IDs (with a theoretical maximum of 4,094).

- They have limited flexibility because a single VLAN can't span multiple IP subnets.

- They have high management overhead associated with them because Ethernet switches need to be reconfigured each time a VLAN is added or removed.

Another problem that customers often experience when contemplating moving their computing resources to the cloud is IP addressing. The issue is that the customer's existing infrastructure typically has one addressing scheme, whereas the datacenter network has an entirely different addressing scheme. So when a customer wants to move one of its servers into the cloud, typically by virtualizing the workload of the existing physical server so the workload can be run as a VM hosted within the cloud provider's datacenter, the customer is usually required to change the IP address of their server so it can fit the addressing scheme of the cloud provider's network. This can pose difficulties, however, because IP addresses are often tied to geographical locations, management policies, and security policies, so changing the server's address when its workload is moved into the cloud may result in routing issues, servers moving out of management scope, or security policies failing to be applied properly.

It would simplify cloud migrations a lot if the customer's servers could keep their existing IP addresses when their workloads are virtualized and moved into the cloud provider's datacenter. That way, the customer's existing routing, management, and security policies should continue to work as before. And that's exactly what network virtualization does!

How network virtualization works

Network virtualization is a new feature of Windows Server 2012 that lets you keep your own internal IP addresses when moving your servers into the cloud. For example, let's say that you have three on-premises physical servers having private IP addresses 192.168.33.45, 192.168.33.46, and 192.168.33.47, and you want to move these servers to the datacenter of a cloud provider called *Fabrikam*. These servers are currently in the 192.168.0.0/16 address space, and Fabrikam's datacenter uses 10.0.0.0/24 for its datacenter network's address space. If Fabrikam has Windows Server 2012 deployed in its datacenter, you're in luck because your servers can keep their existing IP addresses when their workloads are migrated into VMs running on Fabrikam host machines. This means that your existing clients, which are used to accessing servers located on the 192.168.0.0/16 subnet, will be able to continue doing so with no modifications needed to your routing infrastructure, management platform, or network security policies. That's network virtualization at work.

But what if another customer of Fabrikam uses the exact same subnetting scheme for its own virtualized workloads? For example, let's say that Northwind Traders also has been using 192.168.0.0/16 on its private network, and one of the servers it's moved into Fabrikam's datacenter has the exact same IP address (192.168.33.45) as one of the servers that you've moved into Fabrikam's datacenter? No problem! Network virtualization in Windows Server 2012 provides complete isolation between VMs belonging to different customers even if those VMs use the exact same IP addresses!

Network virtualization works by allowing you to assign two different IP addresses to each VM running on a Windows Server 2012 Hyper-V host. These two addresses are:

- The customer address, which is the IP address that the server had when it resided on the customer's premises before it was migrated into the cloud. In the previous example, this might be the 192.168.33.45 address for a particular server that the customer wants to move to the cloud.

- The provider address, which is the IP address assigned by the cloud provider to the server once the server has been migrated to the provider's datacenter. In the previous example, this could be 10.44.2.133, or some other address in the 10.0.0.0/24 address space.

From the customer's perspective, communication with the migrated server is just the same as if the server still resided on the customer's own premises. This is because the VM running the customer's migrated workload can see and use its customer address and thus can be reached by other hosts on the customer's network. The VM cannot see or use its provider address, however, because this address is visible only to the hosts on the cloud provider's network.

Network virtualization thus lets the cloud provider run multiple virtual networks on top of a single physical network in much the same way as server virtualization lets you run multiple virtual servers on a single physical server. Network virtualization also isolates each virtual network from every other virtual network, with the result that each virtual network has the illusion that it is a separate physical network. This means that two or more virtual networks can have the exact same addressing scheme, yet the networks will be fully isolated from one another and each will function as if it is the only network with that scheme.

To make this all happen, network virtualization needs a way of virtualizing IP addresses and mapping them to physical addresses. Network virtualization in Windows Server 2012 offers two ways of accomplishing this:

- **IP rewrite** This approach modifies the customer addresses of packets while they are still on the VM and before they are transmitted onto the physical network.

- **IP encapsulation** In this approach, all the VM's packets are encapsulated with a new header before they are transmitted onto the physical network.

Although IP encapsulation offers better scalability, IP rewrite can provide better performance because it can use the existing capabilities of transferring some of the load to high-end network adapters that support such offloading.

Because network virtualization is intended for datacenters, implementing it requires that you have a VM management framework in place. System Center Virtual Machine Manager 2012 Service Pack 1 provides such a framework and lets you use PowerShell or WMI to create and manage virtual networks.

Benefits of network virtualization

Network virtualization is key to being able to build and provision multi-tenant cloud services, both for shared private clouds, where the "customers" are different business units or departments, and for public cloud scenarios, where the cloud provider offers "space to rent" to all comers. Network virtualization lets you create multi-tenant networks where each network is fully isolated from all other networks, and it does this without any of the limitations of or overhead associated with the job of creating and managing VLANs. This means that cloud providers can use network virtualization to create as many networks as you want—thousands and thousands of them for example if you are a large hosting provider—and then move workloads anywhere you want without having to perform the arduous (and error-prone) task of reconfiguring VLANs.

Network virtualization also provides greater flexibility for VM placement, which helps reduce overprovisioning and fragmentation of resources for the cloud provider. By enabling dynamic VM placement, the cloud provider can make best use of the compute, network, and storage resources within their datacenter and can monitor and control the provisioning of these resources more easily.

Regardless of whether you are a customer looking to migrate your server workloads into the cloud, an enterprise seeking to implement a shared private cloud for provisioning "servers for rent" to different divisions or locations, or a hosting provider wanting to offer cloud hosting services to large numbers of customers, network virtualization in Windows Server 2012 provides the foundation for achieving your goals. Table 2-2 summarizes the benefits of network virtualization to these different parties.

TABLE 2-2 The benefits that network virtualization can provide to customers, enterprises, and hosting providers

Owner	Benefits
The customer who owns the workload that needs to be moved into the cloud	Seamless migration to the cloud Easy to move your three-tier topology to the cloud
An enterprise seeking to deploy a shared private cloud	Easy cloud bursting Preserve your VM settings, IP addresses, and policies Cross premises server-to-server connectivity
A hosting provider wanting to offer secure, multi-tenant "servers for rent" using a shared public cloud	Flexible VM placement requiring no network reconfiguration Create and manage large number of tenant networks

Network virtualization operational challenges

The network virtualization capabilities found in Windows Server 2012 provides a fresh approach to an old problem, and that is primarily that of operator density. Operators, or service providers, are no longer interested in 1:1 solutions. They want more virtual servers per physical server today the same way they wanted more subscribers for a given pool of dial-up modems at the early of days of the World Wide Web. Density typically came at the price of mobility and scalability. Today, of course, this is less of an issue, at least in datacenter virtualization scenarios, as we can have density pushing the limits of hardware while maintaining mobility and scalability.

There was always one difficult problem to solve: how to extend the mobility and scalability of a single datacenter to two or more. This was often required either as datacenters ran out of space or often after a merger or acquisition. Nearly every customer I have worked with in the past five years has or had a datacenter relocation or consolidation project. The problem was now: how do I move these servers to new datacenters while maintaining all the monitoring and security policies associated with their location? The answer usually consisted of storage and network architects sitting down and installing new network and storage equipment which really extended the network subnet(s) from one datacenter to another. This, in a way, was the precursor to network virtualization, and we were able to learn a lot from this. Especially with respect to the newer problems we discovered as a result. Some of the problems we discovered included:

1. **Application behavior**   Moving the VM from one datacenter to another typically introduced network latency. Some applications just did not behave well with the added latency.

2. **Supportability**   It was now difficult for datacenter technicians to effectively know which datacenter a VM was located in by looking at its IP address.

3. **Licensing**   It used to be that some vendors licensed their products to a single IP address. This proved challenging to customers, so certain vendors changed their licensing to be based on the MAC address of the host's NIC. This meant that moving the VM (while keeping its IP) to another datacenter meant it had to keep the same MAC address. Although this is typically possible within a single management domain, this is impossible to predict when that VM was being moved, for instance, to a service provider or a private cloud provider.

Looking back at these problems, I realized the key to avoiding them was to involve the application and server operations. Although this sounds incredibly trivial in theory, it is incredibly difficult to do in practice. How often do you get involved in a project involving network virtualization if you are the corporate custodian or owner of the HR application, for instance?

Server virtualization forced teams to learn to communicate with other teams. Network virtualization will make that even more critical. When you decide to implement network virtualization features found in Windows Server 2012, consider adding teams with operational experience to your team and ensure key application support teams are also consulted.

Adiy Qasrawi
Consultant, Microsoft Consulting Services

Learn more

For an overview of how network virtualization works, see the topic "Hyper-V Network Virtualization Technical Preview" in the TechNet Library at *http://technet.microsoft.com/en-us/library/hh831395.aspx.*

Also, be sure to watch the video "Building secure, scalable multi-tenant clouds using Hyper-V Network Virtualization" from Microsoft's Build conference on Channel 9 at *http://channel9.msdn.com/Events/BUILD/BUILD2011/SAC-442T.*

System Center Virtual Machine Manager 2012 Service Pack 1 is required for implementing network virtualization using Windows Server 2012 Hyper-V hosts. The Community Technology Preview (CTP) of VMM 2012 SP1 is currently available from the Microsoft Download Center at *http://www.microsoft.com/download/en/details .aspx?displaylang=en&id=29220.*

Improved Live Migration

Live Migration was introduced in Windows Server 2008 R2 to provide a high-availability solution for VMs running on Hyper-V hosts. Live Migration uses the Failover Clustering feature to allow running VMs to be moved between cluster nodes without perceived downtime or loss of network connection. Live Migration provides the benefit of increased agility by allowing you to move running VMs to the best host for improving performance, achieving better scaling, or ensuring optimal workload consolidation. Live Migration also helps increase productivity and reduce cost by allowing you to service your host machines without interruption or downtime for your virtualized workloads.

Live Migration in Windows Server 2008 R2 required storing VMs on an Internet Small Computer Systems Interface (iSCSI) or Fibre-Channel SAN. In addition, Live Migration in Windows Server 2008 R2 supported performing only a single Live Migration at a time—multiple simultaneous Live Migrations were not supported.

Now Live Migration in Windows Server 2012 has been improved in several significant ways. First, Live Migrations can be performed much more quickly. In fact, you can even saturate a 10 GB network connection when performing a Live Migration between Windows Server 2012 Hyper-V hosts, something you couldn't do before with Windows Server 2008 R2 Hyper-V hosts.

A second improvement to Live Migration in Windows Server 2012 is that now you can perform multiple Live Migrations simultaneously within the same failover cluster. This means, for example, that if you needed to take down a particular cluster node for immediate servicing, you can migrate all running VMs from that node to a different node quickly and simultaneously in a single operation using either the GUI or a PowerShell command. This can greatly simplify the task of performing maintenance on Hyper-V hosts within your environment.

A third improvement is that Live Migration is now possible even if you don't have a failover clustering infrastructure deployed. In the previous version of Windows Server 2008 R2, Live Migration required installing the Failover Clustering feature, and you also needed to ensure that Cluster Shared Volume (CSV) storage was enabled to ensure the logical unit number (LUN) on which your VM is stored could be accessed by any cluster node at any given time. With Windows Server 2012, however, you have two additional options for Live Migration that can be performed outside a failover clustering environment:

- You can store your VMs on a shared folder on your network, which lets you live-migrate between non-clustered Hyper-V hosts while leaving the VM's files on the share.

- You also can live-migrate a VM directly from one stand-alone Hyper-V host to another without using any shared storage at all.

Let's look at these two Live Migration options in a bit more detail.

Live Migration using a shared folder

With Hyper-V in Windows Server 2012 you can now store all of a VM's files on a shared folder on your network provided the shared folder is located on a file server running Windows Server 2012 (see Figure 2-6). The reason the shared folder must be located on a file server running Windows Server 2012 is because this scenario is supported only through the new capabilities of version 3 of the server message block (SMB) protocol (SMB 3). For more information about SMB 3 and the new continuously available file server capabilities of Windows Server 2012, see the section titled "SMB 3," later in this chapter.

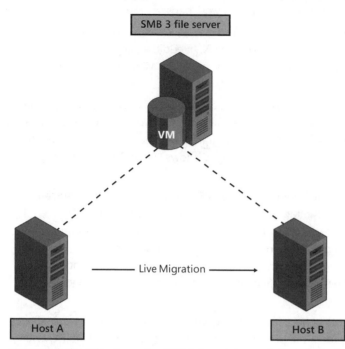

FIGURE 2-6 Live Migration using SMB 3 shared storage but no clustering.

Live Migration using SMB 3 shared storage does not in itself provide high availability unless the file share itself is also highly available. It does, however, also provide the benefit of enhanced VM mobility. And this added mobility can be achieved without the high costs associated SANs and their associated switching fabric. SANs also add extra management overhead in the form of provisioning and managing LUNs. But by simply deploying a Windows Server 2012 file server, you can centralize storage of the VMs in your environment without the added cost and management overhead associated with using a SAN.

Live Migration using SMB 3 shared storage does have a couple of requirements to get it to work, namely the permissions on the share must be configured appropriately, constrained delegation must be enabled in Active Directory directory service, and the path to the shared storage must be configured correctly in the VM's settings. But once everything is set up properly, the procedure for performing Live Migration is essentially unchanged from before.

Experiencing SMB share hosting

Being an infrastructure consultant for the better part of my IT career has included some very deep and thought-provoking discussions about the best ways to accomplish certain goals. Whether the dialogue was comprised of topics such as virtualization, storage, or applications, the common theme throughout was clearly protection of one's digital assets and data. Everyone wanted to design a cost-effective (operative term) disaster recovery solution for their workloads without affecting performance or user impact; however, we all know that you get what you pay for when disaster recovery solutions are concerned.

It was recently told to me that the number two reason for a company implementing a virtualization strategy is disaster recovery. That makes sense to me; however, most of the underlying infrastructure required for a physical server disaster recovery environment is still required in the virtualized world. We still needed the replication of our data through underlying storage. We still needed the like "cold spare" hardware to pick up where our primary servers left off. Don't get me wrong—these solutions are fantastic, but in the end, are quite costly. There needed to be a way to ensure that the smaller IT budgets in the world did not fall to the bottom of the "you get what you pay for in disaster recovery" bucket.

Enter Windows Server 2012. In my opinion, this is truly the first "cloud-ready" piece of software that I have seen capture the entire portfolio of cloud readiness features. Shifting the focus to the mobility of workloads (which is the basis for improving upon current disaster recovery functionality) was clearly a theme when designing this software. The ability to never have to turn your VM off, regardless of scenario, is the holy grail of disaster recovery.

So of course, being an engineer, I wanted to play with this stuff. After installing a couple of Hyper-V and file servers, I decided to test an SMB share hosting my VM files. As generally non-complex as that sounds, it was quite cool to see my associated virtual hard disk (VHD) be linked to a network path.

> Just a tip: For POC setup, make sure you have solid name resolution going on (which often gets overlooked in labs), or alternatively, use IP addresses.

I decided to see what I could do with this share, and without knowing, stumbled upon an improvement to Live Migration. In Windows Server 2012, you can seamlessly migrate a VM hosted on an SMB file share (This needs to be SMB 3—currently Windows Server 2012 only) to any other host in the same domain (given share permissions). I chose to move my machine to another host of mine, and before I was able to Alt-Tab to the documentation and back, my VM had already moved. What I forgot about at the time of migration was that I never did any prerequisite storage configuration on any of the host machines, which made the whole experience much more exciting. It just worked. I couldn't wait to couple this with the other optimization technologies built in to the operating system (de-duplication and compression) for some real gains.

Then, my engineering mind went to the next obviously logical step: "Okay, how can I break this thing?" The demos I had seen on this had shown Live Migration with workloads such as pings and file copies. That just didn't do it for me . . . I wanted my VM to host streaming video. With my setup in place, I streamed not one, but two video files to different clients on my network and monitored them. One stream was a simple AVI file hosted on a file share. The other was a high-definition video file hosted by a server-side transcoder that was streaming to my laptop. I also had a ping going just for kicks. The CPU had settled around 30 percent on the VM once both videos were going, so I was interested to see what the results would be. Once Live Migration kicked in, I was watching for any blip or interruption to the video files, with no result. The best interruption, almost amusingly, was a dropped ping in my command prompt. Being overly satisfied with my little demo environment, I proceeded to watch the rest of my movie.

To sum up, mobility is the key. There is a huge array of other features that Windows Server 2012 comes to the table with. As you're reading the rest of this book, keep in mind the high-level view of cloud readiness and how all of the features in Windows Server 2012 play towards this common goal.
Ted Archer
Consultant, Virtualization and Core Infrastructure

Live Migration without shared storage

Windows Server 2012 also allows you to live migrate VMs between stand-alone Hyper-V hosts without the use of any shared storage. This scenario is also known as Live Migration Without Infrastructure (or Shared Nothing Live Migration), and the only requirements are that the two hosts must belong to the same Active Directory domain and that they must be using processors from the same manufacturer (all AMD or all Intel, for instance). When Live Migration without infrastructure is performed, the entire VM is moved from the first host to the second with no perceived downtime. The process basically works like this (see Figure 2-7):

1. The Virtual Machine Management Service (VMMS; Vmms.exe) on the first host (where the VM originally resides) negotiates and establishes a Live Migration connection with the VMMS on the second host.

2. A storage migration is performed, which creates a mirror on the second host of the VM's VHD file on the first host.

3. The VM state information is migrated from the first host to the second host.

4. The original VHD file on the first host is then deleted and the Live Migration connection between the hosts is terminated.

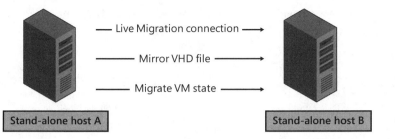

FIGURE 2-7 How Live Migration without shared storage works in Windows Server 2012.

Performing Live Migration

Live Migration can be performed from the GUI or using PowerShell, but first you need to enable Live Migration functionality on your host machines. This can be done by using the Hyper-V console to open the Hyper-V Settings, as shown in Figure 2-8.

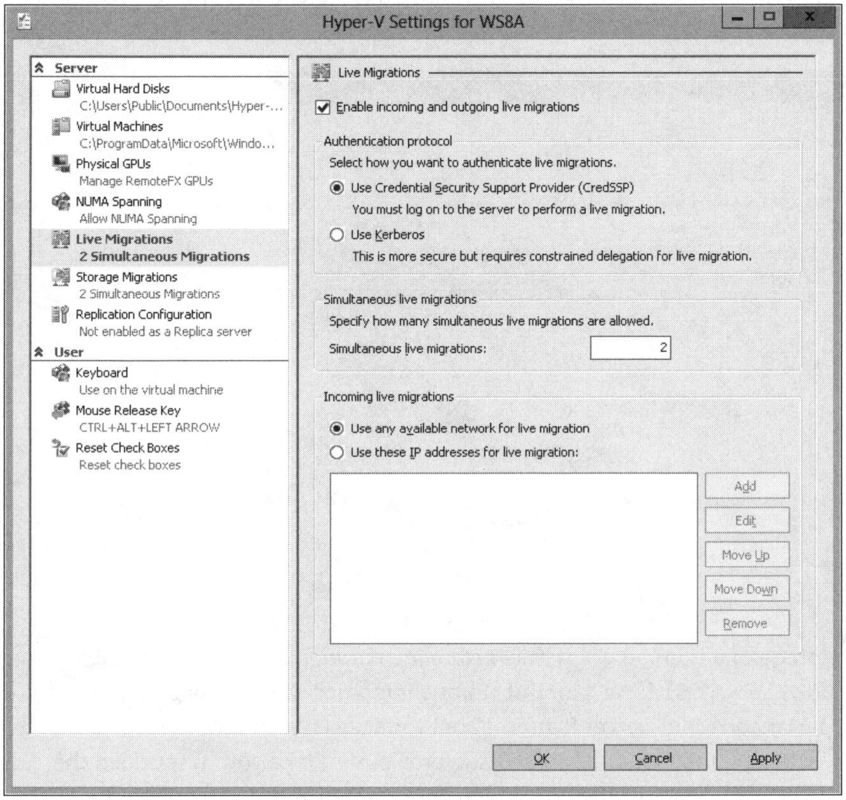

FIGURE 2-8 Enabling Live Migrations in Hyper-V Settings.

The tools that you can use to perform a Live Migration depend on the kind of Live Migration you want to perform. Table 2-3 summarizes the different methods for performing

Live Migrations in failover clustering environments, Live Migrations using SMB 3 shares, and Live Migrations without infrastructure.

TABLE 2-3 Methods for performing different types of Live Migrations

Type of Live Migration	GUI tools	PowerShell cmdlets
VM is on a cluster node and managed by the cluster.	Failover Cluster Manager	Move-ClusterVirtualMachineRole Move-VM
VM is on an SMB 3 share.	Hyper-V Manager	Move-VM
VM is on a stand-alone host.	Hyper-V Manager	Move-VM

Windows Server 2012 gives you great flexibility in how you perform Live Migrations of running VMs, including moving different VM components to different locations on the destination host when performing Live Migrations with or without shared storage. To see this, right-click a running VM in Hyper-V Manager and select Move to start the wizard for moving VMs. The first choice you make is whether to move the VM (and, optionally, its storage) to a different host or to move only the VM's storage, as shown here:

Moving the storage of a running VM is called *storage migration* and is a new capability for Hyper-V in Windows Server 2012. We'll look at storage migration later in Chapter 3, "Highly Available Easy-to-Manage Multi-Server Platform," but for now, let's say that you decide to move the VM by selecting the first option discussed previously. Once you've specified the name of the host you want to move the VM to, you're presented with three options:

- Moving all the VM's files to a single location
- Moving different files of the VM to different locations
- Moving all the VM's files except its VHDs

In each case, the target locations could be a shared folder on a Windows Server 2012 file server or a local directory on the destination host:

If you choose the second option of moving different files of the VM to different locations as shown here, you're presented with additional options for specifying how to move the storage:

Choosing to move the VM's items to different locations lets you specify which items you want to move, including the VHDs, current configuration, snapshot files, and smart paging files for the VM:

Additional wizard pages allow you to specify the exact way in which these items should be moved.

Learn more

For an overview of Live Migration improvements in Windows Server 2012, see the topic "Virtual Machine Live Migration Technical Preview" in the TechNet Library at *http://technet.microsoft.com/en-us/library/hh831435.aspx.*

Enhanced quality of service

In the section titled "Hyper-V extensible switch," earlier in this chapter, we looked at the new bandwidth management capabilities found in Hyper-V, which allows for guaranteeing a minimum amount of bandwidth and/or enforcing a maximum amount of bandwidth for each VM running on a host. This is just one example, however, of the powerful new bandwidth management capabilities built into Windows Server 2012. The term *quality of service (QoS)* refers to technologies used for managing network traffic in ways that can meet SLAs and/or enhance user experiences in a cost-effective manner. For example, by using QoS to prioritize different types of network traffic, you can ensure that mission-critical applications and services are delivered according to SLAs and to optimize user productivity.

As we've previously seen in the earlier section, Hyper-V in Windows Server 2012 lets you specify upper and lower bounds for network bandwidth used by VMs. This is an example of software QoS at work where packet scheduling is implemented by the operating system. But Windows Server 2012 also supports implementing QoS through the use of network adapter hardware that use Data Center Bridging (DCB), a technology that provides performance guarantees for different types of network traffic. DCB is typically found in 10 GbE network adapters and certain kinds of switching fabrics.

The enhanced QoS capabilities included in Windows Server 2012 are particularly useful in shared cloud environments, where the cloud provider wants to ensure that each customer (or business unit for shared private clouds) is able to access the computing, storage, and network resources they need and have paid for or been guaranteed. Customers (and departments of large enterprises) need predictable performance from applications and services they access from the cloud, and the enhanced QoS capabilities in Windows Server 2012 can help ensure this.

But these enhanced QoS capabilities also can provide benefits to the cloud provider. Previously, to ensure that all customers accessing a shared cloud have enough computing, storage, and network resources to meet their needs, cloud providers often overprovisioned VMs on the hosts in their datacenter by running fewer VMs on more hosts, plus extra storage and network resources to ensure that each customer has enough. For example, the cloud provider might use separate networks for application, management, storage, and Live Migration traffic to ensure that each type of workload can achieve the required level of performance. But building and managing multiple physical networks like this can be expensive, and the provider may have to pass the cost on to the customer to ensure profitability.

With the enhanced QoS capabilities in Windows Server 2012, however, cloud providers can ensure that SLAs are met while using their physical host, storage, and network resources more efficiently, which means cost savings from needing fewer hosts, less storage, and a simpler network infrastructure. For example, instead of using multiple overlapping 1 GbE networks for different kinds of traffic, the provider can use a single 10 GbE network backbone (or two for high availability) with each type of traffic carried on it being prioritized through the use of QoS policies.

From the perspective of enterprises wanting to build private clouds and hosting providers wanting to build public clouds, QoS allows replacing multiple physical networks with a single converged network carrying multiple types of traffic with each traffic type guaranteed a minimum amount of bandwidth and limited to a maximum amount of bandwidth. Implementing a QoS solution thus can save enterprises and hosting providers money in two ways: less network hardware is needed and high-end network hardware such as 10 GbE network adapters and switches can be used more efficiently. Note, however, that the converged fabric still needs to be carved up into Management and Production networks for security reasons.

The bottom line is that the old approach of overprovisioning the network infrastructure for your datacenter is inefficient from a cost point of view and now can be superseded by using the new QoS capabilities in Windows Server 2012. Instead of using multiple physical network fabrics like 1 GbE, iSCSI, and Fibre Channel to carry the different kinds of traffic in your multi-tenant datacenter, QoS and other enhancements in Windows Server 2012 now make it possible to use a single converged 10 GbE fabric within your datacenter.

Implementing QoS

There are a number of different ways of implementing software-based control of network traffic in Windows Server 2012. For example:

- You can configure Hyper-V QoS as described previously by enabling bandwidth management in the settings of your VMs to guarantee a minimum amount of bandwidth and/or enforcing a maximum amount of bandwidth for each VM.

- You can use Group Policy to implement policy-based QoS by tagging packets with an 802.1p value to prioritize different kinds of network traffic.

- You can use PowerShell or WMI to enforce minimum and maximum bandwidth and 802.1p or Differentiated Services Code Point (DSCP) marking on filtered packets.

There are additional ways of implementing QoS as well. The method(s) you choose will depend upon the network infrastructure you have and the goals that you are trying to achieve. See the "Learn more" section for more information about QoS solutions for Windows Server 2012.

In terms of which QoS functionality to use in a given scenario, the best practice is to configure Hyper-V QoS for VMs and then create QoS policies when you need to tag traffic for end-to-end QoS across the network.

QoS and the cloud

If you are a hosting provider or a large enterprise that wants to deploy a shared private cloud that provides "servers for rent" to customers or business units, there are several ways that you can configure Hyper-V QoS to assign a minimum bandwidth for each customer or business unit that access applications and services from your cloud:

- **Absolute minimum bandwidth**   In this scenario, you could set different service tiers such as bronze for 100 Mbps access, silver for 200 Mbps access, and gold for 500 Mbps access. Then you can assign the appropriate minimum bandwidth level for customers based on the level of their subscription.

- **Relative minimum bandwidth**   In this scenario, you could assign different weights to different customer workloads such as a weight of 1 for normal priority workloads, 2 for high-priority workloads, and 5 for critical-priority workloads. Then you could assign a minimum bandwidth to each customer based on their workload weight divided by the total weight of all customers accessing your cloud.

Note that minimum bandwidth settings configured in Hyper-V QoS are applied only when there is contention for bandwidth on the link to your cloud. If the link is underused, the configured minimum bandwidth settings will have no effect. For example, if you have two customers, one with gold (500 Mbps) access and the other with silver (200 Mbps) access, and the link between the cloud and these customers is underused, the gold customer will not have 500/200 = 2.5 times more bandwidth than the silver customer. Instead, each customer will have as much bandwidth as they can consume.

Absolute minimum bandwidth can be configured using the Hyper-V Settings in Hyper-V Manager, as shown previously in this chapter. Absolute minimum bandwidth also can be configured from PowerShell by using the *Set-VMSwitch* cmdlet. Relative minimum bandwidth can be configured from PowerShell only by using the *Set-VMSwitch* cmdlet.

As far as configuring maximum bandwidth is concerned, the reason for doing this in cloud environments is mainly because wide area network (WAN) links are expensive. So if you are a hosting provider and a customer accesses its "servers in the cloud" via an expensive WAN link, it's a good idea to configure a maximum bandwidth for the customer's workloads to cap throughput for customer connections to their servers in the cloud.

Data Center Bridging (DCB)

Data Center Bridging (DCB) is an IEEE standard that allows for hardware-based bandwidth allocation for specific types of network traffic. The standard is intended for network adapter hardware used in cloud environments so that storage, data, management, and other kinds of traffic all can be carried on the same underlying physical network in a way that guarantees each type of traffic its fair share of bandwidth. DCB thus provides an additional QoS solution that uses hardware-based control of network traffic, as opposed to the software-based solution described previously.

Windows Server 2012 supports DCB, provided that you have both DCB-capable Ethernet network adapters and DCB-capable Ethernet switches on your network.

Learn more

For an overview of QoS improvements in Windows Server 2012, see the topic "Quality of Service (QoS) overview" and its subtopics in the TechNet Library starting at *http://technet.microsoft.com/en-us/library/hh831679.aspx*.

For the syntax of the *Set-VMSwitch* cmdlet, which can be used for configuring both absolute and relative minimum bandwidth, see *http://technet.microsoft.com/en-us/library/hh848515.aspx*.

For a discussion of how converged networks using QoS and other Windows Server 2012 features can benefit your datacenter, see the post titled "Cloud Datacenter Network Architecture in the Windows Server 2012 era" by Yigal Edery on the Private Cloud Architecture Blog on TechNet at *http://blogs.technet.com/b/privatecloud/archive/2012/03/19/cloud-datacenter-network-architecture-in-the-windows-server-8-era.aspx*.

Resource metering

Resource metering is a new feature of Windows Server 2012 designed to make it easier to build solutions for tracking how cloud services are consumed. Such tracking is important in both enterprise and hosting scenarios. For example, if a hosting provider provides cloud-based applications and services to customers, the hosting provider needs a way of tracking how much resources those customers are consuming to bill them for their use of these resources. Similarly, if a large enterprise has deployed a shared private cloud that is accessed by different business units within the organization, the enterprise needs a way of tracking how much cloud resources each business unit is consuming. This information may be needed for internal billing purposes by the organization, or it may be used to help plan how cloud resources are allocated so that each business unit gets its fair share of the resources they need.

Previously, enterprises or hosting providers who deployed shared private or public cloud solutions using Hyper-V virtualization in Windows Server 2008 and Windows Server 2008 R2 had to create their own chargeback solutions from scratch. Such solutions typically were implemented by polling performance counters for processing, memory, storage, and networking. With the new built-in resource metering capabilities in Windows Server 2012, however, these organizations can use PowerShell to collect and report on historical resource usage of the following metrics:

- Average CPU usage by a VM
- Average physical memory usage by a VM
- Minimum physical memory usage by a VM
- Maximum physical memory usage by a VM
- Maximum amount of disk space allocated to a VM
- Total incoming network traffic for a virtual network adapter
- Total outgoing network traffic for a virtual network adapter

In addition, these metrics can be collected in a consistent fashion even when the VMs are moved between hosts using Live Migration or when their storage is moved using storage migration. And for billing of network usage, you can differentiate between billable Internet traffic and non-billable internal datacenter traffic by configuring network metering port ACLs.

Implementing resource metering

As an example, let's use resource metering to measure resource usage for a VM on our Hyper-V host. We'll start by enabling resource metering for the VM SRV-A using the *Enable-VMResourceMetering* cmdlet, and then we'll verify that resource metering has been enabled by piping the output of the *Get-VM* cmdlet into the *Format-List* cmdlet:

Now we can use the *Measure-VM* cmdlet to report resource utilization data on our VM:

You also can create resource pools for reporting usage for different types of resources such as Processor, Ethernet, Memory or VHD. For example, you could create a new resource pool named PoolOne using the *New-VMResourcePool* cmdlet:

```
Administrator: Windows PowerShell                                    _ □ X
PS C:\Users\Administrator> New-VMResourcePool "PoolOne" -ResourcePoolType Processor

ComputerName          : WS8A
Name                  : PoolOne
ResourcePoolType      : Processor
ParentName            : {Primordial}
IsDeleted             : False
ResourceMeteringEnabled : False


PS C:\Users\Administrator> _
```

Then, once you've enabled resource metering on the new pool using the *Enable-VMResourceMetering* cmdlet, you can use the *Measure-VMResourceMetering* cmdlet to report processor utilization for the pool. You also can use the *Reset-VMResourceMetering* cmdlet to reset the collection of resource metering data.

Resource metering data can be collected, retrieved and reported by combining different PowerShell cmdlets together using pipelines. To configure network metering port ACLs for differentiating different kinds of traffic, you can use the *add-VMNetworkAdapterACL* cmdlet.

Learn more

For an overview of resource metering in Windows Server 2012, see the topic "Hyper-V Resource Metering Technical Preview" in the TechNet Library at *http://technet.microsoft.com/en-us/library/hh831661.aspx*.

For a list of PowerShell cmdlets that can be used for managing Hyper-V in Windows Server 2012, see the topic "Hyper-V Cmdlets in Windows PowerShell" in the TechNet Library at *http://technet.microsoft.com/library/hh848559.aspx*.

Increase scalability and performance

Building cloud solutions, whether with private or public clouds, requires investment of time, energy, and money. To ensure best return on your investment, you need to build your solution on a platform that can scale and perform well to meet the changing demands of your business. This means being able to take advantage of cutting-edge hardware that can provide extreme performance while handling the largest possible workloads. It means being able to use resources effectively at every level, while ensuring that SLAs can be met. It means reducing the chances of mistakes occurring when maintenance tasks are performed. And it means being able to monitor performance effectively to ensure computing, storage, and network resources are used with maximum efficiency.

Windows Server 2012 delivers a virtualization platform that can achieve the highest levels of performance while delivering extreme scalability that enables new scenarios for migrating massive workloads into the cloud. This section examines some new features in Hyper-V and in the underlying operating system that enable such increased scalability and performance.

Expanded processor and memory support

Hyper-V in Windows Server 2008 R2 has been embraced by many organizations as a way of making more efficient use of physical server hardware through virtualization and consolidating server workloads. But limitations in the number of logical processors supported on the host and for VMs, together with limitations of how much physical memory can be supported on the host and assigned to VMs, has meant that Windows Server 2008 R2 lacked sufficient scalability for certain types of mission-critical business applications. For example, large database applications often require large amounts of memory and many logical processors when used to implement business solutions involving online transaction processing (OLTP) or online transaction analysis (OLTA). Until now, the idea of moving such applications into the cloud has been mostly a dream.

Windows Server 2012 changes all this in the following ways:

- Through its increased processor and memory support on the virtualization host by enabling the use of up to 160 logical processors and 2 TB of physical memory per host system
- Through its increased virtual processor and memory support for VMs by enabling the use of up to 32 virtual processors and 1 TB of memory per VM

Increased host processor and memory support

The advent of Windows Server 2012 brings the expansion of processor and memory support in Windows Server 2012. In Windows Server 2008 R2, the host system had limitations of the amount of maximum logical processors (cores, Hyper-Threading, individual CPUs) and memory available for use between the host and the VM. To illustrate this point, note the following:

Windows Server 2008 R2 SP1 had support for up to:

- 64 logical processors per host
- 1 TB of memory per host

- 4 virtual processors per VM

- 64 GB of memory per VM

Windows Server 2012 now has support for up to:

- 160 logical processors per host

- 2 TB of memory per host

- 32 virtual processors per VM

- 1 TB of memory per VM

Please keep in mind that this is largely dependent on the configuration of your hardware and the support of the guest operating system and integrated services that are provided for the VM. The expansion of available processor and memory allocations would allow for your administrators to allocate VM resources as needed. Since many enterprise scale applications continue to consume additional resources to feed the needs of the organization, Microsoft has taken a tone to assist with this demand by increasing this memory and processor support in Windows Server 2012.

One of the points brought to our attention in Windows Server 2008 R2 Hyper-V was the limitation of the hardware portrayal to the VM. With a large number of IT organizations seeking to consolidate their server farms to a handful of servers and virtualize many large infrastructure applications such as Microsoft SQL Server and Microsoft Exchange Server, we decided to move toward larger scalability for these VMs in Windows Server 2012. With Windows Server 2012, the amount of virtual processors that you can have on a SQL Server 2008 virtual machine can go to a max total of 32 virtual CPUs. This is a large increase from the 4 in Windows Server 2008 R2.

Additional RAM is another point that our customers had requested be available to their virtual machines. With hardware able to run multiple terabytes of RAM and physical systems running 32, 64, or 128 GB of RAM, the ability to provide more RAM to the VM became needed as newer, advanced applications took advantage of the larger RAM available. In Windows Server 2012, we move from 64 GB of RAM limitation to 1 TB per VM. This gives the organization the capacity to go to larger memory sizes if the hardware allocation allows.

Patrick Catuncan

Support Escalation Engineer, High Availability, Platforms Core

Virtual NUMA

In addition to its expanded processor and memory support on hosts and for VMs, Hyper-V in Windows Server 2012 also expands support for Non-Uniform Memory Access (NUMA) from the host into the VM. NUMA allows the use of memory by processors to be optimized based on the location of the memory with respect to the processor. High-performance applications like

Microsoft SQL Server have built-in optimizations that can take advantage of the NUMA topology of a system to improve how processor threads are scheduled and memory is allocated.

In previous versions of Hyper-V, VMs were not NUMA-aware, which meant that when applications like SQL Server were run in VMs, these applications were unable to take advantage of such optimizations. Because NUMA was not used in previous versions, it was possible for a VM's RAM to span NUMA nodes and access non-local memory. There is a performance impact when using non-local memory due to the fact that another memory controller (CPU) has to be contacted.

But with VMs now being NUMA-aware in Windows Server 2012, the performance of applications like SQL Server can be significantly better. Note, however, that NUMA support in VMs works in Hyper-V in Windows Server 2012 only when Dynamic Memory has not been configured on the host.

How it works

Virtual NUMA presents a NUMA topology within a VM so that the guest operating system and applications can make intelligent decisions about thread and memory allocation that are reflected in the physical NUMA topology of the host. For example, Figure 2-9 shows a NUMA-capable four-socket host machine with four physical NUMA nodes labeled 1 through 4. Two VMs are running on this host, and two virtual NUMA nodes are presented within each VM, and these virtual NUMA nodes align with physical NUMA nodes on the host based on policy. The result is that NUMA-aware applications like SQL Server installed on the guest operating system of one of these VMs would be able to allocate its thread and memory resources as if it was running directly upon a physical server that had two NUMA nodes.

Virtual NUMA and failover clustering

Virtual NUMA support also extends into high-availability solutions built using failover clustering in Windows Server 2012. This enables the failover cluster to place VMs more appropriately by evaluating the NUMA configuration of a node before moving a VM to the node to ensure the node is able to support the workload of the VM. This NUMA-awareness for VMs in failover clustering environments helps reduce the number of failover attempts which results in increased uptime for your VMs. See Chapter 3 for more information concerning failover clustering enhancements in Windows Server 2012.

Learn more

For an overview of expanded processor and memory support for both hosts and VMs in Windows Server 2012, see the topic "Hyper-V Support for Scaling Up and Scaling Out Technical Preview" in the TechNet Library at *http://technet.microsoft.com/en-us/library/ hh831389.aspx*.

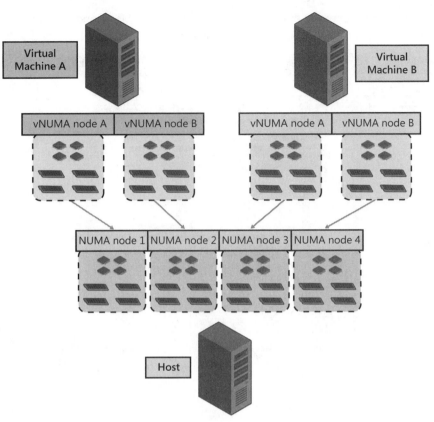

FIGURE 2-9 Example of virtual NUMA at work.

Network adapter hardware acceleration

Besides the increased processor and memory support available for both hosts and VMs, Windows Server 2012 also supports various hardware acceleration features of high-end network adapter hardware to ensure maximum scalability and performance in cloud scenarios. As Figure 2-10 shows, most of these features can be enabled in the Hyper-V Settings of Hyper-V Manager, provided that your network adapter hardware supports these functionalities.

Virtual Machine Queue (VMQ)

Virtual Machine Queue (VMQ) was first available for the Hyper-V role in Windows Server 2008 R2 for host machines that had VMQ-capable network adapter hardware. VMQ employs hardware packet filtering to deliver packets from an external VM network directly to VMs using Direct Memory Access (DMA) transfers. This helps reduce the overhead of routing packets from the host to the VM, which helps improve the performance of the host operating system by distributing the processing of network traffic for multiple VMs among multiple processors. Previously, all network traffic was handled by a single processor.

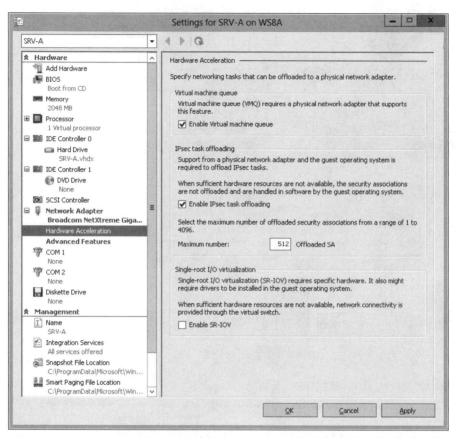

FIGURE 2-10 Enabling use of the hardware acceleration capabilities of high-end network adapter hardware on Hyper-V hosts.

NDIS 6.30 in Windows Server 2012 includes some changes and enhancements in how VMQ is implemented. For example, splitting network data into separate look-ahead buffers is no longer supported.

Although in Windows Server 2008 R2 you had to use System Center Virtual Machine Manager to enable VMQ for a VM on a Hyper-V host, beginning with Windows Server 2012, you can enable VMQ directly from within the VM's settings exposed through Hyper-V Manager, as discussed previously.

IPsec task offload

Internet Protocol Security (IPsec) task offload was first available for servers running Windows Server 2008 that had network adapters that supported this functionality. IPsec task offload works by reducing the load on the system's processors by performing the computationally intensive job of IPsec encryption/decryption using a dedicated processor on the network adapter. The result can be a dramatically better use of the available bandwidth for an IPsec-enabled computer.

Beginning with Windows Server 2012, you can enable IPsec task offload directly from within the VM's settings exposed through Hyper-V Manager, as detailed previously.

Single-root I/O virtualization

Single root I/O virtualization (SR-IOV) is an extension to the PCI Express (PCIe) specification, which enables a device such as a network adapter to divide access to its resources among various PCIe hardware functions. As implemented in the Hyper-V role of Windows Server 2012, SR-IOV enables network traffic to bypass the software switch layer of the Hyper-V virtualization stack to reduce the I/O overhead in this layer. By assigning SR-IOV capable devices directly to a VM, the network performance of the VM can be nearly as good as that of a physical machine. In addition, the processing overhead on the host is reduced.

Beginning with Windows Server 2012, you can enable SR-IOV directly from within the VM's settings exposed through Hyper-V Manager, as shown in Figure 2-11. Before you can do this, however, the virtual switch that the VM uses must have SR-IOV enabled on it, and you also may need to install additional network drivers in the guest operating system of the VM. Note that you can enable SR-IOV on a virtual switch only when you create the switch using the Virtual Switch Manager of Hyper-V Manager or by using the *New-VMSwitch* cmdlet when using PowerShell.

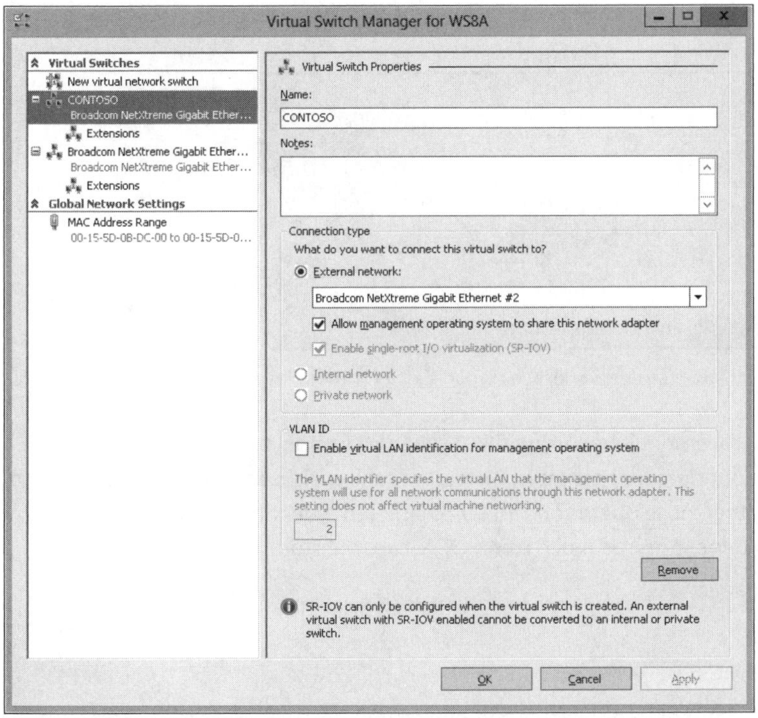

FIGURE 2-11 SR-IOV must be configured on the virtual switch before it can be configured for the VM.

Learn more

For more information about SR-IOV in Windows Server 2012, see the topic "Overview of Single Root I/O Virtualization (SR-IOV)" in the Windows Hardware Development Center on MSDN at *http://msdn.microsoft.com/en-us/library/windows/hardware/hh440148(v=vs.85).aspx*.

Offloaded Data Transfer (ODX)

Another performance and scalability improvement in Windows Server 2012 revolves around storage, in particular when storing VMs on storage arrays. Offloaded Data Transfer (ODX) is a feature of high-end storage arrays that uses a token-based mechanism to read and write data within and between such arrays. Using ODX, a small token is copied between the source and destination servers instead of routing data through the host (see Figure 2-12). So when you migrate a VM within or between storage arrays that support ODX, the only thing copied through the servers is the token representing the VM file, not the underlying data in the file.

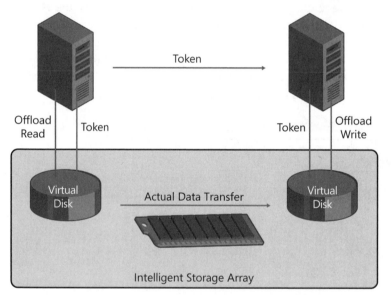

FIGURE 2-12 How offloaded data transfer works in a Hyper-V environment.

The performance improvement when using ODX-capable storage arrays in cloud environments can be astounding. For example, instead of taking about three minutes to create a new 10 GB fixed VHD, the entire operation can be completed in less than a second! Other VM operations that can benefit just as much using ODX-capable storage hardware include:

- Expansion of dynamic VHDs
- Merging of VHDs
- Live Storage Migration

ODX also can provide benefit in nonvirtualized environments, such as when transferring large database files or video files between servers.

Learn more

For more information about ODX support in Windows Server 2012, see the article titled "Rapid and Efficient Data Movement Using Intelligent Storage Arrays Technical Preview" in the TechNet Library at *http://technet.microsoft.com/en-us/library/hh831628.aspx*.

Support for 4 KB sector disks

Windows Server 2012 now includes support for large-sector disks. These disks represent the newest trend in the storage industry whereby the old 512-byte sector format is being replaced by the new 4,096-byte (4 KB) format to meet demand for increased disk capacity. Hyper-V in Windows Server 2012 now supports hosting VHD files on disks that have either the native 4-KB format or the transitional 512-byte emulation (512e) mode.

4K sector support and the real user

With the introduction of Advanced Format storage devices, vendors found the way to increase effectiveness of error correction schemas for large hard drives. The change of format, however, brought certain difficulties.

All versions of Windows up to Windows 7 SP1 support native 512-byte sector read /writes, and via a special emulation method called 512e, can work with bigger sector drives, hiding the physical sector size over logically presented 512-byte values.

However, some file formats are hard-coded to work with physical sectors and won't accept values other than 512 bytes. VHD specification version 1.0 is a sample of such a format. You can connect a brand-new 4 TB disk to Windows 7 or Windows Server 2008 R2, and you can put your media or data on it. You'll fail to create a VHD for Hyper-V or iSCSI. Even if you copy VHD to the drive, you would fail to use it. Windows 8 and Windows Server 2012 bring native support for the Advanced format, as well as the updated VHD and VHDX specifications.

Finally, you can always check the physical sector size via fsutil fsinfo ntfsinfo <drive letter>.

Alex A. Kibkalo
Architect, Microsoft MEA HQ

Learn more

For more information about 4K sector support in Windows Server 2012, see the article titled "Hyper-V Support for Large Sector Disks Technical Preview" in the TechNet Library at *http://technet.microsoft.com/en-us/library/hh831459.aspx*.

Dynamic Memory improvements

Dynamic Memory was introduced for Hyper-V in Windows Server 2008 R2 as a way of enabling virtualization hosts to make more effective use of physical memory allocated to VMs running on the host. Dynamic Memory works by adjusting the amount of memory available to the VM in real time. These adjustments in memory allocation are based on how much memory the VM needs and on how Dynamic Memory has been configured on the VM.

Dynamic Memory provides important scalability and performance benefits, especially for virtual desktop infrastructure (VDI) environments, where at any given time, a subset of the VMs running on the host tend either to be idle or to have a relatively low load. By using Dynamic Memory in such scenarios, you can consolidate greater numbers of VM on your Hyper-V hosts. The result is that you'll need fewer hosts for provisioning virtual desktops to your user population, which means you won't need to procure as much high-end server hardware. In other words, Dynamic Memory can help you save money.

Configuring Dynamic Memory

Dynamic Memory is enabled on a per-VM basis. You can enable and configure Dynamic Memory in the Memory section of the VM's settings in Hyper-V Manager, as shown in Figure 2-13 below. You also can enable and configure Dynamic Memory using PowerShell by using the *Set-VM* cmdlet, which can be used to configure the various properties of a VM. Note that you can enable or disable Dynamic Memory only when the VM is in a stopped state.

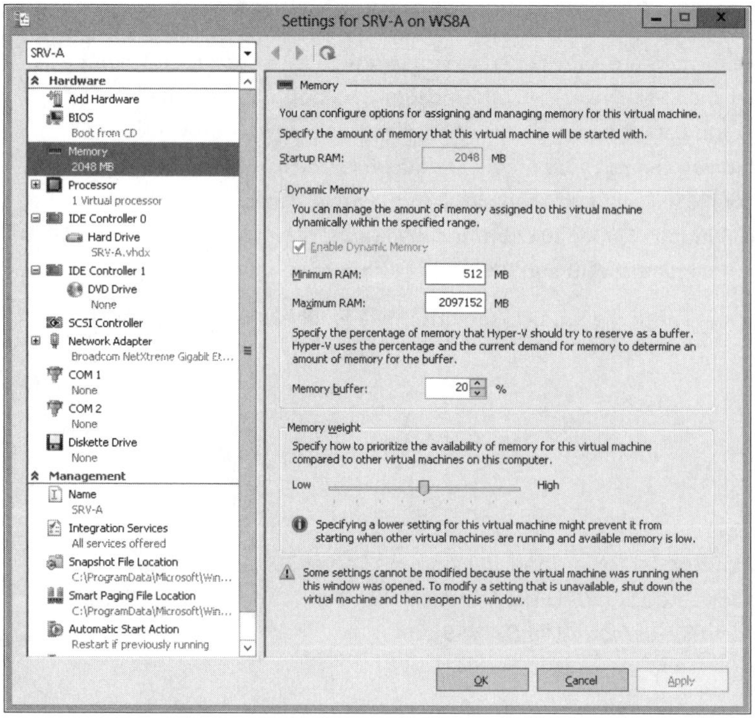

FIGURE 2-13 Configuring Dynamic Memory for a VM.

Configuration options for Dynamic Memory for VMs on Hyper-V hosts running Windows Server 2008 R2 were as follows:

- **Startup RAM**   The amount of memory needed for starting the VM
- **Maximum RAM**   The maximum amount of memory that the VM can use
- **Memory buffer**   An amount of memory (as a percentage of the amount that the VM actually needs to perform its workload) that can be allocated to the VM when there is sufficient memory available on the host
- **Memory weight**   A parameter that determines how available memory on the host is allocated among the different VMs running on the host

Configuration options for Dynamic Memory for VMs on Hyper-V hosts running Windows Server 2012 have been enhanced in several ways:

A new configuration setting called *Minimum Memory* allows you to specify the minimum amount of memory that the VM can use when it is running. The reason for introducing this new setting is because Windows generally needs more memory when starting than it does when idle and running. As a result of this change, you now can specify sufficient startup memory to enable the VM to start quickly and then a lesser amount of memory (the minimum memory) for when the VM is running. That way, a VM can get some extra memory so it can start properly, and then once it's started, Windows reclaims the unneeded memory so other VMs on the host can use the reclaimed memory if needed.

Another change in the way that Dynamic Memory can be configured in Windows Server 2012 is that now you can modify the maximum and minimum memory settings while the VM is running. In Windows Server 2008 R2, the maximum memory setting could be modified only when the VM was in a stopped state. This change gives you a new way of quickly provisioning more memory to a critical VM when needed.

Smart Paging

Specifying a minimum memory for a VM can enable Windows to reclaim some unneeded memory once the VM has started. Then this reclaimed memory can be reallocated towards other VMs on the host. But this raises a question: What if you start as many VMs as you can on a host, allow Windows to reclaim unneeded memory once the VMs are running, then start more VMs using the reclaimed memory, then again allow Windows to reclaim any additional unneeded memory, then try to start more VMs on the host . . . and so on? Eventually, you reach the point where almost all the host's memory is in use and you're unable to start any more VMs. But then you find that one of your running VMs needs to be restarted immediately (for example, to apply a software update). So you try and restart the VM, and it shuts down successfully but it won't start again. Why not? Because there's not enough free memory on the host to meet the Startup RAM criterion for that VM.

To prevent this kind of scenario from happening while enabling Dynamic Memory to work its scalability magic, Hyper-V in Windows Server 2012 introduces a new feature called Smart Paging (see Figure 2-14). Smart Paging allows a VM that's being restarted to use disk resources temporarily on the host as a source for any additional memory needed to restart the VM successfully. Then, once the VM has started successfully and its memory requirements lessen, Smart Paging releases the previously used disk resources because of the performance hit that such use can create.

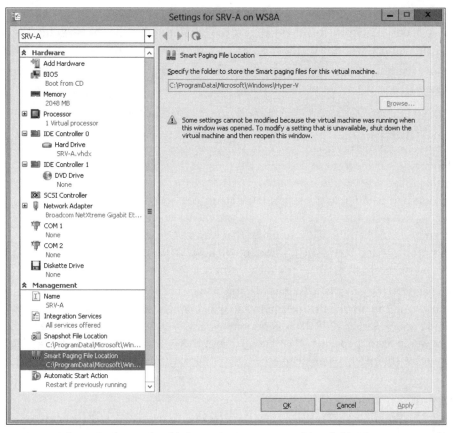

FIGURE 2-14 Smart Paging works with Dynamic Memory to enable reliable VM restart operations.

Smart Paging is used only when a VM is restarted and there is no free physical memory on the host and no memory can be reclaimed from other running VMs. Smart Paging is not used if you simply try and start a VM that's in a stopped state, or if a VM is failing over in a cluster.

Viewing Dynamic Memory at work

Sometimes small changes make a big difference in the usability of a user interface feature. In the Hyper-V Manager of Windows Server 2008 R2, you could monitor in real time how much physical memory was allocated to each VM that had Dynamic Memory enabled on it. This real-time allocation amount is called the *assigned memory*. In addition, you could monitor the memory demand (the total committed memory) and the memory status (whether the current amount of memory assigned to the VM as a buffer is sufficient) for the VM. The problem, though, was that these real-time measurements were displayed as columns in the Virtual Machines pane of Hyper-V Manager, which meant that you had to scroll horizontally to see them.

Hyper-V in Windows Server 2012 adds a series of tabs to the bottom central pane, and by selecting the Memory pane, you can view the assigned memory, memory demand, and memory status for the selected VM quickly (see Figure 2-15).

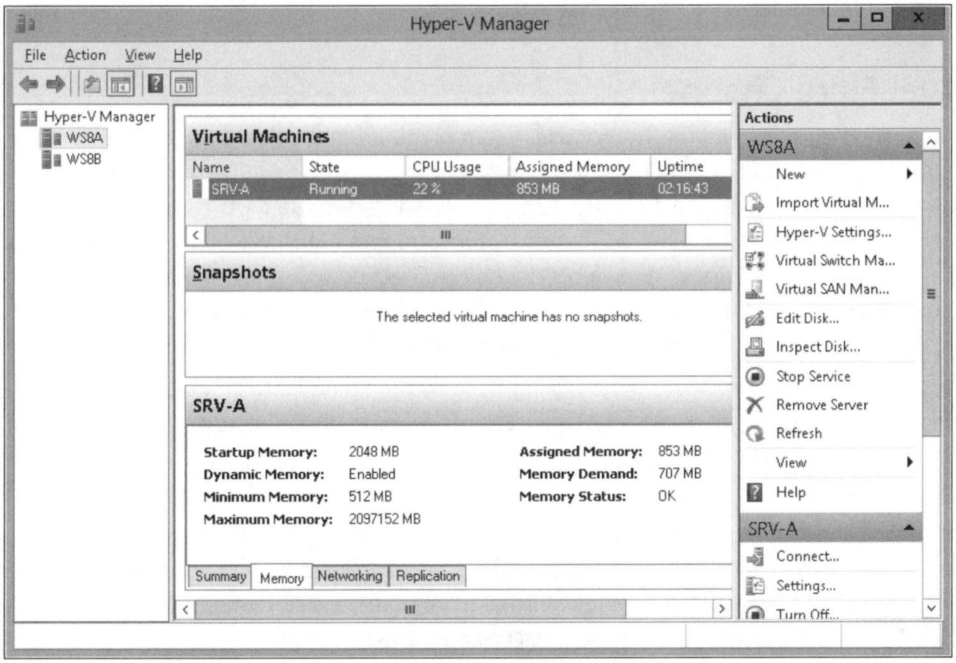

FIGURE 2-15 Using Hyper-V Manager to display real-time changes in memory usage by a VM with Dynamic Memory enabled.

You also can use the *Get-VM* cmdlet in PowerShell to display these same real-time measurements, as shown in Figure 2-16.

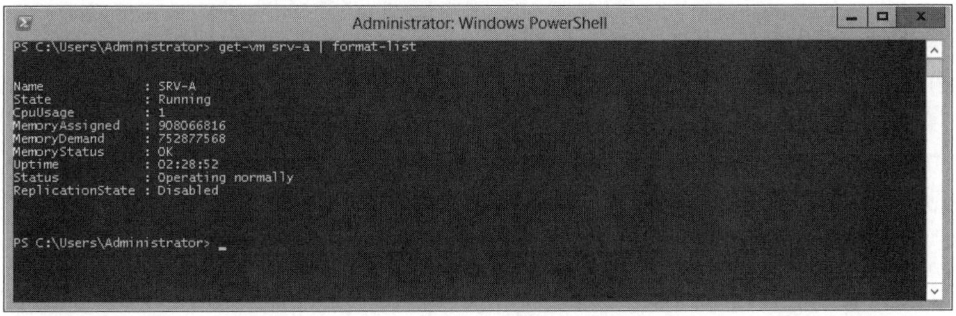

FIGURE 2-16 Using PowerShell to display real-time changes in memory usage by a VM with Dynamic Memory enabled.

Learn more

For more information about Dynamic Memory in Windows Server 2012, see the article titled "Hyper-V Dynamic Memory Technical Preview" in the TechNet Library at *http://technet.microsoft.com/en-us/library/hh831766.aspx.*

For a list of PowerShell cmdlets that can be used for managing Hyper-V in Windows Server 2012, see the topic "Hyper-V Cmdlets in Windows PowerShell" in the TechNet Library at *http://technet.microsoft.com/library/hh848559.aspx.*

Virtual Fibre Channel

Existing technologies often present obstacles when considering the migration of your server workloads into the cloud. An example of this might be if you have an AlwaysOn failover cluster instance running on SQL Server 2012 that's configured to use a Fibre Channel SAN for high performance. You'd like to migrate this workload into the cloud, but Hyper-V in Windows Server 2008 R2 does not support directly connecting to Fibre Channel from within VMs. As a result, you've postponed performing such a migration because you want to protect your existing investment in expensive Fibre Channel technology.

Virtual Fibre Channel removes this blocking issue by providing Fibre Channel ports within the guest operating system of VMs on Hyper-V hosts running Windows Server 2012. This now allows a server application like SQL Server running within the guest operation system of a VM to connect directly to LUNs on a Fibre Channel SAN.

Implementing this kind of solution requires that the drivers for your HBAs support Virtual Fibre Channel. Some HBAs from Brocade and QLogic already include such updated drivers, and more vendors are expected to follow. Virtual Fibre Channel also requires that you connect only to LUNs, and you can't use a LUN as boot media for your VMs.

Virtual Fibre Channel also provides the benefits of allowing you to use any advanced storage functionality of your existing SAN directly from your VMs. You can even use it to cluster guest operating systems over Fibre Channel to provide high availability for VMs. See Chapter 3 for more information about high-availability solutions in Windows Server 2012.

Note that VMs must use Windows Server 2008, Windows Server 2008 R2, or Windows Server 2012 as the guest operating system if they are configured with a virtual Fibre Channel adapter. For more information, see the topic "Hyper-V Virtual Fibre Channel Overview," at *http://technet.microsoft.com/en-us/library/hh831413.aspx.*

Learn more

For more information about Virtual Fibre Channel in Windows Server 2012, see the article titled "Hyper-V Virtual Fibre Channel Technical Preview" in the TechNet Library at *http://technet.microsoft.com/en-us/library/hh831413.aspx.*

SMB 3

Windows Server 2012 introduces SMB 3, version 3 of the Server Message Block (SMB) protocol to provide powerful new features for continuously available file servers. SMB is a network file sharing protocol that allows applications to read and write to files and to request services from services over a network. (Note that some documentation on TechNet and MSDN still refer to this version as SMB 3.)

The improvements in SMB 3 are designed to provide increased performance, reliability, and availability in scenarios where data is stored on file shares. Some of the new features and enhancements in SMB 3 include:

- **SMB Direct** Enables using network adapters capable of Remote Direct Memory Access (RDMA) such as iWARP, Infiniband, or RoCE (RDMA over Converged Ethernet) that can function at full speed and low latency with very little processor overhead on the host. When such adapters are used on Hyper-V hosts, you can store VM files on a remote file server and achieve performance similar to if the files were stored locally on the host.

    SMB Direct makes possible a new class of file servers for enterprise environments, and the new File Server role in Windows Server 2012 demonstrates these capabilities in full. Such file servers experience minimal processor utilization for file storage processing and the ability to use high-speed RDMA-capable NICs including iWARP, InfiniBand, and RoCE. They can provide remote storage solutions equivalent in performance to Fibre Channel, but at a lower cost. They can use converged network fabrics in datacenters and are easy to provision, manage, and migrate.

- **SMB Directory Leasing** Reduces round-trips from client to server because metadata is retrieved from a longer living directory cache. Cache coherency is maintained as clients are notified when directory information changes on the server. The result of using SMB Directory Leasing can be improved application response times, especially in in branch office scenarios.

- **SMB Encryption** Enables end-to-end encryption of SMB data to protect network traffic from eavesdropping when travelling over untrusted networks. SMB Encryption can be configured either on a per-share basis or for the entire file server. It adds no cost overhead and removes the need for configuring IPsec and using specialized encryption hardware and WAN accelerators.

- **SMB Multichannel** Allows aggregation of network bandwidth and network fault tolerance when multiple paths become available between the SMB client and the SMB server. The benefit of this that it allows server applications to take full advantage of all available network bandwidth. The result is that your server applications become more resilient to network failure.

    SMB Multichannel configures itself automatically by detecting and using multiple network paths when they become available. It can use NIC teaming failover but doesn't require such capability to work. Possible scenarios can include:

- Single NIC, but using Receive-Side Scaling (RSS) enables more processors to process the network traffic
- Multiple NICs with NIC Teaming, which allows SMB to use a single IP address per team
- Multiple NICs without NIC Teaming, where each NIC must have a unique IP address and is required for RDMA-capable NICs

- **SMB Scale Out** Allows you to create file shares that provide simultaneous access to data files with direct I/O through all the nodes in your file server cluster. The result is improved use of network bandwidth and load balancing of the file server clients, and also optimization of performance for server applications. SMB Scale Out requires using CSV version 2, which is included in Windows Server 2012, and lets you seamlessly increase available bandwidth by adding cluster nodes.

- **SMB Transparent Failover** Allows administrators to perform hardware or software maintenance of nodes in a clustered file server without interruption to server applications storing their data on file shares. If a hardware or software failure happens on a cluster node, SMB clients will reconnect transparently to another cluster node with no interruption for server applications storing data on these shares.

  SMB Transparent Failover supports both planned failovers (such as maintenance operations) and unplanned failovers (for example, due to hardware failure). Implementing this feature requires the use of failover clustering, that both the server running the application and the file server are running Windows Server 2012, and that the file shares on the file server have been shared for continuous availability.

The implementation of SMB 3 in Windows Server 2012 also includes new SMB performance counters that can provide detailed, per-share information about throughput, latency, and I/O per second (IOPS). These counters are designed for server applications like Hyper-V and SQL Server, which can store files on remote file shares to enable administrators to analyze the performance of the file shares where server application data is stored.

Benefits for Hyper-V

These new capabilities of SMB 3 mean that Hyper-V hosts can store VM files, including the configuration, VHD, and snapshots in file shares on Windows Server 2012 file servers. You can implement this kind of solution for stand-alone Hyper-V servers. You also can implement it for clustered Hyper-V servers where file storage is used as shared storage for the cluster.

The benefits that enterprises can experience from these scenarios include simplified provisioning, management and migration of VM workloads, increased flexibility, and reduced cost.

SMB and PowerShell

You can view and manage many SMB 3 capabilities by using PowerShell. To see what cmdlets are available for doing this, you can use the *Get-Command* cmdlet, as shown in Figure 2-17.

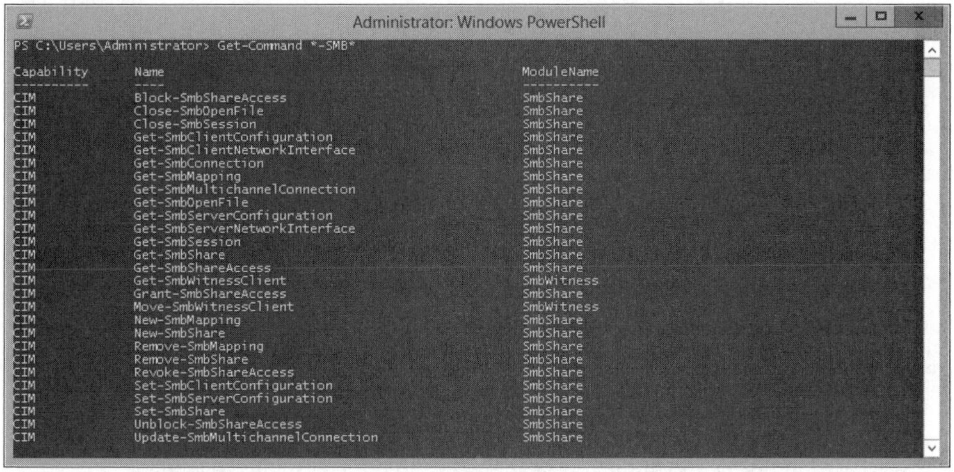

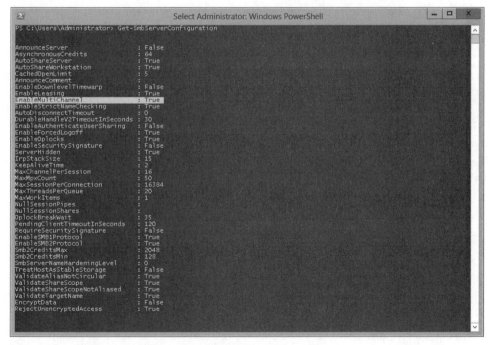

FIGURE 2-17 PowerShell cmdlets for managing SMB features and infrastructure.

For example, Figure 2-18 shows how to use the *Get-SMBServerConfiguration* cmdlet to determine whether SMB Multichannel is enabled on a file server running Windows Server 2012.

FIGURE 2-18 Viewing the configuration settings of the SMB server.

Learn more

For an analysis of the performance capabilities of the new SMB file-sharing protocol over 10 GB Ethernet interfaces, see the blog post titled "SMB 2.2 is now SMB 3.0" on the Windows Server Blog at *http://blogs.technet.com/b/windowsserver/archive/2012/04/19/smb-2-2-is-now-smb-3-0.aspx.*

Windows Server 2012: Enabling the "Storage LAN"

Everyone is familiar with the concept of a SAN. Typically a very expensive disk array, attached to some very expensive fiber channel switches. Then one or more Fibre Channel cables run from the switch to a fairly expensive dual-port HBA.

SANs have long been one of the most expensive and difficult things to manage in the datacenter. Enterprise organizations invest heavily in storage and invest heavily in storage training. Your average Windows administrator is not equipped with the skills required to manipulate and design enterprise storage, yet every server of consequence is typically directly connected to enterprise storage. Configuring HBAs, LUN mapping, and similar tasks is often per-server, manual, and reserved for the select few who have the extra training and experience.

Virtualization improves this, as long as your servers use either iSCSI (which is often regarded as a poor man's SAN), or are self-contained in a VHD. Mapping SAN storage, directly into VMs, is not trivial, quick, or easy.

Windows Server 2012 with the introduction of the continuously available file server, and SMB 3 change this. It allows Windows administrators to disconnect themselves from the traditional SAN and create a new breed of "Storage LAN." Consider this example. In the past, when you deployed a new SQL Server instance, you did one of the following:

- Deploy to a physical host. Install an HBA. Create a SAN LUN. Run the fiber to the server. Map the LUN to the host, and then use the storage for SQL Server.

- Deploy to a VM. Store the VM in a VHD which was stored on, most often a CSV volume, which was on a LUN previously mapped to the host.

- Deploy to a VM. Install an HBA. Create a SAN LUN. Run the fiber to the server. Map the LUN to the host, and then pass the LUN to the VM as a pass-through disk.

Windows Server 2012 changes this by allowing you to replace much of your storage infrastructure with traditional Ethernet. LUNs are replaced with file shares. Here's what this new architecture looks like.

You still have your high-end storage solution; however, instead of running complex storage fabric to every host, you run the storage fabric to a set of high-performance file servers. These file servers present the storage as highly available file shares to be used by any server.

Next, you create an Ethernet segment between your storage file servers and your application servers leveraging technologies such as 10 GB Ethernet (which is standard on most high-end servers), or if you need extremely fast performance (and your storage arrays can even keep up with it), RDMA.

When new servers are brought online, instead of running fiber, provisioning LUNs, and involving your storage administrators, you can simply provision a share or use an existing one. This change allows a Windows administrator to use the skills and tools they already have, and are familiar with, to present highly available, high-performance storage to any application server. You can deploy application workloads such as SQL, and even Hyper-V, which leverage the performance and reliability of enterprise SAN storage without needing to be directly connected to the enterprise SAN fabric.

With technologies such as transparent failover, cluster-aware updating, and storage spaces with thin provisioning, you can now plan for what you need tomorrow, but deploy and manage with what you have today.
Corey Hynes
Architect, holSystems (www.holsystems.com)

Improved VM import

The process used for importing VMs onto Hyper-V hosts has been improved in Windows Server 2012. The goal of these improvements is to help prevent configuration problems from happening that can prevent the import process from completing successfully.

In Hyper-V on Windows Server 2008 R2, when you imported a VM onto a host, the VM and all its files were copied to the host, but they weren't checked for possible configuration problems. However, Hyper-V on Windows Server 2012 now validates the configuration of VM files when they are imported to identify potential problems and, if possible, resolve them.

An additional enhancement to the process of importing VMs in Hyper-V on Windows Server 2012 is that now you can import a VM after manually copying the VM's files to the host. In other words, you don't have to export a VM from one host before you can import it into another host—you can simply copy the files from the first host to the second one and then initiate the import process.

Importing of VMs

Windows Server 2012 has improved the VM import process. This new process helps you resolve configuration problems that would otherwise have prevented you from importing the VM. The Windows Server 2012 improvements to importing a VM also have improved the reliability of importing VMs to other Hyper-V host computers.

The new wizard detects and fixes potential problems, such as hardware or file differences, that might exist when a VM is moved to another host. The import wizard detects and fixes more than 40 types of incompatibilities. This new wizard also creates a temporary copy of the VM configuration file as an added safety step.

With Windows Server 2008 R2 to import a VM to a different host, you first needed to export it. To export the VM, you first needed to turn it off. This caused administrators to schedule downtime prior to exporting the VM. Now, with Windows Server 2012, you can simply copy the VM's files manually to the new host, and then, on the new Windows Server 2012 host, just run through the Import Virtual Machine wizard, point to the newly copied VM, and voila! You have imported it.

In conclusion, the Windows Server 2012 Import wizard is a simpler, better way to import or copy VMs between Hyper-V hosts.

Keith Hill
Support Escalation Engineer, High Availability, Platforms Core

VHDX disk format

VHDX is the new default format for VHDs in Hyper-V in Windows Server 2012. This new format is designed to replace the older VHD format and has advanced capabilities that make it the ideal virtual disk format going forward for virtualized workloads. Some of the features of this new format include the following:

- It supports virtual disks up to 64 TB in size, so you'll be able to use it to virtualize even the largest database workloads and move them into the cloud.
- It aligns to megabyte boundaries to support large sector disks (4 KB sector disks), so you can take advantage of new low-cost commodity storage options.
- It uses large block sizes to provide better performance than the old format could provide.
- It includes a new log to protect from corruption due to power failure, which means the new format has much greater resiliency than the old format.
- You can embed custom user-defined metadata into VHDX files; for example, information about the service pack level of the guest operating system on the VM.

Learn more

For more information about the new VHDX format in Windows Server 2012, see the article titled "Hyper-V Virtual Hard Disk Format Technical Preview" in the TechNet Library at *http://technet.microsoft.com/en-us/library/hh831446.aspx*.

Business continuity for virtualized workloads

No cloud solution would be workable without a viable disaster recovery solution. Virtualized workloads owned by business units in large enterprises or by customers of cloud hosting providers must be backed up regularly to prevent loss of continuity should a disaster occur on the provider's infrastructure. This chapter ends with a look at Hyper-V Replica, a new feature of Hyper-V in Windows Server 2012 that helps ensure that your cloud solutions can be recovered in the event of a disaster.

Hyper-V Replica

While many third-party backup solutions can be used for backing up and recovering VMs running on Hyper-V hosts, the Hyper-V Replica feature in Windows Server 2012 provides an in-box business continuity solution for cloud environments that can efficiently, periodically, and asynchronously replicate VMs over IP-based networks, including slow WAN links and across different types of storage subsystems. The Hyper-V Replica feature does not require any shared storage or expensive storage array hardware, so it represents a low-cost solution for organizations looking to increase the availability of their virtualized workloads and ensure that these workloads can be recovered quickly in the event of a disaster.

Hyper-V, together with Failover Clustering, allows VMs to maintain service availability by moving them between nodes within the datacenter. By contrast, Hyper-V Replica allows VMs to maintain availability across a datacenter where the node hosting the replica is located at a physically separate site. Hyper-V Replica provides host-based replication that allows for failover to a secondary datacenter in the event of a disaster. It's an application-agnostic solution because it operates at a VM level regardless of what guest operating system or applications are installed in the VM. It's a storage-agnostic solution because you can use any combination of SAN, direct attached storage (DAS), or SMB storage for storing your VMs. It also works in both clustered and nonclustered environments, and you can even replicate from a host on a shared cluster to a remote, stand-alone replica host. And it works with Live Migration and Live Storage Migration.

Typical cases for using Hyper-V Replica might include:

- Replicating VMs from head office to branch office or vice versa in large and mid-sized business environments

- Replication between two datacenters owned by a hosting provider to provide disaster recovery services for customers

- Replication from the premises of small and mid-sized businesses to their hosting provider's datacenter

Guidance on configuring the full life cycle of a replicated VM

I've written this particular sidebar because our customers often have not done a deep enough planning for their replica scenario. Essentially, my goal is to remind them that replication one way is easy to set up and great. But once you have recovered a server on your destination, at some point, you may choose to replicate it back to the original location. It is much better to have both ends of replication enabled as replica servers.

When planning your Hyper-V Replica scenario, you should consider the configuration that properly supports the full life cycle of your replicated VM. Take into consideration that both endpoints of your replication relationship should be configured as replica servers. Your replicated VMs from your main office to your branch office is essentially a one-way configuration. If you plan on replicating VMs back to your main office, you need to ensure those Hyper-V servers are configured as replica servers as well.

Consider the step-by-step process you will need to test a replicated VM as part of a recovery effort. By testing a VM prior to failing it over, you can ensure you have chosen the appropriate recovery point. The replica server will first verify that the original VM is not available before allowing a failover copy to be brought online. Once you have recovered all your VMs, you will also need to consider the steps required to bring the services online. In complex environments, you will likely need additional effort to coordinate the order in which you bring VMs and services online. There may be additional Domain Name System (DNS) or firewall changes required to fully return service availability.

Finally, after you have resolved the failure in the Primary datacenter that required you to bring replicated VMs online, you likely will want to replicate your VMs back to the Primary site. It makes sense to configure both endpoints of your replication to be enabled as a replica server as part of their deployment. For example, if your primary site was taken offline by blizzard-related power loss for several days, you may choose to bring online the VM's on your replica server. When your Primary datacenter is back online, you would likely plan to replicate VMs back to it. Of course, you could enable servers as replicas fairly quickly, but proper planning will minimize disaster-related issues and mistakes, especially as you scale out your Hyper-V infrastructure.

Colin Robinson
Program Manager, Enterprise Engineering Center (EEC)

Implementing Hyper-V Replica

Hyper-V Replica can be enabled, configured, and managed from either the GUI or by using PowerShell. Let's briefly look at how to enable replication of a VM by using Hyper-V Manager. Begin by selecting the Replication Configuration section in Hyper-V Settings on the hosts that you plan on replicating VMs to or from. Select the Enable This Computer As A Replica Server check box to enable the host as a replica server and configure the authentication, authorization, and storage settings that control the replication process:

Once you've performed this step on both the primary and replica servers (the primary server hosts the virtualized production workloads, whereas the replica server hosts the replica VMs for the primary server), you then can enable replication on a per-VM basis. To do this, right-click a VM in Hyper-V Manager and select Enable Replication, as shown on the following page.

When the Enable Replication wizard launches, specify the name of the replica server that you want to replicate the selected production VM to:

Specify connection parameters that define the port and authentication method used for performing replication:

Continue through the wizard until you reach the Choose Initial Replication Method page, where you specify how and when the VM first will be copied over to the replica server:

Once you've completed the wizard and clicked Finish, replication will begin. You can view the replication process as it takes place by selecting the Replication tab in the bottom-central pane of Hyper-V Manager:

You also can use the *Measure-VMReplication* cmdlet in PowerShell to view the success or failure of the replication process:

```
                                  Administrator: Windows PowerShell
PS C:\Users\Administrator> Measure-VMReplication

Name  State       Health LRepTime             PReplSize(M) AvgLatency AvgReplSize(M) SuccReplCount
----  -----       ------ --------             ------------ ---------- -------------- -------------
SRV-A Replicating Normal 3/26/2012 9:40:18 PM 0.0039       00:00:40   801.99         11 of 11

PS C:\Users\Administrator>
```

To view all the PowerShell cmdlets for managing the Hyper-V Replica feature, use the *Get-Command* cmdlet, as shown here:

```
                                  Administrator: Windows PowerShell
PS C:\Users\Administrator> Get-Command "*-VMReplication*"

Capability      Name                                    ModuleName
----------      ----                                    ----------
Cmdlet          Get-VMReplication                       Hyper-V
Cmdlet          Get-VMReplicationAuthorizationEntry      Hyper-V
Cmdlet          Get-VMReplicationServer                 Hyper-V
Cmdlet          Measure-VMReplication                   Hyper-V
Cmdlet          New-VMReplicationAuthorizationEntry      Hyper-V
Cmdlet          Remove-VMReplication                    Hyper-V
Cmdlet          Remove-VMReplicationAuthorizationEntry   Hyper-V
Cmdlet          Reset-VMReplicationStatistics           Hyper-V
Cmdlet          Resume-VMReplication                    Hyper-V
Cmdlet          Set-VMReplication                       Hyper-V
Cmdlet          Set-VMReplicationAuthorizationEntry      Hyper-V
Cmdlet          Set-VMReplicationServer                 Hyper-V
Cmdlet          Stop-VMReplication                      Hyper-V
Cmdlet          Suspend-VMReplication                   Hyper-V
```

Guidance on configuring the Hyper-V Replica Broker cluster resource

Customers who have tested Hyper-V Replica in my Enterprise Engineering Center (EEC) lab at Microsoft have often been confused by the following issue. Basically, they successfully install the Hyper-V Replica Broker to the cluster, but they don't find it obvious that they also have to configure the broker. This sidebar describes the necessary steps for that configuration.

After configuring your Hyper-V cluster as a Hyper-V Replica server, you will now have a new cluster resource displayed in your Failover Cluster Manager console. The next step is to configure this new cluster resource. If you look down near the bottom of the Failover Cluster Manager, you will see that your new cluster resource is listed and is Online.

Now we have to configure the Replication settings to be used by the cluster. Within Failover Cluster Manager, highlight the newly created broker, select Resources at the bottom, and choose Replication Settings. These settings will be configured once here, and all nodes of the cluster will share this replication configuration based on what you do here:

The options you configure for the broker (and, in turn, the whole cluster) are exactly like setting up one server. First, select the Enable This Cluster as a Replica Server check box:

The same choices are available for the cluster, such as Authentication And Ports, as well as Authorization And Storage. Make your desired configuration here and click OK.

You are now done with the Host configuration of settings for a Replica cluster.
Colin Robinson
Program Manager, Enterprise Engineering Center (EEC)

Learn more

For more information about Hyper-V Replica, see the article titled "Hyper-V Replica Technical Preview" in the TechNet Library at *http://technet.microsoft.com/en-us/library/hh831716.aspx*.

For more information about Hyper-V Replica scenarios, see the article titled "Maintaining Business Continuity of Virtualized Environments with Hyper-V Replica: Scenario Overview" in the TechNet Library at *http://technet.microsoft.com/en-us/library/hh831783.aspx*.

For a detailed look at how Hyper-V Replica works and how to implement it, see the Understanding and Troubleshooting Guide (UTG) titled "Understand and Troubleshoot Hyper-V Replica in Windows Server '8' Beta," which is available from the Microsoft Download Center at *http://www.microsoft.com/download/en/details.aspx?id=29016*.

For information about another kind of business continuity solution for Windows Server 2012, see the Understanding and Troubleshooting Guide (UTG) titled "Understand and Troubleshoot Microsoft Online Backup Service in Windows Server '8' Beta," which is available from the Microsoft Download Center at *http://www.microsoft.com/download/en/details.aspx?id=29005*.

There's more

In this short book, we can't cover every reason why Windows Server 2012 provides the ideal foundation for building your cloud solutions, and one thing we haven't talked about yet is security. For example, Windows Server 2012 enables Identity Federation using Active Directory Federation Services (AD FS), which provides a common identity framework between on-premises and cloud environments. Using AD FS like this provides easier access to cloud resources and single sign-on (SSO) for both on-premises and cloud-based applications. Windows Server 2012 also includes support for cross-premises connectivity between on-premises servers and "servers in the cloud" hosted by IaaS providers. It does this by providing virtual private network (VPN) site-to-site functionality using the remote access server role.

More security enhancements in Windows Server 2012 can make it easier for you to build your cloud infrastructure, but we need to move on, so let's just end with a sidebar from a couple of our experts at Microsoft.

Embedding security into your private cloud design plan

One of the most common misconceptions seen in the industry today is to think that the private cloud obviates security concerns, and therefore, security isn't a critical design and planning consideration. There are many security challenges specific to cloud computing. These are based on cloud essential characteristics defined by the National Institute of Standards and Technology (NIST). According to the NIST definition of cloud computing, the core characteristics of a cloud are *resource pooling, on-demanding self-service, rapid elasticity, broad network access,* and *measured services.*

In a private cloud environment, there are important security concerns related to each of these essential cloud characteristics, and you need to address those concerns during the design and planning phase. Otherwise, security won't be embedded into the project from a foundational perspective. If you don't integrate security into every aspect of your private cloud architecture, you'll increase the chances that later on, you will find breaches that were not predicted due to the lack of due diligence planning.

Some cloud architects may think that these essential characteristics of cloud computing only apply to a public cloud infrastructure; this is not true. Large enterprises already have network segmentation and different levels of authentication and authorization according to organizational structure or business unit. When evolving from a physical datacenter to a private cloud, these core security design points need be in place: segmentation, isolation, and security across organizational and divisional boundaries.

During the private cloud design and planning phase, you need to be sure to address the following security concerns as they relate to the essential security characteristics of the private cloud.

Resource pooling

When the cloud characteristic under consideration is resource pooling, the security concern may be that the consumer (user/tenant) requires that the application is secure and that the data is safe even in catastrophic situations. Possible strategies for addressing these concerns can include:

- Implementing data isolation between tenants
- Applying Authentication, Authorization, and Access Control (AAA)
- Using the Role Based Access Control (RBAC) model

On-demand self-service

When the cloud characteristic under consideration is on-demand self-service capabilities, the security concern may be control of who has the authority to demand, provision, use, and release services from and back to the shared resource pool. Possible strategies for addressing these concerns can include:

- Implementing least privilege and RBAC
- Implementing a well-documented cleanup process
- Explicitly addressing how cleanup is accomplished in the SLA you have with private-cloud tenants

Rapid elasticity

When the cloud characteristic under consideration is rapid elasticity, the security concern may be that rogue applications can execute a Denial of Service (DoS) attack that may destabilize the datacenter by requesting a large amount of resources. Possible strategies for addressing these concerns can include:

- Monitoring resources to alert and prevent such scenarios
- Implementing policy-based quotas

Broad network access

When the cloud characteristic under consideration is broad network access, the security concern may be that users will have access to private cloud applications and data from anywhere, including unprotected devices. Possible strategies for addressing these concerns can include:

- Implementing endpoint protection
- As part of the defense in depth approach, making sure to have a security awareness training in place that covers this scenario
- Applying AAA

It is the cloud architect's responsibility to bring these concerns to the table during the planning and design phase of the project.

Note: for comprehensive coverage of Microsoft's Private Cloud Security architecture, please see the article "A Solution for Private Cloud Security" on TechNet Wiki at *http://social.technet.microsoft.com/wiki/contents/articles/6642.a-solution-for-private-cloud-security.aspx.*
Yuri Diogenes
Senior Technical Writer, SCD iX Solutions/Foundations Group - Security

Tom Shinder
Principal Knowledge Engineer, SCD iX Solutions Group – Private Cloud Security

Up next

The next chapter will examine how you can use Windows Server 2012 as a highly available, easy-to-manage multi-server platform that provides continuous availability, ensures cost efficiency, and provides management efficiency for your organization's move into the cloud.

CHAPTER 3

Highly available, easy-to-manage multi-server platform

This chapter introduces some new features and capabilities of Windows Server 2012 that can help make your IT operations more efficient and cost-effective. With enhancements that help ensure continuous availability and improvements that make server management more efficient and help drive down costs, Windows Server 2012 provides a highly available and easy-to-manage multi-server platform that is ideal for building the infrastructure for your organization's private cloud.

Understanding Microsoft's high-availability solutions

Windows Server and other Microsoft products offer a wide range of high-availability options, affecting everything from infrastructure to applications. Here is a brief overview of the different technologies and some guidelines for when to use each of them in order to eliminate every single point of failure, providing the datacenter with continual availability for both planned and unplanned downtime.

Hardware

Before implementing high availability for servers and services, it is important to ensure that the datacenter and physical infrastructure can also maintain availability when any single component fails or must be taken offline for maintenance.

The datacenter itself should have backup power sources, such as generators or batteries, and every server should have redundant power supplies connected to separate power strips on different circuits.

There should be redundancy throughout the network fabric, including switches, routers, and hardware load balancers. Network interface cards (NICs) should be teamed, and there should be duplicate paths for all networks, including any connections to the Internet.

The storage should use redundant array of independent disks (RAID) technologies to recover from the loss of any disk, and the data should be replicated or mirrored to a secondary array. Multipath I/O (MPIO) should be deployed to provide multiple communication routes to the storage. If Internet Small Computer Systems Interface (iSCSI) storage is used, the iSCSI target itself should be clustered to reduce downtime.

Even when every component in the datacenter is highly available, it is important to realize that a natural disaster could take out the entire site, so also consider having a secondary datacenter for disaster recovery using multisite clustering or replication.

Server infrastructure

Once the datacenter is prepared, it is important to ensure that all critical server infrastructure components are highly available. First, make sure that there are multiple instances of each server role to provide redundancy for all services.

Within Active Directory, there are different high-availability options for different roles. Active Directory supports backup and restore, multisite load balancing, and recovery of deleted objects through the Active Directory Recycle Bin. Additionally, read-only domain controllers can be deployed in less secure locations or branch offices. Active Directory Certificate Services (AD CS) supports Failover Clustering, and Active Directory Federation Services (AD FS) supports cross-site replication and SQL mirroring for its database. Active Directory Lightweight Directory Services (AD LDS) also supports cross-site replication, as well as backup and restore. The Active Directory Rights Management Services (AD RMS) servers use SQL high availability for its database (either using Failover Clustering or log shipping) and Network Load Balancing (NLB) for the licensing server.

The Domain Name System (DNS) uses a round-robin algorithm to send clients to different DNS servers. This provides simple load balancing by presenting redundant servers.

NLB is a software-based solution that provides high availability and scalability by distributing traffic to multiple redundant servers. It is used for server roles with identical data on each node that does not regularly change, such as a website hosted on Internet Information Services (IIS). If a node becomes unavailable, they can be redirected automatically to a different server that contains the same information.

Failover Clustering is the high-availability solution for most other server roles. This is done by interconnecting multiple servers that monitor each other and maintain the data for the service on shared storage, which is accessible by every node. The services and virtual machines (VMs) can move between different servers while seeing the same information on the storage area network (SAN). Automatic failure detection and recovery minimizes unplanned downtime due to crashes, and failover and live migration capabilities reduce or eliminate downtime during planned maintenance. Some of the workloads that Failover Clustering is recommended for include DFS-Namespace Server, DHCP Server, Distributed Transaction Coordinator, Exchange, File Server, Hyper-V, Hyper-V Replica Broker, iSCSI Target Server, iSNS Server, Messaging Queuing, SQL, and WINS. Additionally, Failover Clustering is extensible, so it is possible to cluster any generic application, script, or service, and advanced integration is possible for almost any application through writing a custom resource dynamic-link library (DLL).

Microsoft Hyper-V primarily uses Failover Clustering as its high-availability solution, but VMs can also maintain service continuity through NLB, replication, or backup and restore. In Windows Server 2012, the Hyper-V Replica provides in-box replication of VMs to other Hyper-V hosts in the environment for disaster recovery. It is even possible to support Failover Clustering within Hyper-V VMs, which is known as "guest clustering." The individual VMs form the different cluster nodes, and applications running inside those VMs can move to different nodes, providing a great high-availability option when doing maintenance of the VM, such as adding memory or updating the guest operating system.

Server applications

Several of the most common enterprise applications have their own high-availability solutions. Some of them use Failover Clustering, while others have their own implementations. For server roles that do not have a native solution, remember that it is always possible to place the application inside a VM that is running on a failover cluster. The Windows Server 2012 Failover Clustering feature of VM Monitoring allows the cluster to monitor the health of any service inside a VM, allowing it to restart the service, restart the VM, or move the VM to a different node in the cluster, while alerting the administrator that there is a problem.

File servers use traditional Failover Clustering and have been enhanced in Windows Server 2012 with the Continuously Available File Server technology, which presents client access points across multiple nodes. Additionally, there is the DFS-Replication service, which copies files to different location, providing redundancy.

Microsoft's IIS web server supports Failover Clustering for the FTP and WWW role, and NLB for most other roles. Additionally, IIS has the Application Request Routing

(ARR) module, which performs load balancing for Hypertext Transfer Protocol (HTTP) traffic, and the ARR component can be made highly available by using NLB.

Microsoft Exchange Server, Microsoft Lync Server, Microsoft SQL Server, and Microsoft SharePoint Server also have a variety of high-availability options for both planned and unplanned downtime. Each of the System Center 2012 components also has a rich high-availability story, not only being made highly available, but also offering high-availability features and enhancements to Windows Server Failover Clustering and NLB.

Additionally, third-party backup and restore technologies, along with replication solutions, should be considered. Backup and restore provides high-availability data by keeping multiple copies of that information that can be recovered when needed; however, some data loss can happen if a failure occurred after the last time the data was backed up. Replication continually pushes copies of the data to other servers or locations, so data can be accessed if the primary location becomes unavailable.

Conclusion

There are many different high-availability solutions to select, ranging from the hardware to infrastructure roles to server applications to management utilities. Always remember to provide redundancy and eliminate every single point of failure; then it can be possible to have continuous availability for your datacenter and its services.

Symon Perriman
Technical Evangelist

Continuous availability

Guaranteeing continuous availability of applications and services is essential in today's business world. If users can't use the applications they need, the productivity of your business will be affected. And if customers can't access the services your organization provides, you'll lose their business. Although previous versions of Windows Server have included features like Failover Clustering and NLB that help you ensure the availability of business-critical applications and services, Windows Server 2012 adds a number of improvements that can greatly help ensure application uptime and minimize service disruptions.

Key availability improvements include enhancements to Failover Clustering such as greater scalability, simplified updating of cluster nodes, and improved support for guest clustering. The new SMB 3.0 Transparent Failover capability lets you perform maintenance on your cluster nodes without interrupting access to file shares on your cluster. Storage Migration now allows you to transfer the virtual disks and configuration of VMs to new locations while the VMs are still running. Windows NIC Teaming now provides an in-box solution for implementing fault tolerance for the network adapters of your servers. Improvements to Chkdsk greatly reduce potential downtime caused by file system corruption on mission-critical servers. Easy conversion between installation options provides increased flexibility for how you configure servers in your environment, whereas Features On Demand lets you install Server Core features from a remote repository instead of the local disk. And DHCP failover improves resiliency by allowing you to ensure continuous availability of Dynamic Host Configuration Protocol (DHCP) services to clients on your network.

In the following sections, we'll dig deeper into each of these capabilities and features. And we'll continue to benefit from the insights and tips from insiders working at Microsoft and from select experts who have worked with Windows Server 2012 during the early stages of the product release cycle.

Combining host and guest clustering for continuously available workloads

A major investment area in Windows Server 2012 is the notion of continuous availability. This refers to the combination of infrastructure capabilities that enable VMs and workloads to remain online despite failures in compute, network, or storage infrastructure. Designing infrastructure and workloads for continuous availability requires analyzing and providing resiliency for each layer of the supporting architecture. The physical compute, storage, and network architecture providing the private cloud fabric is the first area of interest. Next, guest clustering or clustering of the VMs providing the workload functionality is an additional layer of resiliency that can be used. Together, these technologies can be deployed to provide continuous availability during both planned and unplanned downtime of the host infrastructure or the guest infrastructure.

At the fabric level or physical infrastructure layer, a Windows Server 2012 infrastructure provides continuous availability technologies for compute, network, and storage. For storage, Windows Server 2012 introduces Storage Spaces, a new technology for providing highly available storage using commodity hardware. Using either Storage Spaces or SAN-based storage, Windows Server 2012 also introduces Scale-Out File Server Clusters. With Scale-Out File Server Clusters, two or more clustered file servers use Cluster Shared Volumes Version 2 (CSV2) to enable a single share to be scaled out across file servers, providing very high-speed access and high availability of the file share. This file share can be used as the storage location for VMs because Windows Server 2012 supports storing VMs on SMB 3 file shares. With the combination of Storage Spaces, Scale-Out File Clusters, and SMB 3 Multi-Channel access, any component of the Windows Server 2012 storage infrastructure could fail, but access to the file share or VM will be maintained. This combination provides continuous availability of the storage infrastructure.

For the network infrastructure, Windows Server 2012 introduces built-in network adapter teaming that supports load balancing and failover (LBFO) for servers with multiple network adapters. Regardless of brands or speeds of network adapters in your server, Windows Server 2012 can take those adapters and create a network adapter "team." The team can then be assigned an IP address and will remain connected, provided that at least one or more of the network adapters has connectivity. When more than one network adapter is available in a team, traffic can be load-balanced across them for higher aggregate throughput. Use of NIC teaming at the host level, combined with redundancy of the switch/routing infrastructure, provides continuous availability of the network infrastructure.

For the compute infrastructure, Windows Server 2012 continues to use Windows Failover Clustering with Hyper-V host clusters. The scalability of Hyper-V hosts and clusters has been increased dramatically, up to 64 nodes per cluster. Host clusters enable the creation of highly available virtual machines (HAVMs). Hyper-V host clusters use the continuously available storage infrastructure to store the HAVMs. For planned downtime, HAVMs (as well as non-HA VMs) can be live-migrated to another host with no downtime for the VMs. For unplanned downtime, a VM is moved to or booted on another node in the cluster automatically. Clusters can be updated automatically using Cluster Aware Updating, which live-migrates all VMs off the node to be updated so that there is no downtime during host maintenance and updating. Together, these technologies enable continuous availability of the compute and virtualization infrastructure.

Although these technologies provide a robust physical infrastructure and virtualization platform, the key availability requirement is for the workloads being hosted. A VM may still be running, but its workload may have an error, stop running, or suffer from some other downtime-causing event. To enable continuous availability for workloads, Windows Server 2012, like Windows Server 2008 R2, also support guest clustering, or creating a failover cluster consisting of VMs. A common example is creating a guest cluster of SQL VMs so that the advanced error detection and failover of database instances between cluster nodes can be used even when the nodes are virtualized. Previously, the only shared storage supported for guest clusters was iSCSI. With Windows Server 2012, Fibre Channel shared storage for VMs are enabled by the introduction of the virtual Fibre Channel host bus adapter (HBA) for VMs. This feature enables Fibre Channel–based storage to be zoned and presented directly into VMs. The VMs can then use this as shared storage for guest failover clusters.

The combination of host and guest clustering can provide continuous availability of the workload despite the failure of any layer of the architecture. In the case of a SQL guest cluster, if there is a problem in SQL such as a service or other failure, the database instance can fail over to another node in the guest cluster. If one of the network connections of the underlying physical host is lost, NIC teaming enables the SQL VM to remain accessible. Anti-affinity rules can be configured such that the SQL guest cluster VMs will not all be running on the same physical node; therefore, if a physical node fails, the SQL databases will fail over to another SQL node in the guest cluster running on one of the other nodes in the host cluster. If one of the disks where the SQL VM or its data is being stored fails, Storage Spaces and the Scale-Out File Cluster maintain uninterrupted access to the data.

These examples show that with proper design, the combination of host and guest clustering in conjunction with other Windows Server 2012 features like NIC teaming, enables continuous availability of VMs and their workloads.
David Ziembicki
Senior Architect, U.S. Public Sector, Microsoft Services

Failover Clustering enhancements

Failover Clustering is a feature of Windows Server that provides high availability for server workloads. File servers, database servers, and application servers are often deployed in failover clusters so that when one node of the cluster fails, the other nodes can continue to provide services. Failover Clustering also helps ensure workloads can be scaled up and out to meet the demands of your business.

Although the Failover Clustering feature of previous versions of Windows Server provided a robust solution for implementing high-availability solutions, this feature has been significantly enhanced in Windows Server 2012 to provide even greater scalability, faster failover, more flexibility in how it can be implemented, and easier management. The sections that follow describe some the key improvements to Failover Clustering found in Windows Server 2012. Note that some other cluster-aware features, such as concurrent Live Migrations and Hyper-V Replica, were discussed previously in Chapter 2, "Foundation for building your private cloud."

Increased scalability

Failover Clustering in Windows Server 2012 now provides significantly greater scalability compared to Windows Server 2008 R2 by enabling you to do the following:

- Scale out your environment by creating clusters with up to a maximum of 64 nodes, compared to only 16 nodes in the previous version.

- Scale up your infrastructure by running up to 4,000 VMs per cluster and up to 1,024 VMs per node.

These scalability enhancements make Windows Server 2012 the platform of choice for meeting the most demanding business needs for high availability.

CSV2 and scale-out file servers

Version 1 of Cluster Shared Volumes (CSV) was introduced in Windows Server 2008 R2 to allow multiple cluster nodes to access the same NTFS-formatted volume simultaneously. A number of improvements have been made to this feature in Windows Server 2012 to make it easier to configure and use a CSV and to provide increased security and performance.

For example, a CSV now appears as a single consistent file namespace called the *CSV File System* (CSVFS), although the underlying file system technology being used remains NTFS. CSVFS also allows direct I/O for file data access and supports sparse files, which enhances performance when creating and copying VMs. From the security standpoint, a significant enhancement is the ability to use BitLocker Drive Encryption to encrypt both traditional failover disks and CSVs. And it's also easier now to back up and restore a CSV with in-box support for CSV backups provided by Windows Server Backup. Backups of CSV volumes no longer require redirected I/O in version 2. The volume snapshots can be taken on the host that currently owns the volume, unlike version 1, where they were taken on the node requesting the backup. Configuring a CSV can now be performed with a single right-click in the Storage pane of Failover Cluster Manager.

CSV2 also supports the SMB 3.0 features described in the previous chapter, making possible scale-out file servers that can host continuously available and scalable storage. Scale-out file servers are built on top of the Failover Clustering feature of Windows Server 2012 and the SMB 3.0 protocol enhancements. Scale-out file servers allow you to scale the capacity of your file servers upward or downward dynamically as the needs of your business change. This means you can start with a low-cost solution such as a two-node file server, and then later add additional nodes (to a maximum of four) without affecting the operation of your file server.

Scale-out file servers can be configured by starting the High Availability Wizard from Failover Cluster Manager. Begin by selecting File Server from the list of cluster roles (formerly called clustered services and applications):

Then, on the next page of the wizard, select the File Server For Scale-Out Application Data option, as shown here, and continue through the wizard:

When the wizard executes, a series of steps is performed to create the scale-out file server. These steps are summarized in a report that the wizard generates:

Scale-out file servers have a few limitations that general-use file servers don't have. Specifically, scale-out file servers don't support:

- File Server Resource Management (FSRM) features like Folder Quotas, File Screening, and File Classification
- Distributed File Services Replication (DFS-R)
- NFS
- Data deduplication

Easier cluster migration

The Migrate A Cluster Wizard makes it easy to migrate services and applications from a cluster running Windows Server 2008, Windows Server 2008 R2, or Windows Server 2012. The wizard helps you migrate the configuration settings for clustered roles, but it doesn't migrate settings of the cluster, network, or storage, so you need to make sure that your new cluster is configured before you use the wizard to initiate the migration process. In addition, if you want to use new storage for the clustered roles you're migrating, you need to make sure that this storage is available to the destination cluster before running the wizard. Cluster migration also now supports Hyper-V and allows you to export and re-import VMs as part of the migration process.

Now support is also included for copying the configuration information of multiple VMs from one failover cluster to another, making it easier to migrating settings between clusters. And you can migrate configuration information for applications and services on clusters running Windows Server 2008, Windows Server 2008 R2, and Windows Server 2012.

Improved Cluster Validation

Cluster validation has been improved in Windows Server 2012 and is much faster than in the previous version of Failover Clustering. The Validate A Configuration Wizard, shown in Figure 3-1, simplifies the process of validating hardware and software for the servers that you want to use in your failover cluster. New validation tests have been added to this wizard for the Hyper-V role and VMs (when the Hyper-V role is installed) and for verification of CSV requirements. And more detailed control is now provided so that you can validate an explicitly targeted logical unit number (LUN).

Simplified cluster management

The Failover Clustering feature is now fully integrated with the new Server Manager of Windows Server 2012, making it easier to discover and manage the nodes of a cluster. For example, you can update a cluster by right-clicking the cluster name, which in Figure 3-2 has been added to the server group named Group 1.

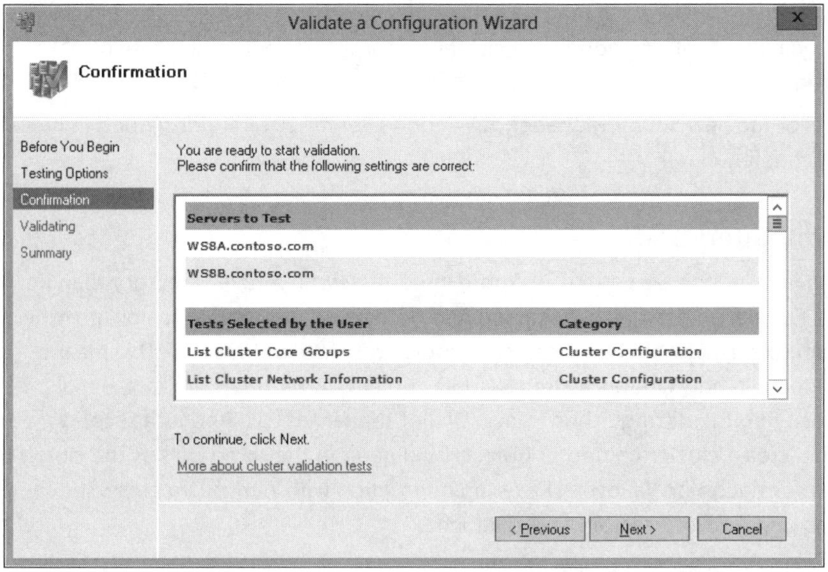

FIGURE 3-1 Validating a failover cluster using the Validate A Configuration Wizard.

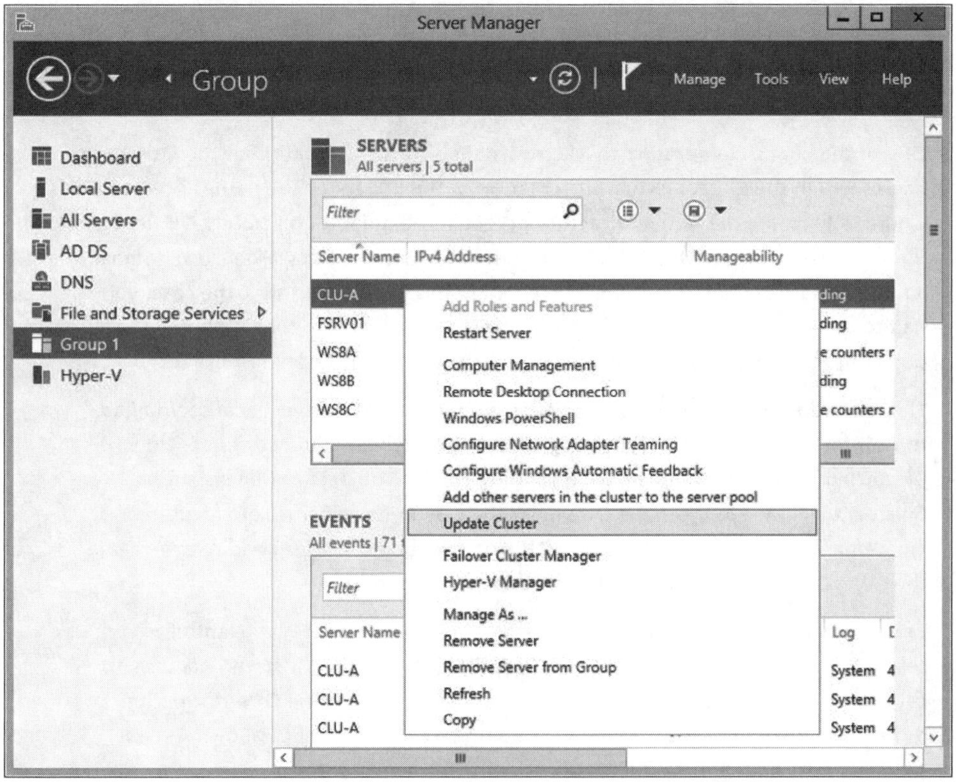

FIGURE 3-2 You can perform cluster-related tasks from the new Server Manager.

Server groups simplify the job of managing sets of machines such as the nodes in a cluster. A single-click action can add all the nodes in a cluster to a server group to facilitate remote multi-server management.

The capabilities of the new Server Manager of Windows Server 2012 are described in more detail later in this chapter.

Active Directory integration

Failover Clustering in Windows Server 2012 is more integrated with Active Directory than in previous versions. For example, support for delegated domain administration is now provided to enable intelligent placement of cluster computer objects in Active Directory. This means, for example, that you can now create cluster computer objects in targeted organizational units (OUs) by specifying the distinguished name (DN) of the target OU. And as a second example, you could create cluster computer objects by default in the same OUs as the cluster nodes. For more information on Failover Clustering integration with Active Directory, see the sidebar "Clustering and Active Directory improvements."

Clustering and Active Directory improvements

In Windows Server 2012, Failover Clustering is more integrated with Active Directory. There are improvements made based on past experiences that administrators were running into.

One of the big call generators to Microsoft Support is the creation of the Cluster or names within the Cluster. When the creation of the Cluster or the names occurs, it would only create the Active Directory object in the default Computers OU. In many domain environments, the default Computers OU is locked down because domain administrators did not want objects created in this OU. When this is the case, you had to pull in a domain administrator to pre-create objects in the OU where the object needed to be, set permissions on the object, and do a few other tasks.

This tended to be a long, drawn-out process if there were issues because you had to wait for someone else to fix your problems before you could continue. Now, Clustering is smarter about where it is going to place objects. When creating a Cluster, it will look in the same OU where the cluster node names are located and create the Cluster Name in the same OU. So now you no longer need to pre-create the objects in a separate OU—Cluster is doing it for you.

Let's take this a step further. Say in your domain environment, you wanted to separate the physical machines (OU called Physical) and the Clustered names (OU called Clusters). This is not a problem because you can pass the OU information during the creation of the Cluster. When doing this through the Failover Cluster Manager interface, you would input the name in this fashion:

```
Type the name you want to use when administering the cluster.

Cluster Name:    "CN=MyCluster,OU=Cluster,DC=Contoso,DC=com"
```

If you wanted to do this in Windows PowerShell, the command would be:

`New-Cluster –Name "CN=MyCluster,OU=Clusters,DC=Contoso,DC=Com"`

Another call generator is the accidental deletions of the Virtual Computer Object from Active Directory. When a name comes online, Failover Clustering checks the *objectGUID* that it has for it to match it with the one in Active Directory. If this account is deleted, it would fail to come online. You had to go through a utility such as ADRESTORE.EXE, restore it from the Recycle Bin (if enabled), do an Active Directory Restore, or simply delete the resource and create it again.

This is no longer the case in Windows Server 2012 Failover Clustering because we have built-in "repair" functionality for just these instances. If the name has been removed from Active Directory, the resource will still come online. It will still log an event about the resource so that you are notified. However, it will give you time so that you can repair the object and not experience downtime. There is a "repair" option you can select where it will go into Active Directory and re-create the object for you.

Failover Clustering is no longer dependent on a writeable domain controller. In some environments where perimeter networks are in place, the perimeter network will usually contain a Read Only Domain Controller (RODC). Failover Clustering will now work with those environments because the requirement has been removed.

Along those same lines, we can talk about virtualized environments. For many companies, moving to virtualized environments is proving to be cost effective. However, there were "gotchas." In some cases, cluster design was not planned to consider the need for a writable domain controller.

So, let's say you want to virtualize all your domain controllers and make them highly available by placing them all in a cluster and storing them on CSVs. In the event that all nodes of the cluster are down, you are placed in a catch-22 situation: Cluster services and CSVs depend on a writable domain controller for domain authentication in the beginning, but your virtualized domain controllers need the cluster services running in order to start. The Cluster Service would not start because it could not get to the domain controller, and the domain controller would not start because the Cluster was down!

In Windows Server 2012 Failover Clustering, this has changed. The Cluster Service will now start using a special internal local account. All other nodes in the Cluster will start and join as it is using this special account. The CSVs would also come online. It is almost like we have our own hidden domain just for ourselves to use. Because the Cluster Service is started and the CSVs are online, the domain controllers can start.

We have made big strides in the way we integrate in Active Directory, and all of it is for the better. Cluster administrators spoke, and Microsoft listened.
John Marlin
Senior Support Escalation Engineer

Task Scheduler integration

Failover Clustering in Windows Server 2012 is also integrated into the Task Scheduler, which allows you to configure tasks you want to run on clusters in three ways:

- ClusterWide tasks are scheduled to run on all nodes in the cluster.
- AnyNode tasks are scheduled to run on a single, randomly selected cluster node.
- ResourceSpecific tasks are scheduled to run only on the cluster node that currently owns the specified resource.

You can configure clustered tasks by using PowerShell. Table 3-1 lists the cmdlets available for this purpose. For more information on any of these cmdlets, use Get-Help <cmdlet>.

TABLE 3-1 PowerShell Cmdlets for Configuring Clustered Tasks

PowerShell Cmdlet	Description
Register-ClusteredScheduledTask	Creating a new clustered scheduled task
Unregister-ClusteredScheduledTask	Delete a clustered scheduled task
Set-ClusteredScheduledTask	Update existing clustered task
Get-ClusteredScheduledTask	Enumerating existing clustered tasks

VM priority

Efficient automatic management of clustered VMs and other clustered roles is now possible in Windows Server 2012 by assigning a relative priority to each VM in the cluster. Once this has been configured, the cluster will then automatically manage the VM or other clustered role based on its assigned priority.

Four possible priorities can be assigned to a clustered VM or clustered role:

- High
- Medium (the default)
- Low
- No Auto Start

Assigning priorities to clustered VMs or other clustered roles lets you control both the start order and placement of each VM or other role in the cluster. For example, VMs that have higher priority are started before those having lower priority. The benefit of this is to allow you to ensure that the most important VMs are started first and are running before other VMs are started. In addition, support for preemption is included so that low-priority VMs can be automatically shut down in order to free up resources so that higher-priority VMs can successfully start. And although Hyper-V in Windows Server 2012 now supports concurrent Live Migrations, the order in which VMs queued for Live Migration but not yet migrated can also be determined on the basis of priority.

VMs that have higher priority are also placed on appropriate nodes before VMs with lower priority. This means, for example, that VMs can be placed on the nodes that have the best available memory resources, with memory requirements being evaluated on a per-VM basis. The result is enhanced failover placement, and this capability is also Non-Uniform Memory Access (NUMA)–aware.

Figure 3-3 shows Failover Cluster Manager being used to manage a two-node cluster that has two cluster roles running on it: a scale-out file server and a VM. Right-clicking the clustered VM and selecting Change Startup Priority allows you to change the priority of the VM from its default Medium setting to High.

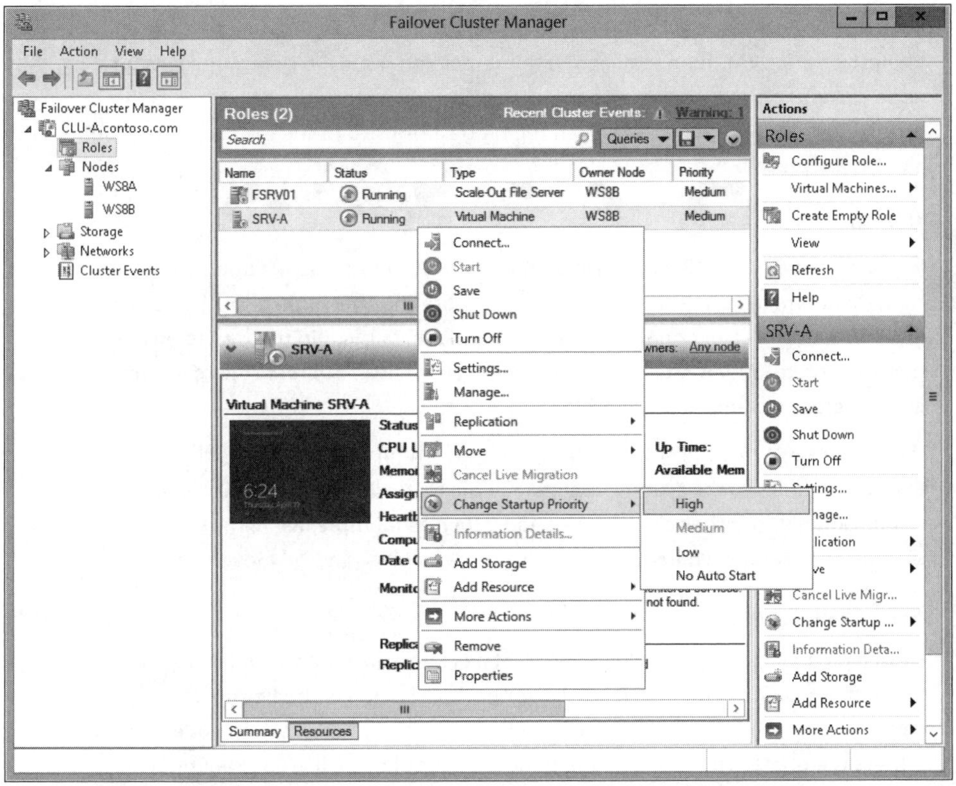

FIGURE 3-3 Using Failover Cluster Manager to configure the priority of a clustered VM.

Failover Clustering placement policies for Hyper-V

Windows Server Failover Clustering provides a critical piece of Hyper-V infrastructure not just for high availability, but also for mobility. A key concept of a virtualized or private cloud environment is to abstract workloads from their underlying physical resources, and Failover Clustering enables this by allowing the movement and placement of VMs between different physical hosts using live migration with no perceived downtime. There are a few placement best practices that can allow you to optimize the cluster for different Hyper-V scenarios.

Default failover policy

When there is a failure of a node, VMs are distributed across the remaining cluster nodes. In previous versions of Windows Server, any resource would be distributed to the nodes hosting the fewest number of VMs. In Windows Server 2012, enhancements in this logic have been made to redistribute the VMs based on the most commonly constrained resource, host memory. Each VM is placed on the node with the freest memory resources, and the memory requirements are evaluated on a per-VM basis, including checks to see if the VM is NUMA-aware.

If a cluster node hosting several VMs crashes, the Cluster Service will find the highest-priority VM, then look across the remaining nodes to determine which node currently has the freest memory. The VM is then started on that node. This process repeats for all the VMs, from the highest priority to the lowest priority, until all VMs are placed.

VM Priority

In Windows Server 2012, each VM running on a cluster can be assigned a priority: High, Medium, or Low. This can be used to ensure that the high-priority VMs are given preferential treatment for cluster operations. This could be used to ensure that the organization's most critical services or key infrastructure roles can come online before less important workloads.

If a cluster node hosting several VMs crashes, the high-priority VMs will start first, then the medium-priority VMs, then finally the low-priority ones. This same logic will be applied for other cluster operations, such as multiple live migrations or Node Maintenance Mode, where the high-priority VMs will always be moved first.

Preferred Owners

From earlier versions of Windows Server, it has been possible to configure the preference for node failover order for each VM. This can be helpful in an environment where it is important for certain VMs to stay on certain nodes, such as if there is a primary datacenter where the VMs should usually run (the Preferred

Owners), and a backup datacenter available for a disaster recovery for the VMs if the primary site is unavailable.

If a cluster node hosting several VMs crashes, a high-priority VMs will attempt to move to the first node in the list of Preferred Owners. If that node is not available, then the VM will attempt to move to the second node in the Preferred Owners list. If none of those Preferred Owners are available, then it will move to the first node that is on the Possible Owners list.

Possible Owners

The Possible Owners setting for each VM also existed in earlier versions of Windows Server. It enables VMs to move to and start on a cluster node when none of the Preferred Owners are available. This can be used in an environment when VMs should still run on a host, even when none of the Preferred Owners are available. In a multisite cluster, the nodes at the backup site would be assigned as a Possible Owner, but not as a Preferred Owner. In this scenario, the VMs would fail over to the secondary site only when none of the nodes at the primary site (Preferred Owners) are available.

If a cluster node hosting several VMs crashes, a high-priority VMs will attempt to move to the first node in the list of Preferred Owners. If none of those Preferred Owners are available, then it will move to the first node that is on the Possible Owners list. If the first node in the Possible Owners list is not available, then it will move to the next node on the list. If none of the nodes in either the Preferred Owners nor Possible Owners lists are available, then the VM will move to any other node, but remain offline. Depending on Failback policies, the VM can move back to a Preferred Owner or Possible Owner and start as soon as one of those nodes becomes available.

Failback

Another setting for each VM that continues to be important in Windows Server 2012 is the option to move the VM back to Preferred Owners or Possible Owners, starting from the most Preferred Owner. This feature is helpful if you wish to keep certain VMs on the same hosts, and return those VMs to the host once it recovers from a crash.

If a cluster node recovers from a crash and rejoins cluster membership, any VMs that are not running on a Preferred Owner will be notified that this node is now available for placement. Starting with the high-priority VMs that are running on a Possible Owner (or are offline on another node), each VM will determine if this node is a better host, then live-migrate (or start) the VM on that Preferred Owner.

Persistent Mode

One problem that is often seen in highly virtualized environments is a "boot storm," which happens when simultaneously starting a large number of VMs. Starting a VM requires more host resources than standard running operations, so starting a lot of VMs can sometimes overload the host, affecting its performance, or even causing it to crash (if certain host reserves are not set). As a safety precaution, during failover or when a node is restarted, the number of VMs that will start simultaneously is limited (High priority first), and the rest will be queued up to start on that node. Even when these VMs are simultaneously starting, they are slightly staggered to help spread out the demands on the host. There are still some settings that can be configured to avoid these "boot storms."

Persistent Mode was introduced in Windows Server 2008 R2 and provides the ability to keep a VM on the last host it was deliberately placed on (either by an administrator or a System Center Virtual Machine Manager placement policy). If an entire cluster crashes, each VM will wait for the node is was previously hosted on to come online before starting up, still honoring high-priority VMs first. This prevents all of the VMs across the cluster from trying to start up on the first node(s) that come online, helping to avoid a "boot storm." There is a default amount of time the cluster service will wait for the original node to rejoin the cluster. If the node does not join within this period, the VM will be placed on the most Preferred Owner, ensuring that the VM will still come online, while having given that new host an opportunity to start its own VMs.

Auto-Start

There may be cases when there are unimportant VMs that should not be started after a cluster failover or a crash, giving the other VMs an opportunity to fail over and come online quickly. The Auto-Start property has also existed in previous versions of Windows Server, and if it is disabled, the VM will not be automatically started when it is placed on a node.

This can be useful in highly virtualized environments when it is important to keep hosts and critical infrastructure VMs running, while not worrying about constraining resources or "boot storms" caused by VMs that do not need to be continually available, yet are still hosted on the cluster. These VMs can be started later by the administrator or automatically using a script.

Anti-Affinity

The final placement policy has also existed before Windows Server 2012, but looks at other VMs, rather than the hosts. The cluster property, AntiAffinityClassName (AACN), enables custom tagging of a VM so that different VMs may share or have different AACNs. VMs that share the same AACN will distribute themselves across different hosts automatically. This can be useful to separate tenets or VMs with the same infrastructure roles across different nodes in the cluster. For example, having all the virtualized DNS servers or guest cluster nodes on the same host would be a single point of failure if that node crashes, so spreading these VMs out across different hosts helps maintain continual service availability.

If there is a cluster with four nodes and four VMs that have the AntiAffinityClass-Name of "blue," then by default, each node would host one of the "blue" VMs. If there are more "blue" VMs with the same AACN than there are nodes in the cluster, then there will be more than 1 "blue" VM on each node, but they will still distribute themselves as evenly as possible.

Conclusion

Using these policies, it is possible to optimize the placement of VMs on a Windows Server 2012 Failover Cluster. Always remember to configure the priority to the VMs so that high-priority VMs are placed first, and consider how VM placement will look when any one of the nodes becomes unavailable.

Symon Perriman
Technical Evangelist

Virtual machine monitoring

Ensuring high availability of services running in clustered VMs is important because service interruptions can lead to loss of user productivity and customer dissatisfaction. A new capability of Failover Cluster Manager in Windows Server 2012 is the ability to monitor the health of clustered VMs by determining whether business-critical services are running within VMs running in clustered environments. By enabling the host to recover from service failures in the guest, the cluster service in the host can take remedial action when necessary in order to ensure greater uptime for services your users or customers need.

You enable this functionality by right-clicking the clustered VM and selecting Configure Monitoring from the More Actions menu item, as shown here:

You then select the service or services you want to monitor on the VM, and if the selected service fails, the VM can either be restarted or moved to a different cluster node, depending on how the service restart settings and cluster failover settings have been configured:

You can also use PowerShell to configure VM monitoring. For example, to configure monitoring of the Print Spooler service on the VM named SRV-A, you could use this command:

```
Add-ClusterVMMonitoredItem -vm SRV-A -service spooler
```

For VM monitoring to work, the guest and host must belong to the same domain or to domains that have a trust relationship. In addition, you need to enable the Virtual Machine Monitoring exception in Windows Firewall on the guest:

If PowerShell Remoting is enabled in the guest, then you don't need to enable the Virtual Machine Monitoring exception in Windows Firewall when you configure VM monitoring using PowerShell. You can enable PowerShell Remoting by connecting to the guest, opening the PowerShell console, and running this command:

```
Enable-PSRemoting
```

Then, to configure monitoring of the Print Spooler service on the guest, you would open the PowerShell console on the host and run these commands:

```
Enter-PSSession
Add-ClusterVMMonitoredItem -service spooler
Exit-PSSession
```

VM monitoring can monitor the health of any NT Service such as the Print Spooler, IIS, or even a server application like SQL Server. VM monitoring also requires the use of Windows Server 2012 for both the host and guest operating systems.

Node vote weights

The quorum for a failover cluster is the number of elements that need to be online in order for the cluster to be running. Each element has a "vote," and the votes of all elements determine whether the cluster should run or cease operations. In the previous version of Failover Clustering in Windows Server 2008 R2, the quorum could include nodes, but each node was treated equally and assigned one vote. In Windows Server 2012, however, the quorum settings can be configured so that some nodes in the cluster have votes (their vote has a weight of 1, which is the default), whereas others do not have votes (their vote has a weight of 0).

Node vote weights provide flexibility that is particularly useful in multisite clustering scenarios. By appropriately assigning a weight of 1 or 0 as the vote for each node, you can ensure that the primary site has the majority of votes at all times.

Note also that a hotfix has been released that allows you to backport this feature to Windows Server 2008 R2 SP1 failover clusters; see *http://support.microsoft.com/kb/2494036/*.

Dynamic quorum

Another new feature of Failover Clustering in Windows Server 2012 is the ability to change the quorum dynamically based on the number of nodes currently in active membership in the cluster. This means that as nodes in a cluster are shut down, the number of votes needed to reach quorum changes instead of remaining the same, as in previous versions of Failover Clustering.

Dynamic quorum allows a failover cluster to remain running even when more than half of the nodes in the cluster fail. The feature works the following quorum models:

- Node Majority
- Node and Disk Majority
- Node and File Share Majority

It does not work, however, with the Disk Only quorum model.

Node drain

When a failover cluster node needs to be taken down for maintenance, the clustered roles hosted on that node first need to be moved to another node in the cluster. Some examples of the kind of maintenance you might need to perform on a cluster node might be upgrading the hardware on the node or applying a service pack.

In the previous version of Failover Clustering in Windows Server 2008 R2, taking down a node for maintenance was a manual process that required placing the node into a Paused state and then manually moving the applications and services running on the node to another node on the cluster.

However, Failover Clustering in Windows Server 2012 now makes performing maintenance on cluster nodes much easier. A new feature called node drain now lets you automate the moving of clustered roles off from the node scheduled for maintenance onto other nodes running on the cluster.

Draining a node can be done either manually by a single click in the Failover Cluster Manager console (as shown in Figure 3-4), or you can script it with PowerShell for automation purposes by using the Suspend-ClusterNode cmdlet.

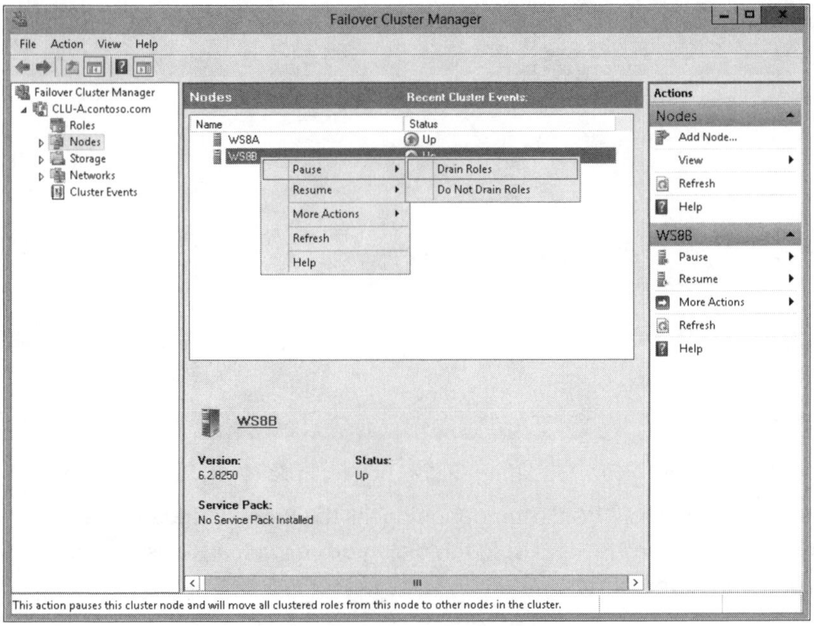

FIGURE 3-4 Initiating a node drain to take down a node for maintenance.

Initiating the node drain process does the following:

1. Puts the node into the Paused state to prevent roles hosted on other nodes from being moved to this node

2. Sorts the roles on the node according to the priority you've assigned them (assigning priorities to roles is another new feature of Failover Clustering in Windows Server 2012)

3. Moves the roles from the node to other nodes in the cluster in order of priority (VMs are live-migrated to other hosts)

Once the process is completed, the node is down and is ready for maintenance.

Cluster-Aware Updating

Cluster-Aware Updating (CAU) is a new feature of Windows Server 2012 that lets you automatically apply software updates to the host operating system in clustered servers with little or no downtime. CAU thus both simplifies update management of cluster nodes and helps ensure your cluster remains available at all times.

CAU functionality works seamlessly with your Windows Server Update Services (WSUS) infrastructure and is installed automatically on each cluster node. CAU can be managed from any server that has the Failover Cluster feature installed but does not belong to the cluster whose nodes you wish to update.

As shown previously in Figure 3-2, you can use Server Manager to initiate the process of updating a cluster. Selecting the Update Cluster menu item opens the Cluster-Aware Updating dialog box and connects to the cluster you selected in Server Manager:

```
CLU-A - Cluster-Aware Updating                                      _ □ x

Connect to a failover cluster:                                            ?
CLU-A                                              ▼    Connect

Cluster nodes:                                         Cluster Actions
Node name    Last Run status    Last Run time
WS8A         Not Available      Not Available         ⇨ Apply updates to this cluster
WS8B         Not Available      Not Available         ⇨ Preview updates for this cluster
                                                       Create or modify Updating Run Profile
                                                       Generate report on past Updating Runs
                                                       Configure cluster self-updating options

                                                       Manage this cluster

Last Cluster Update Summary | Log of Updates in Progress
Cluster name:        CLU-A
Last Updating Run:   Not Available
Last updating status: Not Available
```

You can also open the Cluster-Aware Updating dialog box from Failover Cluster Manager.

Clicking the Preview Updates For This Cluster option opens the Preview Updates dialog box, and clicking Generate Update Preview List in this dialog box downloads a list of the updates available for nodes in the cluster:

```
CLU-A - Preview Updates                                             _ □ x

To see the updates that would currently be applied to each node, click Generate Update Preview List. Generating
the list might take a few minutes. Important: The preview list includes only an initial set of updates. The list does not
include updates that might become applicable only after the initial updates are installed.

Select Plug-in:  WindowsUpdateAge ▼   Plug-in arguments: [                    ]

Node Name        Update ID                              Update Title
WS8B             62d2d6a6-ac1e-4d90-9889-5c08...        Update for Windows Server 8 Bet...
WS8B             497e7ac2-0aaf-4b85-9616-8afa6...       Update for Windows Server 8 Bet...
WS8B             d3075d19-4e5a-4058-99d6-30c0...        Security Update for Windows Ser...




Select an item above to see more detailed information about it.

                              Generate Update Preview List    Close
```

Closing the Preview Updates dialog box returns you to the Cluster-Aware Updating dialog box where clicking the Apply Updates To This Cluster option starts the Cluster-Aware Updating Wizard:

Once you've walked through the steps of this wizard and clicked Next, the update process begins. The way the whole process works is like this:

Cluster nodes are scanned to determine which updates they require in the following way:

1. Nodes are prioritized according to the number of workloads they have running on them.

2. The node with the fewest workloads is then drained to place it into maintenance mode. This causes the workloads running on the node to be moved automatically to other active nodes in the cluster (see the section "Node drain," earlier in this chapter).

3. The Windows Update Agent on this node downloads the necessary updates from either Windows Update or from your WSUS server if you have one deployed in your environment.

4. Once the node has been successfully updated, the node is resumed and becomes an active node in the cluster again.

5. The process is then repeated on each remaining node in the cluster in turn, according to priority.

CAU employs an updating run profile to store the settings for how exceptions are handled, time boundaries for the update process, and other aspects of the node updating process. You can configure these settings by clicking the Create Or Modify Updating Run Profile option in the Cluster-Aware Updating dialog box shown previously. Doing this opens the Updating Run Profile Editor, as shown here:

Why CAU?

Since Failover Clustering was first introduced back in Microsoft Windows NT 4.0 Service Pack 3, there has been an issue with updating the nodes of the cluster. With Windows NT, because we could have only 2 nodes, the problem was relatively easy to solve. You could put the individual nodes into separate update groups, or create a custom batch file or script to move everything off a single node, update it, and then repeat on the other side at a later time. As clustering has improved, and we have added the number of nodes you can have in a cluster, updating gets more and more complex. With Windows 2008 R2 allowing up to 16 nodes in a cluster, maintaining an update methodology that keeps all resources online as much as possible in large clusters is cumbersome and replete with possible errors. This contributes to the most common issue I see at customer sites when I am brought in to review clusters or troubleshoot what went wrong in a failure. This issue is that the hotfixes or drivers installed are different versions in a cluster.

The answer to this in Windows Server 2012 is CAU, which allows all nodes in the cluster to be updated, one at a time, while maintaining the availability of applications. By having an update process that is aware of all nodes in the cluster and can move the resources around, we are able to maintain availability and still update all nodes of the cluster. This also helps reduce the human error element when relying on someone to follow the best practice of moving resources off and pausing a node—this action is automated in CAU. With CAU, we can coordinate and install updates and hotfixes on all nodes, moving the groups around to maintain availability and still get everything up to date. Because CAU also integrates with normal Windows updating, you can control what updates are applied using WSUS and only approve the updates that are appropriate for your environment.

Matthew Walker
Premier Field Engineer

Guest clustering

Failover Clustering of Hyper-V can be implemented in two ways:

- Host clustering, in which the Failover Clustering feature runs in the parent partition of the Hyper-V host machines. In this scenario, the VMs running on the hosts are managed as cluster resources and they can be moved from one host to another to ensure availability of the applications and services provided by the VMs.

- Guest clustering, in which the Failover Clustering feature runs in the guest operating system within VMs. Guest clustering provides high availability for applications and services hosted within VMs, and it can be implemented either on a single physical server (Hyper-V host machine) or across multiple physical servers.

Host clustering helps ensure continued availability in the case of hardware failure or when you need to apply software updates to the parent partition. Guest clustering, by contrast, helps maintain availability when a VM needs to be taken down for maintenance. Implementing guest clustering on top of host clustering can provide the best of both worlds.

Guest clustering requires that the guest operating systems running in VMs have direct access to common shared storage. In previous versions of Windows Server, the only way to provision such shared storage in a guest clustering scenario was to have iSCSI initiators running in the guest operating systems so they could connect directly with iSCSI-based storage. Guest clustering in previous versions of Windows Server did not support using Fibre Channel SANs for shared storage. VMs running Windows Server 2008 R2 in a guest clustering scenario can use Microsoft iSCSI Software Target 3.3, which can be downloaded from the Microsoft Download Center. Figure 3-5 illustrates the typical way guest clustering was implemented in Windows Server 2008 R2.

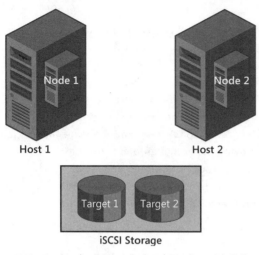

FIGURE 3-5 Implementing guest clustering with Failover Clustering in Windows Server 2008 R2 using iSCSI Software Target.

In Windows Server 2012, iSCSI Software Target is now an in-box feature integrated into Failover Clustering, making it easier to implement guest clustering using shared iSCSI storage. And by starting the High Availability Wizard from the Failover Clustering Manager console, you can add the iSCSI Target Server as a role to your cluster quickly. You can also do this with PowerShell by using the Add-ClusteriSCSITargetServerRole cmdlet.

But iSCSI is now no longer your only option as far as shared storage for guest clustering goes. That's because Windows Server 2012 now includes an in-box Hyper-V Virtual Fibre Channel adapter that allows you to connect directly from within the guest operating system of a VM to LUNs on your Fibre Channel SAN (see Figure 3-6). The new virtual Fibre Channel adapter supports up to four virtual HBAs assigned to each guest with separate worldwide names (WWNs) assigned to each virtual HBA and N_Port ID Virtualization (NPIV) used to register guest ports on the host.

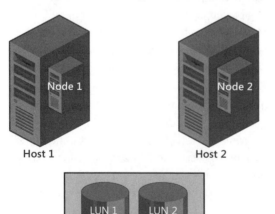

FIGURE 3-6 Failover Clustering in Windows Server 2012 now allows VMs to connect directly to a Fibre Channel SAN.

Configuring Fibre Channel from the guest

Before you configure Fibre Channel as the shared storage for VMs in a guest cluster, make sure that you have HBAs installed in your host machines and connected to your SAN. Then, open the Virtual SAN Manager from the Hyper-V Manager console and click Create to add a new virtual Fibre Channel SAN to each host:

Provide a name for your new virtual Fibre Channel and configure it as needed. Then open the settings for each VM in your guest cluster and select the Add Hardware option to add the virtual Fibre Channel adapter to the guest operating system of the VM:

Then simply select the virtual SAN you created earlier, and once you're done, each VM in your guest cluster can use your SAN for shared storage:

Guest clustering in Windows Server 2012 also supports other new Failover Cluster features, such as CAU, node drain, Storage Live Migration, and much more.

Guest clustering vs. VM monitoring

Guest clustering in Windows Server 2012 is intended for server applications that you currently have clustered on physical servers. For example, if you currently have Exchange Server or SQL Server deployed on host clusters, you will have the additional option of deploying them on guest clusters (which can themselves be deployed on host clusters) for enhanced availability when you migrate your infrastructure to Windows Server 2012.

VM monitoring by contrast can enhance availability for other server roles in your environment, such as your print servers. You can also combine VM monitoring with guest clustering for even greater availability.

Guest Clustering: key differences between the Windows Server 2008 R2, Windows Server 2012, and VMware approaches

When we speak about clusters, we usually draw a picture of a few servers and a shared disk resource, required to build a cluster. Hence, for certain applications, like Exchange Server 2010, SQL Server 2012, or System Center 2012, clustering architecture may not require a shared disk resource; there are still plenty of scenarios where shared disks are essential to build a cluster.

In Windows Server 2008 R2, Hyper-V doesn't provide a way to share a single virtual hard disk (VHD) or pass-through disk between VMs. It also doesn't provide native access to Fibre Channel, so you can't share a LUN. The only way to build guest clusters in Windows Server 2008 R2 is to use an iSCSI initiator. You can build a cluster with up to 16 nodes. You can freely live-migrate guest clusters and use dynamic memory in that machine.

In VMware vSphere, you can add the emulated LSI Logic SAS and Parallel controllers to provide a shared VMDK or a LUN to two VMs. No, you can't create a cluster of more than two nodes on vSphere with built-in disk sharing support. Note that the usage of vSphere advanced techniques like VMotion or FT are not supported for guest clusters in VMware environment. The same applies to hosts, with overcommitted memory.

Windows Server 2012 Hyper-V brings synthetic Fibre Channel interface to VMs, building clusters without limitation for the number of nodes. Here, 16-node guest clusters of Windows Server 2008 R2 and 64-node guest clusters of Windows Server 2012 come to reality.
Alex A. Kibkalo
Architect, Microsoft MEA HQ

Enhanced PowerShell support

Failover Clustering in Windows Server 2012 also includes enhanced PowerShell support with the introduction of a number of new cmdlets for managing cluster registry checkpoints, creating scale-out file servers, monitoring health of services running in VMs, and other capabilities. Table 3-2 lists some of the new PowerShell cmdlets for Failover Clustering.

TABLE 3-2 New PowerShell Cmdlets for Failover Clustering

PowerShell cmdlet	Purpose
Add-ClusterCheckpoint	Manages cluster registry checkpoints, including cryptographic checkpoints
Get-ClusterCheckpoint	
Remove-ClusterCheckpoint	
Add-ClusterScaleOutFileServerRole	Creates a file server for scale-out application data
Add-ClusterVMMonitoredItem	Monitors the health of services running inside a VM
Get-ClusterVMMonitoredItem	
Remove-ClusterVMMonitoredItem	
Reset-ClusterVMMonitoredState	
Update-ClusterNetworkNameResource	Updates the private properties of a Network Name resource and sends DNS updates
Test-ClusterResourceFailure	Replaces the Fail-ClusterResource cmdlet

Learn more

For more information about the various Failover Clustering improvements in Windows Server 2012, see the following topics in the TechNet Library:

- "What's New in Failover Clustering" at *http://technet.microsoft.com/en-us/library/hh831414.aspx*.

- "Failover Clustering Technical Preview" at *http://technet.microsoft.com/en-us/library/hh831806.aspx*.

- "Cluster-Aware Updating Technical Preview" at *http://technet.microsoft.com/en-us/library/hh831810.aspx*.

- "High-Performance, Continuously Available File Share Storage for Server Applications Technical Preview" at *http://technet.microsoft.com/en-us/library/hh831399.aspx*.

- "iSCSI High-Availability Block Storage Technical Preview" at *http://technet.microsoft.com/en-us/library/hh831340.aspx*.

For more information on CAU, download the "Understand and Troubleshoot Cluster-Aware Updating (CAU) in Windows Server '8' Beta" topic from *http://www.microsoft.com/download/en/details.aspx?id=29015*.

For additional information concerning Failover Clustering improvements in Windows Server 2012, see the Failover Clustering and Network Load Balancing Team Blog at *http://blogs.msdn.com/b/clustering/*.

SMB Transparent Failover

Windows Server 2012 includes the updated version 3.0 of the Server Message Block (SMB) file-sharing protocol. Some of the features of SMB 3.0 were described in the previous chapter. SMB Transparent Failover is a new feature that facilitates performing maintenance of nodes in a clustered file server without interrupting server applications that store data on Windows Server 2012 file servers. SMB Transparent Failover can also help ensure continuous availability by transparently reconnecting to a different cluster node when a failure occurs on one node. For information about other SMB 3.0 features that can help increase reliability, availability, manageability, and high performance for your business-critical applications, see Chapter 2.

Learn more

For more information about SMB Transparent Failover, see the topic "High-Performance, Continuously Available File Share Storage for Server Applications Technical Preview" in the TechNet Library at *http://technet.microsoft.com/en-us/library/hh831399.aspx*.

For additional information, see the blog post "SMB 2.2 is now SMB 3.0" on the Windows Server Blog at *http://blogs.technet.com/b/windowsserver/archive/2012/04/19/smb-2-2-is-now-smb-3-0.aspx*.

Storage migration

Storage migration is a new feature of Hyper-V in Windows Server 2012 that lets you move all of the files for a VM to a different location while the VM continues running. This means that with Hyper-V hosts running Windows Server 2012, it's no longer necessary to take a VM offline when you need to upgrade or replace the underlying physical storage. We briefly looked at storage migration in Chapter 2 in the context of performing a Live Migration without shared storage, so here we'll dig a bit deeper and look at how storage migration actually works.

When you initiate a storage migration for a VM, the following takes place:

1. A new VHD or VHDX file is created in the specified destination location (storage migration works with both VHD and VHDX).

2. The VM continues to both read and write to the source VHD, but new write operations are now mirrored to the destination disk.

3. All data is copied from the source disk to the destination disk in a single-pass copy operation. Writes continue to be mirrored to both disks during this copy operation, and uncopied blocks on the source disk that have been updated through a mirrored write are not recopied.

4. When the copy operation is finished, the VM switches to using the destination disk.

5. Once the VM is successfully using the destination disk, the source disk is deleted and the storage migration is finished. If any errors occur, the VM can fail back to using the source disk.

Moving a VM from test to production without downtime

A VM that is in a test environment typically lives on a Hyper-V server, usually nonclustered, and usually not in the best location or on the best hardware. A VM that is in production typically lives on a cluster, on good hardware, and is in a highly managed and monitored datacenter.

Moving from one to the other has always involved downtime—until now.

Hyper-V on Windows Server 2012 enables some simple tasks that greatly increase the flexibility of the administrator when it comes to movement and placement of running VMs. Consider this course of events.

I create a VM on a testing server, configure it, get signoff, and make the VM ready for production. With Hyper-V shared nothing Live Migration, I can migrate that VM to a production cluster node without taking the VM offline. The process will copy the VHDs using storage migration, and then once storage is copied, perform a traditional live migration between the two computers. The only thing the computers need is Ethernet connectivity. In the past, this would have required an import/export operation.

Now that the VM is running on my node, I need to cluster it. This is a two-step process. First, using storage migration, I can move the VHD of the VM onto my CSV volume for the cluster. I could also move it to the file share that is providing storage for the cluster, if I'm using Hyper-V over SMB. Regardless of the configuration, the VHD can be moved to a new location without any downtime in the VM. In the past, this would have taken an import/export of the VM, or, at minimum, shutdown and manual movement of the VHD file.

Finally, I can fire up my Failover Cluster Manager and add the VM as a clustered object. Windows Server 2012 lets you add running VMs to a failover cluster without needing to take the VMs offline to do this.

There you have it: start the VM on the stand-alone test server, move the VM to the cluster and cluster storage, and finally create the cluster entry for the VM, all without any downtime required.
Corey Hynes
Architect, holSystems (www.holsystems.com)

Storage migration of unclustered VMs can be initiated from the Hyper-V Manager console by selecting the VM and clicking the Move option. Storage migration of clustered VMs cannot be initiated from the Hyper-V Manager console; the Failover Clustering Manager console must be used instead. You can also perform storage migrations with PowerShell by using the Move-VMStorage cmdlet.

Storage Migration: real-world scenarios

Storage Migration simply adds greater flexibility on when your VMs can be moved from one storage volume to another. This becomes critical as we move from high-availability clusters to continuously available clusters. This, of course, adds tremendous agility, allowing IT to better respond to changing business requirements.

Let's consider two kinds of scenarios: out of space and mission-critical workloads.

Out of space

You just ran out of space on the beautiful shiny storage enclosure you bought about 12 months ago. This can happen due to many reasons, but the common ones include the following:

- Unclear business requirements when the enclosure was acquired
- Server sprawl or proliferation, which is a very common problem in most established virtualization environments

That storage enclosure probably has hundreds or thousands of VMs and performing the move during the shrinking IT maintenance windows are simply not realistic. With Live Storage Migration, IT organizations can essentially move the VMs to other storage units outside of typical maintenance windows.

Mission-critical workloads

The workload associated with your most mission-critical VMs is skyrocketing. You bought a new high-performance SAN to host this workload, but you can't take the VMs down to move them to the new SAN.

This is a common problem in organizations with very high uptime requirements or organizations with very large databases, where the move to the new storage volume would simply take too long.

Adiy Qasrawi
Consultant, Microsoft Consulting Services (MCS)

Learn more

For more information about Storage Migration in Windows Server 2012, see the topic "High-Performance, Continuously Available File Share Storage for Server Applications Technical Preview" in the TechNet Library at *http://technet.microsoft.com/en-us/library/hh831399.aspx*.

For additional information, see the blog post "Windows Server 8 – Truly Live Storage Migration" on the Team blog of MCS @ Middle East and Africa at *http://blogs.technet.com/b/meamcs/archive/2012/03/23/windows-server-8-truly-live-storage-migration.aspx*.

Also see the following posts by Ben Armstrong on his Virtual PC Guy blog:

- "Doing a Simple Storage Migration with Windows Server 8" at *http://blogs.msdn.com/b/virtual_pc_guy/archive/2012/03/12/doing-a-simple-storage-migration-with-windows-server-8.aspx*.

- "Using PowerShell to Storage Migrate with Windows Server 8" at *http://blogs.msdn.com/b/virtual_pc_guy/archive/2012/03/13/using-powershell-to-storage-migrate-with-windows-server-8.aspx*.

- "How does Storage Migration actually work?" at *http://blogs.msdn.com/b/virtual_pc_guy/archive/2012/03/14/how-does-storage-migration-actually-work.aspx*.

- "Storage Migration + PowerShell + Windows 8 = Magic" at *http://blogs.msdn.com/b/virtual_pc_guy/archive/2012/03/15/storage-migration-powershell-windows-8-magic.aspx*.

- "Doing an Advanced Storage Migration with Windows 8" at *http://blogs.msdn.com/b/virtual_pc_guy/archive/2012/04/02/doing-an-advanced-storage-migration-with-windows-8.aspx*.

- "Doing an Advanced Storage Migration with Windows 8 in PowerShell" at *http://blogs.msdn.com/b/virtual_pc_guy/archive/2012/04/03/doing-an-advanced-storage-migration-with-windows-8-in-powershell.aspx*.

Windows NIC Teaming

Windows NIC Teaming is the name for the new network adapter teaming functionality included in Windows Server 2012. Network adapter teaming is also known as load balancing and failover (LBFO) and enables multiple network adapters on a server to be grouped together into a team. This has two purposes:

- To help ensure availability by providing traffic failover in the event of a network component failure

- To enable aggregation of network bandwidth across multiple network adapters

Previously, implementing network adapter teaming required using third-party solutions from independent hardware vendors (IHVs). Beginning with Windows Server 2012, however, network adapter teaming is now an in-box solution that works across different NIC hardware types and manufacturers.

Windows NIC Teaming supports up to 32 network adapters in a team in three modes:

- **Static Teaming** Also called *Generic Teaming* and based on IEEE 802.3ad draft v1, this mode is typically supported by server-class Ethernet switches and requires manual configuration of the switch and the server to identify which links form the team.

- **Switch Independent** This mode doesn't require that the team members connect to different switches; it merely make it possible.

- **LACP** Also called *dynamic teaming* and based on IEEE 802.1ax, this mode is supported by most enterprise-class switches and allows automatic creation of a team using the Link Aggregation Control Protocol (LACP), which dynamically identifies links between the server and a specific switch. To use this mode, you generally need to enable LACP manually on the port of the switch.

Configuring NIC teaming

NIC teaming can be enabled from Server Manager or using PowerShell. For example, to use Server Manager to enable NIC teaming, you can begin by right-clicking the server you want to configure and selecting Configure NIC Teaming:

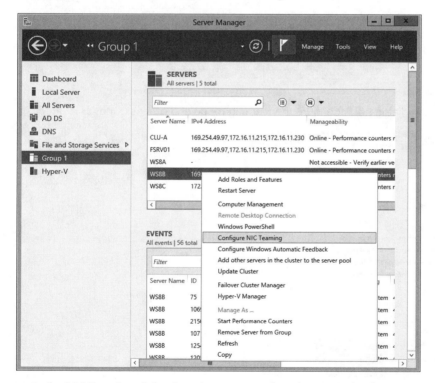

In the NIC Teaming dialog box that opens, select the network adapters you want to team. Then right-click and select Add To New Team:

In the New Team dialog box, configure the teaming mode and other settings as desired:

Clicking OK completes the process and, if successful, the new team will be displayed in the Teams tile of the NIC Teaming dialog box:

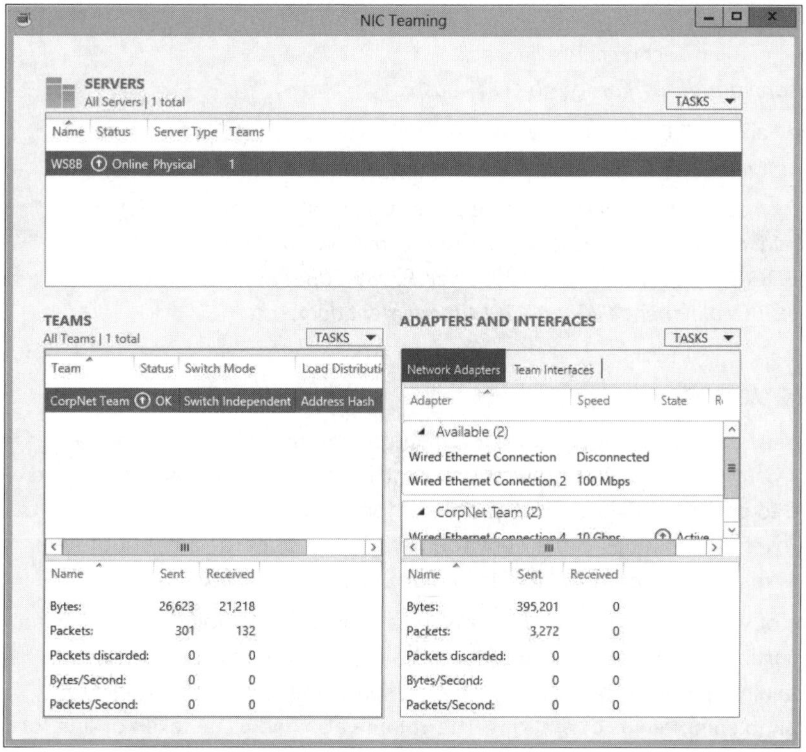

To configure and manage NIC teaming using PowerShell, use cmdlets such as New-NetLbfoTeam to add a new team or Get-NetLbfoTeam to display the properties of a team. The cmdlets for managing NIC teaming are defined in the PowerShell module named NetLbfo, and as Figure 3-7 shows, you can use the Get-Command cmdlet to display all the cmdlets defined in this module.

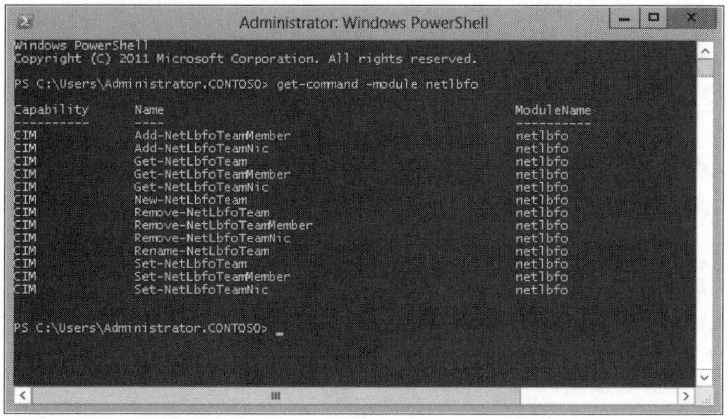

FIGURE 3-7 Obtaining a list of cmdlets for configuring and managing NIC teaming.

Learn more

For more information about NIC teaming in Windows Server 2012, see the following topics in the TechNet Library:

Network Adapter Teaming Technical Preview at *http://technet.microsoft.com/en-us/library/hh831732.aspx*.

Load Balance and Failover (LBFO) overview at *http://technet.microsoft.com/en-us/library/hh831648.aspx*.

For additional information, download the white paper titled "NIC Teaming (LBFO) in Windows Server 8 Beta" from *http://download.microsoft.com/download/E/1/3/E13C9AD6-B4D6-4041-97E0-6BDC48273BC7/Windows%20Server%208%20Beta%20NIC%20Teaming%20(LBFO)%20Deployment%20and%20Management.docx*.

Chkdsk improvements

Today's businesses must be able to manage larger and larger amounts of data. At the same time, the capacity of hard disk drives has grown significantly, whereas the price of very large drives has continued to decline. This has posed problems for organizations that have tried to deploy multi-terabyte disk volumes in their environments because of the amount of time Chkdsk takes to analyze and recover from file system corruption when it occurs.

In earlier versions of Windows Server, the time taken to analyze a disk volume for potential corruption was proportional to the number of files on the volume. The result was that for server volumes containing hundreds of millions of files, it sometimes took many hours (or even days) for Chkdsk to complete its operations. The volume also had to be taken offline for Chkdsk to be run against it.

In Windows Server 2012, however, Chkdsk has been redesigned so that the analysis phase, which consumes most of the time it takes Chkdsk to run, now runs online as a background task. This means that a volume whose file system indicates there may be file corruption can remain online instead of needing to be taken offline for analysis. If analysis by Chkdsk determines that the file system corruption was only a transient event, no further action need be taken. If Chkdsk finds actual corruption of the file system, the administrator is notified in the management consoles and via events that the volume needs repair. The suggested repair process may require that the volume be remounted, and the server may need to be rebooted to complete the repair process.

The result of this redesign of Chkdsk is to reduce the time it takes to analyze and repair a corrupt large disk volume is reduced from hours (or days) to minutes or even seconds. Additional improvements to NTFS in Windows Server 2012 include enhanced self-healing, which automatically repairs many issues without the need of running Chkdsk. The overall result of such improvements is to ensure continuous availability even for servers having very large disk volumes with hundreds of millions of files stored on them.

Learn more

For more information about Chkdsk improvements in Windows Server 2012, see the topic "Multiterabyte Volumes Technical Preview" in the TechNet Library at *http://technet.microsoft.com/en-us/library/hh831536.aspx.*

Easy conversion between installation options

Windows Server 2008 and Windows Server 2008 R2 offered an alternative installation option called Windows Server Core that included only a subset of the server roles, features, and capabilities found in the full installation option. Server Core included only those services and features needed to support common infrastructure roles such as domain controllers, DNS servers, and DHCP servers. By eliminating unnecessary roles and features, and also most of the graphical user interface (GUI; the Server Core user interface only presents a command-line interface), the result is a minimal Windows Server installation that has a smaller disk footprint, a smaller attack service, and requires less servicing (fewer software updates) than the full installation.

A limitation of how installation options were implemented in Windows Server 2008 and Windows Server 2008 R2 is that you cannot switch an installation between the full and Server Core options. So if you have a DNS server with a full installation of Windows Server 2008 R2, the only way to change this into a DNS server with a Server Core installation is to reinstall the operating system on the machine.

Starting with Windows Server 2012, however, you can now switch between Server Core and GUI installations. For example, if you have deployed a GUI installation of Windows Server 2012 and you want to remove the GUI management tools and desktop shell to convert it into a Server Core installation, you can do this easily by running the following PowerShell command:

```
Uninstall-WindowsFeature Server-Gui-Mgmt-Infra -restart
```

When you run this command, it first collects data for the system and then starts the removal process:

Once the GUI and management tools and desktop shell have been removed, the server restarts, and when you log on, you are presented with the bare-bones Server Core user interface:

The process can be reversed by running the following command to convert the Server Core installation back into a GUI one:

```
Install-WindowsFeature Server-Gui-Mgmt-Infra,Server-Gui-Shell –Restart
```

Minimal Server Interface

In addition to the Server Core and GUI installation options, Windows Server 2012 can be configured in a third form called *Minimal Server Interface*. This form is not available when you install Windows Server 2012, but you can configure it using Server Manager or using PowerShell.

There are several reasons you may want to configure the Minimal Server Interface. First, it can function as a compatibility option for applications that do not yet support Microsoft's recommended application model but still want some of the benefits of running Server Core. Second, administrators who are not yet ready to use remote command-line-based management can install the graphical management tools (the same ones they would install on a Windows client) alongside the Minimal Server Interface or Server Graphical Shell.

The Minimal Server Interface is similar to the GUI installation, except that the following are not installed:

- Desktop
- Start screen
- Windows Explorer
- Windows Internet Explorer

However, the following management tools are available on the Minimal Server Interface:

- Server Manager
- Microsoft Management Console (MMC) and snap-ins
- Subset of Control Panel

Benefits for organizations

A key benefit of the easy conversion between installation options available in Windows Server 2012 is the added flexibility you gain by being able to convert between the GUI and Server Core installation options. For example, you could deploy your servers with the GUI option to make them easier to configure. Then you could convert some of them to Server Core to reduce footprint, enable greater consolidation ratios of VMs, and reduce your servicing overhead. You can also select the Minimal Server Interface for application compatibility needs or as a compromise for administrators who are not yet ready to administer without a GUI.

Learn more

For more information about easy conversion between installation options in Windows Server 2012, see the following topics in the TechNet Library:

- "Server Core and Full Server Integration Overview" at
  http://technet.microsoft.com/en-us/library/hh831758.aspx.
- "Windows Server Installation Options" at
  http://technet.microsoft.com/en-us/library/hh831786.aspx.
- "Windows Server 8: Server Applications and the Minimal Server Interface" at
  http://blogs.technet.com/b/server-cloud/archive/2012/01/11/windows-server-8-server-applications-and-the-minimal-server-interface.aspx.

Also see the Server Core Blog on TechNet at *http://blogs.technet.com/b/server_core/*.

Managing servers without the Metro start menu

So you miss the Start menu, the good old Start menu? Well, if that's the case, you're doing it wrong. If you miss the Start menu, it's probably because you've been running a full Windows desktop on your server and logging on to the console of the server to do work. That's wrong on a few levels. You should not use the console, and unless there is a very compelling reason, you should not have a full Windows desktop on the server.

Sounds easy, and Microsoft have been telling us this for years. In reality, though, it's not that simple. Server Core does not run everything, and there are a lot of custom and third-party software packages that need a GUI to be configured. They may not even support remote management. So this idea of running Server Core everywhere to reduce updates, decrease attack surface, and increase performance is great—it's just not always achievable.

Enter Windows Server 2012. Windows Server 2012 has gone a long way toward bringing us close to this ideal scenario. Windows Server 2012 introduces a new level of user interface, which bridges the gap between Server Core and a full desktop. It allows you to migrate from Server Core to a full desktop and back again.

Annoyed by not having a traditional Start menu? Guess what—you don't need it, and you will never use it. Here is what you should do instead.

First of all, install with a full server desktop and configure your drivers, hardware, etc. using the full GUI you are used to. When you are done, remove the GUI by running the PowerShell command Remove-WindowsFeature User-Interfaces-Infra. This will take you to a Server Core configuration. You can now use your remote administration tools as you did in the past, as well as remote PowerShell.

If you find that you need access to an MMC snap-in, or access to the entire set of control panel apps, you can raise the server one level by running Install-WindowsFeature Server-GUI-MGMT-Infra. This gives you full GUI access, accessible from a command line. You can run MMC.exe and use any snap-in. You can run any control panel app. You just don't have Explorer.exe. This should be more than enough to do any advanced driver configuration (you have Device Manager or configure any third-party application). If you do need a full desktop, you can always add the User-Interfaces-Infra that you removed earlier.

Finally, Server Manager has gotten a complete overhaul. There's more to this than can be discussed here, but it further reduces the need for the Start menu. Personally, once I learned how to navigate the new Server Manager, I found myself configuring all my servers with Server-GUI-MGMT-Infra only, starting Server Manager, and doing all my traditional server management from that location only. The tools menu gives you one-click access to all installed administrative tools.

This is not about getting "around" the lack of the traditional Start menu. It's all about learning to use the rich new tools that are there. Once you do, you'll forget the Start menu ever existed.
Corey Hynes
Architect, holSystems (www.holsystems.com)

Features On Demand

Installations of previous versions of Windows Server included binaries for all server roles and features even if some of those roles and features were not installed on the server. For example, even if the DNS Server role was not installed on a Windows Server 2008 R2 installation, the system drive of the server still included the binaries needed to install that role, should it be needed later.

In Windows Server 2012, you can remove the binaries for roles or features that aren't needed for your installation. For example, if you won't be installing the DNS Server role on a particular server, you can remove the binaries for this role from the server's system drive. Being able to remove binaries used to install roles and features allows you to reduce the footprint of your servers significantly.

Completely removing features

Binaries of features can be removed by using PowerShell. For example, to completely remove a feature including its binaries from a Windows Server 2012 installation, use the Uninstall-WindowsFeature cmdlet.

If you later decide you want to install the feature whose binaries you have removed from the installation, you can do this by using the Install-WindowsFeature cmdlet. When you use this cmdlet, you must specify a source where Windows Server 2012 installation files are located. To do this, you can either include the Source option to specify a path to a Windows Imaging (WIM) mount point, or you can leave out this option and let Windows use Windows Update as the source location.

Learn more

For more information about Features On Demand in Windows Server 2012, see the topic "Windows Server Installation Options" in the TechNet Library at *http://technet.microsoft.com/en-us/library/hh831786.aspx*.

DHCP Server Failover

DHCP servers are a critical part of the network infrastructure of most organizations. Therefore, ensuring that a DHCP server is always available to assign IP addresses to hosts on every subnet is essential.

In previous versions of Windows Server, two approaches could be used to ensure the availability of DHCP servers. First, two DHCP servers can be clustered together using Failover Clustering so that the second server could take over the load should the first one fail. The problem with this approach, however, is that clusters are often using shared storage that can be a single point of failure for the cluster. Providing redundant storage is a solution, but it can add significant cost to this approach. Configuring a failover cluster is also not a trivial task.

The other approach is to use split scope approach in which 70 percent to 80 percent of the addresses in each scope are assigned to the primary DHCP server, while the remaining 30 percent to 20 percent are assigned to the secondary DHCP server. This way, if a client can't reach the primary server to acquire an address, it can get one from the secondary server. This approach also has problems, however, because it does not provide for continuity of IP addressing, is prone to possible overlap of scopes due to incorrect manual configuration, and is unusable when the scope is already highly used.

The DHCP Server role in Windows Server 2012 solves these problems by providing a third approach to ensuring DHCP server availability. This approach is called *DHCP failover*, and it enables two DHCP servers to replicate lease information between them. That way, one of the DHCP servers can assume responsibility for providing addresses to all the clients on a subnet when the other DHCP server becomes unavailable.

Learn more

For more information about DHCP failover in Windows Server 2012, see the following topics in the TechNet Library:

- "Dynamic Host Configuration Protocol (DHCP) overview" at *http://technet.microsoft.com/en-us/library/hh831825.aspx*.
- "Step-by-Step: Configure DHCP for Failover" at *http://technet.microsoft.com/en-us/library/hh831385.aspx*.

You can also download the "Understand and Troubleshoot DHCP Failover in Windows Server '8' Beta" from *http://www.microsoft.com/download/en/details.aspx?id=29008*.

Cost efficiency

Keeping costs in line is an important consideration for many organizations, and Windows Server 2012 includes new features and enhancements that can help relieve the pressure faced by IT budgets. Features like Hyper-V virtualization, discussed in the previous chapter, already enable businesses to reduce costs by creating private clouds and by virtualizing workloads, applications, and services. And features such as in-box NIC teaming, described earlier in this chapter, can help reduce cost by eliminating the need for purchasing costly, vendor-specific solutions.

The following sections highlight other features of the new platform that can help your organization. For example, Storage Spaces lets you store application data on inexpensive file servers with similar performance to what you've come to expect from expensive SAN solutions. Thin provisioning and trim allow just-in-time allocations of storage and let you reclaim storage when it is no longer needed, which enables organizations to use storage infrastructures in a more cost-efficient fashion. And the enhanced Network File System (NFS) functionality included in Windows Server 2012 lets you save money by running VMware ESX on VMs that are using Server for NFS as a data store instead of more expensive SAN technologies.

Storage Spaces

SANs are a traditional "heavy iron" technology often used for storing large amounts of data, but they tend to be very expensive to acquire and fairly complex to manage. A new feature of Windows Server 2012 called *Storage Spaces* is designed to change the storage task for enterprises by providing an in-box storage virtualization that can use low-cost commodity storage devices.

Storage Spaces is designed to address a simple question: How can you pool together commodity storage devices so you can provision storage as you need it? The result is Storage Spaces, and by combining this feature with the new scale-out file server and other capabilities of Windows Server 2012, the result is a highly available storage solution that has all the power and flexibility of a SAN but is considerably cheaper and also easier to manage.

Storage Spaces terminology

Storage Spaces can virtualize storage to create what are called storage pools. A *storage pool* is an aggregation of unallocated space on physical disks installed in or connected to servers. Storage pools are flexible and elastic, allowing you to add or remove disks from the pool as your demand for storage grows or shrinks.

Once you've created a storage pool using Storage Spaces, you can provision storage from the pool by creating virtual disks. A virtual disk behaves exactly like a physical disk except that it can span multiple physical disks within the storage pool. Virtual disks can host simple volumes or volumes with resiliency (mirroring or parity) to increase the reliability or performance of the disk. A virtual disk is sometimes called a *LUN*.

Configuring a storage pool

Configuring a storage pool using Storage Spaces requires that you have at least one unallocated physical disk available (a disk with no volumes on it). If you want to create a mirrored volume, you'll need at least two physical disks; a parity volume requires at least three physical disks. Pools can consist of a mixture of disks of different types and sizes. Table 3-3 shows the different types of disks supported by Storage Spaces. These disks could be installed inside servers on your network or within just-a-bunch-of-disks (JBOD) enclosures.

TABLE 3-3 Types of Disks Supported by Storage Spaces

Type of drive	Stand-alone file servers	Clustered file servers
SATA	Supported	
SCSI	Supported	
iSCSI	Supported	Supported
SAS	Supported	Supported
USB	Supported	

You can use Server Manager or PowerShell to configure your storage pools, virtual disks, and volumes. To create a new storage pool using Server Manager, select Storage Pools under File And Storage Services. The primordial pool contains unallocated physical disks on the servers you are managing.

To create a new storage pool, click Tasks in the Storage Pools tile and select New Storage Pool:

The New Storage Pool Wizard is started, and after specifying a name for your new pool, you can select which physical disks you want to include in your pool. We'll select all three available Serial Attached SCSI (SAS) disks for our pool, with the first two disks used for storage and the third designated as a "hot spare" disk that Storage Spaces can bring online automatically if it needs to, such as if one of the other two disks fails:

New Storage Pool Wizard

Select physical disks for the storage pool

Before You Begin
Storage Pool Name
Physical Disks
Confirmation
Results

Select unused physical disks for the storage pool, and choose whether volumes can automatically allocate free space from the physical disks. To reserve physical disks for use by specific volumes, select manual allocation.

Physical disks:

☑	Name	Capacity	Bus	RPM	Model	Allocation	
☑	PhysicalDisk1	699 GB	SAS	1		Data Store ▾	
☑	PhysicalDisk2	699 GB	SAS	1		Data Store ▾	
☑	PhysicalDisk3	932 GB	SAS	1		Hot Spare ▾	

Data Store
Manual
Hot Spare

Total selected capacity: 2.27 TB

< Previous   Next >   Create   Cancel

On completing the wizard, you have the option of creating a new virtual disk when the wizard closes:

New Storage Pool Wizard

View results

Before You Begin
Storage Pool Name
Physical Disks
Confirmation
Results

You have successfully completed the New Storage Pool Wizard.

Task	Progress	Status
Gather information		Completed
Create storage pool		Completed
Add hot spare drives		Completed
Update cache		Completed

ⓘ You can now create one or more virtual disks in this storage pool.

☑ Create a virtual disk when this wizard closes

< Previous   Next >   Close   Cancel

The New Virtual Disk Wizard lets you provision storage from your new pool to create virtual disks that span one or more physical disks within your pool:

New Virtual Disk Wizard

Select the server and storage pool

Before You Begin
Storage Pool
Virtual Disk Name
Storage Layout
Provisioning
Size
Confirmation
Results

Server:

Server Name	Status	Cluster Role	Owner Node
WS8B	Online	Cluster Node	

Storage pool:

Pool Name	Capacity	Free Space	Subsystem
CONTOSO Pool	1.59 TB	1.59 TB	Storage Spaces

< Previous   Next >   Create   Cancel

After you have selected a pool and specified a name for your new virtual disk, you can choose whether to create a simple virtual disk or one with resiliency:

New Virtual Disk Wizard

Select the storage layout

Before You Begin
Storage Pool
Virtual Disk Name
Storage Layout
Provisioning
Size
Confirmation
Results

Layout:

Simple
Mirror
Parity

Description:

Data is duplicated on two or three physical disks. This increases reliability, but reduces capacity by 50 to 66.

< Previous   Next >   Create   Cancel

Next, you will select either fixed or thin as the provisioning type (thin provisioning is discussed later in this chapter):

You'll also need to specify the size of your new virtual disk. Once you've finished provisioning your new virtual disk, you can create volumes on it using the New Volume Wizard by selecting a server and virtual disk and specifying size, drive letter, and file system settings for the volume.

Once you've finished creating your storage pools, virtual disks, and volumes, you can manage them using the Storage Pool page of Server Manager:

Provisioning and managing storage using PowerShell

Although the new Server Manager user interface in Windows Server 2012 provides a very convenient and intuitive workflow to provision and manage storage, interaction with PowerShell is required to access many of the advanced features afforded by the new Storage Management application programming interface (API). For example, you can easily create a virtual disk in the user interface; however, the wizard only allows setting the following parameters:

- Underlying storage pool name
- Virtual disk name
- Resiliency setting (Simple, Mirror, or Parity)
- Provisioning type (Thin or Fixed)
- Virtual disk size

In contrast, when creating a virtual disk via PowerShell, you can specify additional parameters to tune both resiliency and performance:

- Number of columns: The number of columns the virtual disk contains
- Number of data copies: Number of complete copies of data that can be maintained
- Disk interleave: Number of bytes forming a stripe
- Physical disks to use: Specific disks to use in the virtual disk

For example, assume that I have an existing pool with the following attributes:

- Friendly Name: Pool01
- Disks: nine 450-GB disks (each allocated as Data Store)
- Pool Capacity: 3.68 TB

If I then create a simple 200-GB virtual disk via the user interface named VDiskSimpleUI, the resulting virtual disk uses eight columns and maintains one copy of the data. But when creating the virtual disk via PowerShell, I can force the stripping across all nine of the disks and optimize performance as follows:

```
New-VirtualDisk -StoragePoolFriendlyName Pool01 -ResiliencySettingName Simple -Size 200GB
-FriendlyName VDiskSimplePS -ProvisioningType Fixed -NumberOfDataCopies 1 -NumberOfColumns 9
```

And creating a mirrored 200-GB virtual disk via the user interface named VDiskMirrorUI produces a virtual disk with four columns and two data copies. But with PowerShell, I can create a slightly different configuration, increasing the data protection (and also the disk footprint):

```
New-VirtualDisk -StoragePoolFriendlyName Pool01 -ResiliencySettingName Mirror -Size 200GB
-FriendlyName VDiskMirrorPS -ProvisioningType Fixed -NumberOfDataCopies 3 -NumberOfColumns 3
```

The results and differences of these various permutations can be easily displayed via PowerShell:

```
Get-VirtualDisk | ft FriendlyName, ResiliencySettingName, NumberOfColumns,
NumberOfDataCopies, @{Expression={$_.Size / 1GB}; Label="Size(GB)"}, @{Expression={$_.
FootprintOnPool / 1GB}; Label="PoolFootprint(GB)"} -AutoSize
```

Here is some output from running this command:

```
FriendlyName    ResiliencySettingName NumberOfColumns
NumberOfDataCopies Size(GB) PoolFootprint(GB)

------------    --------------------- ---------------  ----------------
-- -------- -----------------

VDiskSimpleUI Simple                                8              1
200               200

VDiskMirrorUI Mirror                                4              2
200               400

VDiskSimplePS Simple                                9              1
200.25            200.25

VDiskMirrorPS Mirror                                3              3
200.25            600.75
```

Some additional tips:

- The number of columns multiplied by the number of data copies cannot exceed the number of disks in the underlying pool.
- 256 MB of each physical disk is consumed when adding to a pool.
- Default resiliency settings:
  - Simple: Striping with no redundancy using a default stripe size of 64 K
  - Mirror: Two-way mirroring with a 64-K default stripe size
  - Parity: Striping with parity using a default column width of 3 (i.e., three disks per row with two containing data and the other containing parity) and a default stripe size of 64 K
- Although not enforced, it is recommended that pools with more than 24 disks use Manual allocation (as opposed to the auto allocation default of Data Store)
- Clustering tips:
  - Clustering virtual disks requires the underlying hardware to support persistent reservations.
  - Clustered Storage Spaces require fixed provisioning.

- Removing a clustered Storage Pool from Failover Clustering will cause the underlying pool to be marked Read Only.

- PowerShell links:
  - New-VirtualDisk:
    http://technet.microsoft.com/en-us/library/hh848643.aspx

  - New-StoragePool:
    http://technet.microsoft.com/en-us/library/hh848689.aspx

Joshua Adams
Senior Program Manager, Enterprise Engineering Center (EEC)

Learn more

For more information about Storage Spaces in Windows Server 2012, see the following topics in the TechNet Library:

- "Storage Spaces Overview" at
  http://technet.microsoft.com/en-us/library/hh831739.aspx.

- "Storage Management Overview" at
  http://technet.microsoft.com/en-us/library/hh831751.aspx.

- "File and Storage Services overview" at
  http://technet.microsoft.com/en-us/library/hh831487.aspx/.

You can also download the "Understand and Troubleshoot Storage Spaces in Windows Server '8' Beta" from *http://www.microsoft.com/download/en/details.aspx?id=29002.*

Thin Provisioning and Trim

Thin provisioning is a new capability in Windows Server 2012 that integrates with supported storage technologies, including the built-in Storage Spaces feature to allow just-in-time allocation of storage. Trim capability complements thin provisioning by enabling the reclaiming of provisioned storage that is no longer needed.

Thin provisioning is designed to address several issues with traditional models for provisioning storage used by enterprises:

- The challenges associated with forecasting your organization's future storage needs makes it hard to pre-allocate storage capacity to meet changing demand for storage.

- Pre-allocated storage is often underused, which leads to inefficiencies and unnecessary expenditures.

- Managing an enterprise storage system can often add considerable overhead to the overall cost of managing your IT infrastructure.

The goals of thin provisioning technologies are to address these different needs and deliver the following business benefits:

- Maximizing how the organization's storage assets are used
- Optimizing capital and operational expenditures for managing storage assets
- Provisioning storage with high availability, scalability, performance, and resilience

Learn more

For more information about thin provisioning and trim in Windows Server 2012, see the topic "Thin Provisioning and Trim Storage Technical Overview" in the TechNet Library at *http://technet.microsoft.com/en-us/library/hh831391.aspx*.

You can also download a white paper titled "Thin Provisioning in Windows Server 8: Features and Management of LUN Provisioning," which is available from the Windows Hardware Development site on MSDN at *http://msdn.microsoft.com/en-us/library/windows/hardware/hh770514.aspx*.

Server for NFS data store

Server for NFS has been enhanced in Windows Server 2012 to support continuous availability. This makes possible new scenarios, such as running VMware ESX VMs from file-based storage over the NFS protocol instead of using more expensive SAN storage. This improvement enables Windows Server 2012 to provide continuous availability for VMware VMs, making it easier for organizations to integrate their VMware infrastructure with the Windows platform.

Using Server for NFS as a data store for VMware VMs requires using VMware ESX 4.1. You also need a management server with VMware vSphere Client version 4.1 installed. You can use PowerShell to provision and configure shared files on your Server for NFS data store.

Learn more

For more information about Server for NFS Data Store Technical Preview in Windows Server 2012, see the topic "Server for NFS Data Store Technical Preview" in the TechNet Library at *http://technet.microsoft.com/en-us/library/hh831653.aspx*.

The most robust virtualization solution on the market

Competitive product analysis is a process that architects and engineers are often expected to participate in. Whether it is for internal strategic decision making or external solution design, the objective remains consistent: to determine what products accomplish certain goals and include specific features for the least possible cost. Having certain features or overcoming certain business challenges can often make or break the product's chances of being a part of the solution design win, and therefore they can be detrimental to the survival of the product itself.

One of the most abundant competitive product analyses occurring in the last five years or so has been around server virtualization and the competing software vendors (mainly because this discussion scales from small businesses to very large organizations). As an architect, I can't tell you how many times I was pulled into customer discussions to talk about the comparisons between Hyper-V and VMWare vSphere (and ultimately tell them which one was better for their company). The result of the discussion, prior to today, has often leaned away from the Hyper-V solution. Customers wanted a more feature-rich solution that could scale into large-enterprise environments easily.

Clearly noticing their need to stay in the game (relating to my first point of being detrimental to product survival), Microsoft has equalized the game (and even greatly surpassed its competition in some cases) with the release of Windows Server 2012 and the included version of Hyper-V clustering. Features such as Live Migration and failover placement have been greatly enhanced while components such as VM priorities (which allow granular control of VM importance in the environment), Storage Migration, and Hyper-V Replica have been added as game-changers in the virtualization world. All of these features, when used together, help to complete the "continuous availability" puzzle for your VMs.

Another important point to note is the significant rework that Microsoft has done with the management of their clustered environment. With clusters now capable of scaling to 64 nodes encompassing 4,000 VMs, a more streamlined management solution was needed. Improvements to cluster manager that include features such as CAU have been added. CAU allows online and automatic updating of your Hyper-V host machines, while automatically relocating your VMs back and forth. This allows the administrator to fully update their Hyper-V environment without impacting any running services. (Note: This does not include guest operating systems.)

As you can clearly see by the content of the surrounding chapters, Hyper-V has become the most robust virtualization solution on the market. With integration already in place in the vast majority of IT organizations, there will be little reason (technical or financial) to be considering any other virtualization solution in the near future.
Ted Archer
Consultant, Virtualization and Core Infrastructure

Management efficiency

Provisioning and managing servers efficiently is an essential ingredient for cloud computing. Whether you are a mid-sized organization implementing a dedicated private cloud, a large enterprise deploying a shared private cloud, or a hoster managing a multitenant public cloud, Windows Server 2012 provides both the platform and the tools for managing your environment.

The new Server Manager of Windows Server 2012 can simplify the job of managing multiple remote servers across your organization. Enhancements to Active Directory can make your Active Directory environment much easier to deploy and manage than with previous versions of Windows Server. Domain controllers can now be safely cloned in order to save time when you need to deploy additional capacity, and restoring domain controller snapshots no longer disrupts your Active Directory environment. Foundational to successful cloud computing is automation, and version 3.0 of PowerShell in Windows Server 2012 includes numerous enhancements that extend its capabilities and improve its usefulness in server administration.

The new Server Manager

Server Manager has been redesigned in Windows Server 2012 to facilitate managing multiple remote servers from a single administration console. Server Manager uses the remote management capabilities of Windows Management Instrumentation (WMI), PowerShell, and the Distributed Component Object Model (DCOM) for connecting to remote servers to manage them. By default, servers running Windows Server 2012 are enabled for remote management, making it easy to provision and configure remote servers using Server Manager or PowerShell. For example, in previous versions of Windows Server, you needed either physical access to a server or a Remote Desktop connection to the server if you wanted to add or remove a role or feature on the server. With Windows Server 2012, however, you can provision roles and features quickly and easily on remote servers from a central location by using Server Manager.

Server Manager is also included in the Remote Server Administration Tools (RSAT) for Windows 8, which enables administrators to manage their organization's server infrastructure from a client workstation running Windows 8. Server Manager can also be used to manage servers running Windows Server 2008 R2, Windows Server 2008, or Windows Server 2003, provided that remote management has been suitably configured on these systems.

Using Server Manager

The dashboard section of Server Manager shows you the state of your servers at a glance. The dashboard uses a 10-minute polling cycle so it's not a live monitoring solution like the System Center Operations Manager, but it does give you a general picture of what's happening with each server role in your environment. For example, in the following screenshot, the tile for the DNS role indicates an alert in the Best Practices Analyzer results for the DNS Server role:

Clicking the alert brings up the details of the alert, indicating a possible problem with the configuration of one of the DNS servers in the environment:

The Local Server section of Server Manager lets you view and configure various settings on your local server. You can also perform various actions on the local server, or on other servers in the available pool, by using the Manage and Tools menus. For example, you can add new roles or features to a server by selecting Add Roles And Features from the Manage menu:

The Select Destination Server page of the new Add Roles And Features Wizard lets you select either a server from the server pool or an offline VHD as your destination server. The ability to provision roles and features directly to offline VHDs is a new feature of Windows Server 2012 that helps administrators deploy server workloads in virtualized data centers:

The All Servers section of Server Manager displays the pool of servers available for management. Right-clicking a server lets you perform different administrative tasks on that server:

To populate the server pool, right-click All Servers in Server Management and select Add Server from the shortcut menu. Doing this opens the Add Servers dialog box, which lets you search for servers in Active Directory, either by computer name or IP address or by importing a text file containing a list of computer names or IP addresses. Once you've found the servers you want to add to the pool, you can double-click them to add them to the Selected list on the right:

Servers are often better managed if they are grouped together according to their function, location, or other characteristics. Server Manager lets you create custom groups of servers from your server pool so that you can manage them as a group instead of individually. To do this, select Create Server Group from the Manage menu at the top of Server Manager. Doing this opens the Create Server Group dialog box, which lets you specify a name for the new server group and select multiple servers from your server pool to add to the group:

Once you've added servers to your new group, you can select multiple servers in your group and perform actions on them such as restarting:

The Tools menu at the top of Server Manager can be used to start other management tools, such as MMC consoles. However, as the new Server Manager of the Windows Server platform evolves toward a true multiserver management experience, such single-server MMC consoles will likely become tightly integrated into Server Manager. With Windows Server 2012, such integration is already present for two roles: Remote Desktop Services and file and storage management. For example, by selecting File And Storage Services, you can manage the file servers, storage pools, volumes, shares, and iSCSI virtual disks in your environment:

Learn more

For more information about the new Server Manager, see the following topics in the TechNet Library:

- "Automation and Management Technical Preview" at
  http://technet.microsoft.com/en-us/library/hh831586.aspx.

- "Manage multiple, remote servers with Server Manager" at
  http://technet.microsoft.com/en-us/library/hh831456.aspx.

- "Remote, Multiserver Management: scenario overview" at
  http://technet.microsoft.com/en-us/library/hh831378.aspx.

- "Unified Remote Management for File Services Technical Preview" at
  http://technet.microsoft.com/en-us/library/hh831838.aspx.

Simplified Active Directory administration

Active Directory is foundational to the IT infrastructure of most organizations today, and Windows Server 2012 includes new capabilities and enhancements that help you deploy and manage your Active Directory environment. Whether you have a traditional datacenter or are migrating to the cloud, the new features and functionality of Active Directory in Windows Server 2012 will make your job easier.

Deploying domain controllers

The process for deploying domain controllers is faster and more flexible in Windows Server 2012. The Dcpromo.exe wizard of previous versions of Windows Server has been replaced with a new Active Directory Domain Services Configuration Wizard that is built upon PowerShell (see Figure 3-8). This redesign provides a number of benefits. For example, you can now install the AD DS server role binaries remotely using Server Manager or with the new AD DS PowerShell cmdlets. You can also install the binaries on multiple servers at the same time. Adprep.exe has now been integrated into the Active Directory installation process to make it easier to prepare your existing Active Directory environment for upgrading to Windows Server 2012. And the Active Directory Domain Services Configuration Wizard performs validation to ensure that the necessary prerequisites have been met before promoting a server to a domain controller.

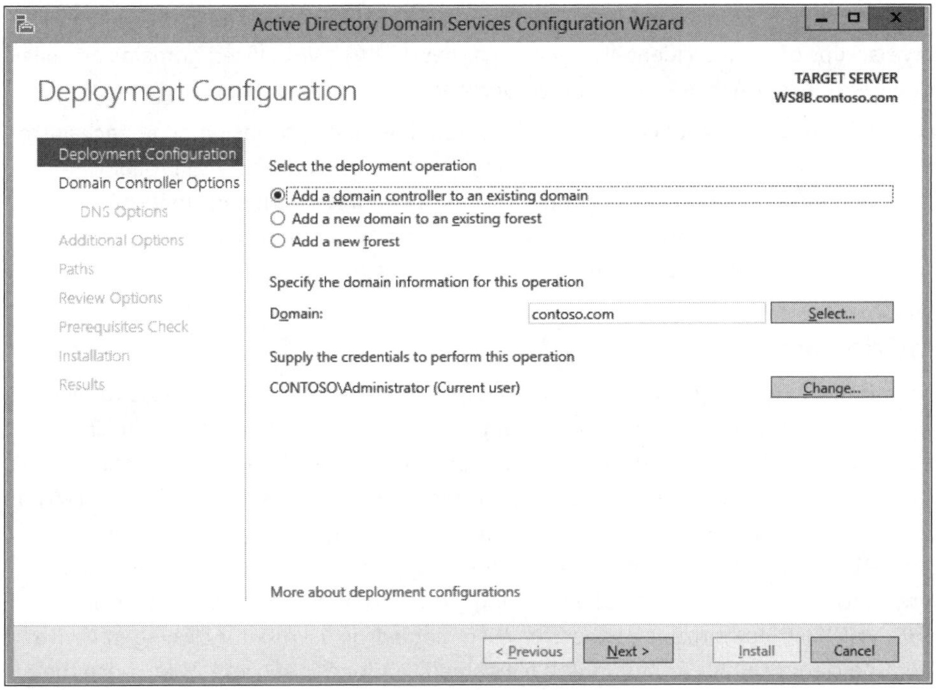

FIGURE 3-8 The Active Directory Domain Services Configuration Wizard replaces Dcpromo.exe and is built upon PowerShell.

Of course, everything you can do using the Configuration Wizard can also be done directly using PowerShell. Figure 3-9 lists the PowerShell cmdlets available in the ADDSDeployment module. These cmdlets can be scripted to automate the deployment and configuration of domain controllers within your datacenter or across your private cloud.

```
Administrator: Windows PowerShell                                    _  □  X

PS C:\Users\Administrator> get-command -module ADDSDeployment

Capability      Name                                              ModuleName
----------      ----                                              ----------
Cmdlet          Add-ADDSReadOnlyDomainControllerAccount            ADDSDeployment
Cmdlet          Install-ADDSDomain                                 ADDSDeployment
Cmdlet          Install-ADDSDomainController                       ADDSDeployment
Cmdlet          Install-ADDSForest                                 ADDSDeployment
Cmdlet          Test-ADDSDomainControllerInstallation             ADDSDeployment
Cmdlet          Test-ADDSDomainControllerUninstallation           ADDSDeployment
Cmdlet          Test-ADDSDomainInstallation                        ADDSDeployment
Cmdlet          Test-ADDSForestInstallation                        ADDSDeployment
Cmdlet          Test-ADDSReadOnlyDomainControllerAccountCreation   ADDSDeployment
Cmdlet          Uninstall-ADDSDomainController                     ADDSDeployment


PS C:\Users\Administrator> _
```

FIGURE 3-9 The PowerShell cmdlets available in the ADDSDeployment module.

Virtualizing domain controllers

In previous versions of Windows Server, virtualizing a domain controller by running it in a VM was risky. Because of how Active Directory replication works, reverting a virtualized domain controller to an earlier state by applying a snapshot could cause Active Directory replication to fail. Because snapshots are commonly used in Hyper-V environments for performing quick and dirty backups of VMs, accidentally applying a snapshot to a virtualized domain controller could easily wreck your Active Directory environment.

Windows Server 2012 prevents such situations from happening by including a mechanism that safeguards your Active Directory environment if a virtualized domain controller is rolled back in time by using a snapshot. Note that although this now means that snapshots can be taken and used with virtualized domain controllers, Microsoft still recommends that snapshots not be used for this purpose.

Cloning domain controllers

When your business grows, you may need to deploy additional domain controllers to meet the expanding needs of your organization. Being able to rapidly provision new domain controllers is important, particularly in cloud environments where elasticity is essential. In Windows Server 2012, you can now safely deploy cloned virtual domain controllers instead of having to go through the time-consuming process of deploying a sysprepped server image, adding the AD DS role, and promoting and configuring the server as a domain controller. All you need to do is export the VM of an existing virtual domain controller or make a copy of its VHD/VHDX file, authorize the exported VM or copied virtual disk for cloning in Active Directory, and create an XML configuration file named DCCloneConfig.xml. Then, once the destination VM is deployed and has started, the cloned domain controller provisions itself as a new domain controller.

Cloning virtualized domain controllers like this can make it much easier for you to scale out your Active Directory environment. For example, if you have a branch office that is rapidly growing and has an existing virtualized domain controller on site, you can simply clone that domain controller to support the growing needs of your branch office infrastructure.

Another scenario where cloning virtualized domain controllers can be useful is helping ensure business continuity. For example, if a disaster happens and you lose some domain controllers in your organization, you can restore the level of capacity needed quickly by cloning more domain controllers.

Other improvements

The Active Directory Administrative Center (ADAC) was first introduced in Windows Server 2008 R2 as a central management console for Active Directory administrators. ADAC is built on PowerShell and has been enhanced in Windows Server 2012 to provide a rich graphical user interface for managing all aspects of your Active Directory environment (see Figure 3-10).

FIGURE 3-10 The Active Directory Administrative Center in Windows Server 2012.

A number of improvements have been made to ADAC in Windows Server 2012 to make it easier to manage your Active Directory infrastructure. For example:

- The Active Directory Recycle Bin, first introduced in Windows Server 2008 R2, has been enhanced in Windows Server 2012 with a new GUI to make it easier for you to find and restore deleted objects.

- Fine-grained password policies, also first introduced in Windows Server 2008 R2, have been enhanced in Windows Server 2012 with a new GUI as well, making it possible to view, sort, and manage all password policies in a given domain.

- Windows PowerShell History Viewer helps you quickly create PowerShell scripts to automate Active Directory administration tasks by viewing and utilizing the PowerShell commands underlying any actions performed using the user interface of ADAC. For example, Figure 3-11 shows the PowerShell commands that were run when ADAC was used to create a new organizational unit for the marketing department of Contoso.

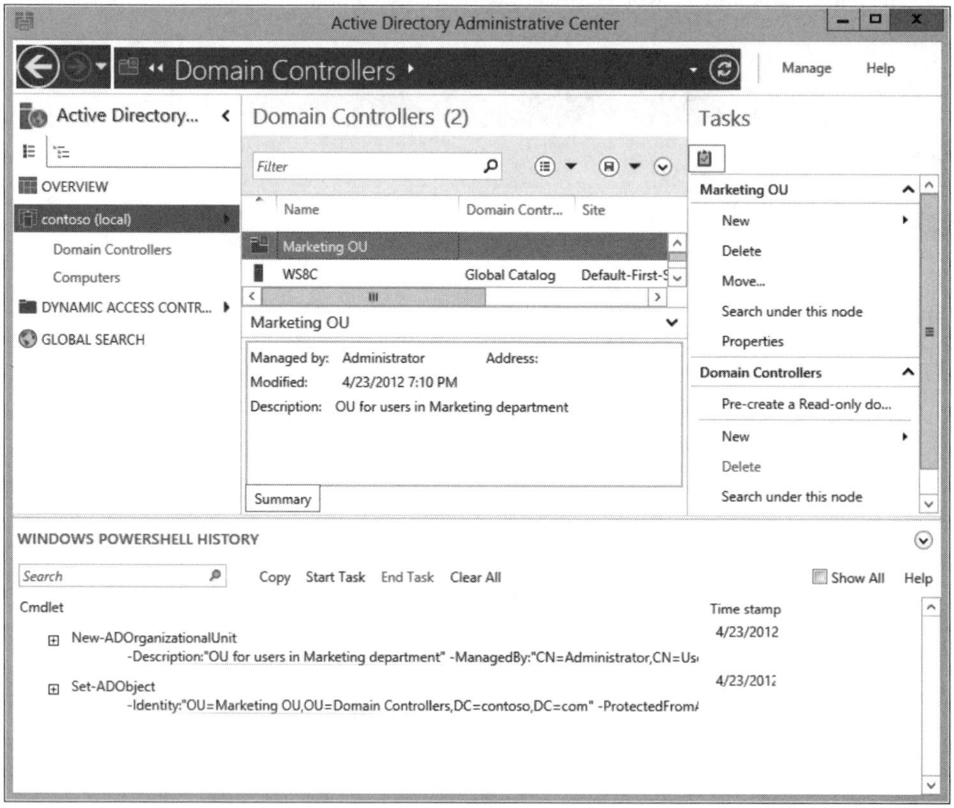

FIGURE 3-11 The Windows PowerShell History Viewer can provide you with commands you can use to create your own PowerShell scripts for managing Active Directory.

Learn more

For more information about the new features and enhanced capabilities of Active Directory in Windows Server 2012, see the following topics in the TechNet Library:

- "What's new in Active Directory Domain Services (AD DS)" at *http://technet.microsoft.com/en-us/library/hh831356.aspx*.

- "Easier to Manage and Deploy Active Directory: scenario overview" at *http://technet.microsoft.com/en-us/library/hh831816.aspx*.

- "Deploy Active Directory Domain Services (AD DS) in your Enterprise" at *http://technet.microsoft.com/en-us/library/hh472160.aspx*.

- "Active Directory Domain Services (AD DS) Virtualization" at *http://technet.microsoft.com/en-us/library/hh831734.aspx*.

- "Active Directory Administrative Center Enhancements" at *http://technet.microsoft.com/en-us/library/hh831702.aspx*.

You can also download the following guides from the Microsoft Download Center:

- "Understand and Troubleshoot AD DS Simplified Administration in Windows Server '8' Beta" at *http://www.microsoft.com/download/en/details.aspx?id=29019*.

- "Understand and Troubleshoot Virtualized Domain Controller (VDC) in Windows Server '8' Beta" at *http://www.microsoft.com/download/en/details.aspx?id=29001*.

For additional information on Active Directory improvements in Windows Server 2012, see the Ask the Directory Services Team blog at *http://blogs.technet.com/b/askds/*.

PowerShell 3.0

PowerShell has become the de facto platform for automating the administration of Windows-based environments. Built on top of the common language runtime (CLR) and the Microsoft .NET Framework, PowerShell has brought a whole new paradigm to how computers running Windows are configured and managed in enterprise environments.

A new version 3.0 of PowerShell is now included in Windows Server 2012. PowerShell 3.0 is built upon the Windows Management Framework 3.0, which includes a new WMI provider model that reduces dependency on COM, a new API for performing standard Common Information Model (CIM) operations, and the capability of writing new PowerShell cmdlets in native code. Windows Management Framework 3.0 also includes improvements that make WinRM connections more robust so they can support long-running tasks and be more resilient against transient network failure.

PowerShell 3.0 includes many new features that bring added flexibility and power for managing cloud and multiserver environments. Many of these key new capabilities are discussed next.

New cmdlets

Windows Server 2012 includes hundreds of new PowerShell cmdlets that help you manage almost every aspect of your private cloud environment. Note that many cmdlets are only available when the appropriate server role or feature is installed. For a complete list of PowerShell modules included with Windows Server 2012, see *http://technet.microsoft.com/en-us/library/hh801904.aspx*.

Show-Command

PowerShell 3.0 includes a new cmdlet called *Show-Command* that displays a GUI for a command with a simpler overview of any PowerShell cmdlet. This capability can make it much easier to understand the syntax of a cmdlet, as opposed to using the Get-Help cmdlet. For example, if you want to understand the syntax of the Install-ADDSDomain cmdlet used to promote a server to a domain controller, you can type **Get-Command Install-ADDSDomain** in the PowerShell console to open the dialog box shown in Figure 3-12.

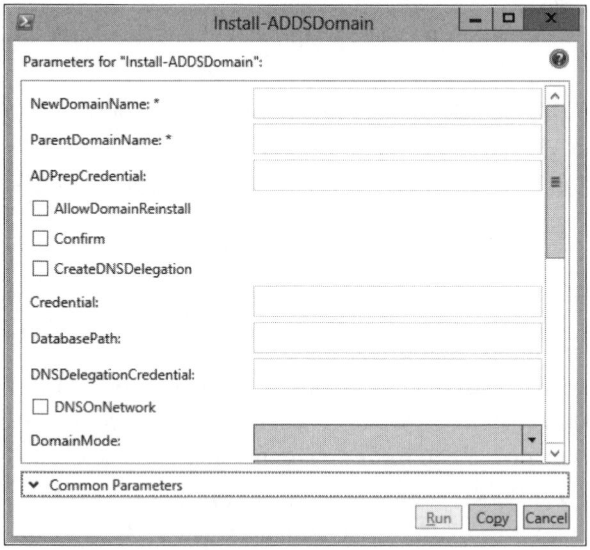

FIGURE 3-12 Example of using the Show-Command cmdlet.

For more information on the capabilities of the Get-Command cmdlet, see the blog post titled "Running show-command for a cmdlet" on the PowerShell blog at *http://blogs.msdn.com/b/powershell/archive/2012/04/13/running-show-command-for-a-cmdlet.aspx*.

Disconnected sessions

PowerShell 3.0 now supports persistent user-managed sessions (PSSessions) that are not dependent upon the session in which they were created. By using the New-PSSession cmdlet, you can create and save a session on a remote server and then disconnect from the session.

The PowerShell commands in the session on the remote server will then continue to execute, even though you are no longer connected to the session. If desired, you can reconnect later to the session from the same or a different computer.

To work with disconnect sessions, you simply do the following:

1. Enable remoting.

2. Create a PSSession to the remote computer.

3. Invoke some PowerShell commands on the remote computer.

4. Verify the completion of the commands on the remote computer.

PowerShell workflows

PowerShell workflows let you write workflows in PowerShell or using Extensible Application Markup Language (XAML) and then run your workflows as if they were PowerShell cmdlets. This enables PowerShell to use the capabilities of the Windows Workflow Foundation to create long-running management activities that can be interrupted, suspended, restarted, repeated, and executed in parallel.

PowerShell workflows are especially valuable in cloud computing environments because they help you automate administrative operations by building in repeatability and by increasing robustness and reliability. They also help increase your servers-to-administrators ratio by enabling a single administrator to execute a PowerShell workflow that runs simultaneously on hundreds of servers.

For a detailed discussion of how to construct PowerShell workflows using both new PowerShell 3.0 syntax and XAML, see the blog post titled "When Windows PowerShell Met Workflow" on the PowerShell blog at *http://blogs.msdn.com/b/powershell/archive/2012/03/17/when-windows-powershell-met-workflow.aspx*.

Scheduled Jobs

PowerShell 2.0 introduced the concept of background jobs, which can be scheduled to run asynchronously in the background. PowerShell 3.0 now includes cmdlets like Start-Job and Get-Job that can be used to manage these jobs. You can also easily schedule jobs using the Windows Task Scheduler. This means that you, as the administrator, can now have full control over when PowerShell scripts execute in your environment.

For a detailed look at how you can create and manage background jobs in PowerShell 3.0, see the blog post titled "Scheduling Background Jobs in Windows PowerShell 3.0" on the PowerShell blog at *http://blogs.msdn.com/b/powershell/archive/2012/03/19/scheduling-background-jobs-in-windows-powershell-3-0.aspx*.

PowerShell Web Access

PowerShell Web Access lets you manage the servers in your private cloud from anywhere, at any time, by running PowerShell commands within a web-based console. PowerShell Web Access acts as a gateway to provide a web-based PowerShell console that you can use to manage remote computers. This lets you run PowerShell scripts and commands even on computers that don't have PowerShell installed. All your computer needs is an Internet connection and a web browser that supports JavaScript and accepts cookies.

To use PowerShell Web Access, begin by installing it using the Add Roles And Features Wizard, which you can start from Server Manager:

Installing PowerShell Web Access also installs the .NET Framework 4.5 features and the Web Server (IIS) server role, if these are not already installed on the server. You can also install PowerShell Web Access with PowerShell by using the Install-WindowsFeature cmdlet.

Next, configure PowerShell Web Access on your server. You can do this by running the Install-PswaWebApplication cmdlet. You'll need to have already installed a server certificate on your server. If you are trying this in a test environment, however, you can use a self-signed test certificate, as shown here:

```
Administrator: Windows PowerShell                                          _ □ x

PS C:\Users\Administrator.CONTOSO> Install-PswaWebApplication -useTestCertificate
WARNING: Using a test certificate in a production environment is not recommended due to security reasons. This should
be used only for internal testing of Windows PowerShell Web Access. The test certificate will expire in 90 days.
Creating application pool pswa_pool...

Name                    State        Applications
----                    -----        ------------
pswa_pool               Started

Creating web application pswa...

Path                : /pswa
ApplicationPool     : pswa_pool
EnabledProtocols    : http
PhysicalPath        : C:\Windows\Web\PowerShellWebAccess\wwwroot


Creating self-signed certificate...


Creating HTTPS binding...

IPAddress : 0.0.0.0
Port      : 443
Host      :
Store     : My
Sites     : Microsoft.IIs.PowerShell.Framework.ConfigurationAttribute


PS C:\Users\Administrator.CONTOSO> _
```

Once you've configured PowerShell Web Access, you need to grant users access explicitly by adding authorization rules. You can use the Add-PswaAuthorizationRule cmdlet to do this:

```
Administrator: Windows PowerShell                                          _ □ x

PS C:\Users\Administrator.CONTOSO> Add-PswaAuthorizationRule -UserName CONTOSO\Administrator -ComputerName WS8B.contoso.
com -ConfigurationName AdminsOnly

Id    RuleName       User                        Destination            ConfigurationName
--    --------       ----                        -----------            -----------------
0     Rule 0         CONTOSO\Administrator       WS8B.contoso.com       AdminsOnly

PS C:\Users\Administrator.CONTOSO> Get-PswaAuthorizationRule

Id    RuleName       User                        Destination            ConfigurationName
--    --------       ----                        -----------            -----------------
0     Rule 0         CONTOSO\Administrator       WS8B.contoso.com       AdminsOnly

PS C:\Users\Administrator.CONTOSO> _
```

Administrators can then run PowerShell scripts and commands against servers they have been authorized to manage by accessing the gateway from a remote computer. They do this by opening the URL *https://<server_name>/pswa* in a web browser:

For more information on setting up and using PowerShell Web Access, see the topic titled "Deploy Windows PowerShell Web Access" in the TechNet Library at *http://technet.microsoft .com/en-us/library/hh831611.aspx*.

Managing non-Windows systems and devices

You can now use PowerShell cmdlets to manage any standard-compliant CIM-capable systems, which means you can manage non-Windows servers and even hardware devices using PowerShell just as you manage Windows. For a detailed overview of this capability, see the blog post titled "Standards-based Management in Windows Server '8' on the Windows Server Blog at *http://blogs.technet.com/b/windowsserver/archive/2012/03/30/standards-based-management-in-windows-server-8.aspx*.

Other improvements

Some other improvements in PowerShell 3.0 include the following;

- Delegated administration using RunAs allows commands to be executed using a delegated set of credentials so that users having limited permissions can run critical jobs.
- Improved cmdlet discovery and automatic module loading make it easier to find and run any cmdlets installed on your computer.

- Show-Command, a cmdlet and ISE Add-On that helps you quickly find the right cmdlet, view its parameters in a dialog box, and run the command.

- Simplified language syntax that make PowerShell commands and scripts seem a lot less like code and feel more like natural language. For example, the construct $_. is no longer necessary.

- The Get-ChildItem cmdlet has new parameters, making it easier to search for files with particular attributes.

- PowerShell now automatically loads a module when a cmdlet is run from that module.

- The PowerShell 3.0 Integrated Scripting Environment (ISE) includes new features that make it easier to code in PowerShell. Examples of these features include Intellisense, brace-matching, syntax coloring, Most Recently Used list, snippets, and the ISE Script Explorer.

- With PowerShell 3.0, you are no longer restricted to the help content that shipped with Windows Server 2012. Help is now published on the web as downloadable CAB files.

Learn more

For more information about PowerShell 3.0 in Windows Server 2012, see the following topics in the TechNet Library:

- "What's New in Windows PowerShell 3.0" at *http://technet.microsoft.com/en-us/library/hh857339.aspx.*

- "Deploy Windows PowerShell Web Access" at *http://technet.microsoft.com/en-us/library/hh831611.aspx.*

- "Windows PowerShell Support for Windows Server '8' Beta" at *http://technet.microsoft.com/en-us/library/hh801904.aspx.*

For additional information on PowerShell 3.0, see the Windows PowerShell Blog at *http://blogs.msdn.com/b/powershell/.*

Up next

The next chapter will examine how you can use Windows Server 2012 to deploy web applications on premises and in the cloud so that they are flexible, scalable, and elastic.

CHAPTER 4

Deploy web applications on premises and in the cloud

- Scalable and elastic web platform **155**

- Support for open standards **182**

- Up next **186**

This chapter examines some of the new features and capabilities of version 8 of the Internet Information Services (IIS) web platform in Windows Server 2012. IIS 8 provides the foundation for hosting web applications, both on premises and in cloud environments, and provides a scalable and elastic platform that fully supports open industry standards.

Scalable and elastic web platform

Web hosting platforms like IIS are the foundation for cloud computing, and they need both scalability and elasticity to be effective. A platform has scalability if it allows additional resources such as processing power, memory, or storage to be provisioned to meet increasing demand. For example, if users of applications running on your web server farm are complaining about delays and slow performance, you may need to add more servers to your farm to scale outward. Or you might upgrade your existing servers by adding more memory to scale them upward. Elasticity, on the other hand, means allowing such additional resources to be provisioned automatically on demand.

Whether you are an enterprise hosting line of business (LoB) applications or a cloud hosting provider managing a multi-tenant public cloud, IIS 8 in Windows Server 2012 can enhance both the scalability and elasticity of your hosting environment. IIS 8 provides increased scale through improved Secure Sockets Layer (SSL) scalability, better manageability via centralized SSL certificate support, Non-Uniform Memory Access (NUMA)–aware scalability to provide greater performance on cutting-edge hardware, and other new features and enhancements.

NUMA-aware scalability

High-end server hardware is rapidly evolving. Powerful servers that are too expensive today for many smaller businesses to acquire will soon be commonplace.

NUMA, which until recently was available only on high-end server hardware, will probably be a standard feature of commodity servers within the next two years. NUMA was designed to overcome the scalability limits of the traditional symmetric multi-processing (SMP) architecture, where all memory access happens on the same shared memory bus. SMP works well when you have a small number of CPUs, but it doesn't when you have dozens of them competing for access to the shared bus. NUMA alleviates such bottlenecks by limiting how many CPUs can be on any one memory bus and connecting them with a high-speed interconnection.

Previous chapters of this book have discussed two other ways that Windows Server 2012 can take advantage of the increased scalability possible for NUMA-capable hardware: the NUMA-aware placement of virtual machines (VMs) on a failover cluster, and Virtual NUMA, by which the guest operating system of VMs can take advantage of the performance operations of an underlying NUMA-capable host machine. The NUMA-aware scalability of IIS 8 means that web application servers running in Windows Server 2012 can now experience near-optimal out-of-the-box performance on NUMA hardware.

Understanding NUMA-aware scalability

A significant percentage of recent server hardware has NUMA architecture. These machines use multiple bus systems, one for each socket. Each socket has multiple CPUs and its own memory. A socket with the attached memory and I/O system comprises a NUMA node. Accessing data that is located in a different NUMA node is more expensive than accessing memory on the local node. When we tested IIS 7.5 on NUMA hardware, we noticed that an increasing number of CPU cores did not result in increased performance beyond a certain number of cores. In fact, the performance actually degraded for certain scenarios. This was happening because the process scheduling is not NUMA-aware, and because of that, the cost of memory synchronization on NUMA hardware outweighed the benefits of additional cores. The goal behind the NUMA-Aware Scalability feature is to ensure that IIS 8 can take advantage of modern NUMA hardware and provide optimal performance on servers with a high number of CPU cores.

To get the best performance on NUMA hardware for a web workload, a Hypertext Transfer Protocol (HTTP) request packet should traverse through the fastest I/O path to the CPU. This also means that the packet should be served by a CPU socket, which is the same I/O hub as the network interface card (NIC) receiving the packet. This configuration is very specific to hardware architecture, and there is no programmatic way to know which NIC and sockets are on the same I/O hub.

One of the design goals of this feature is to provide near-optimal settings out of the box without much user configuration. Understanding the finer details of NUMA hardware (for example, the hardware schematic, NIC, and CPU layout) and configuring it correctly can be pretty difficult and time consuming for average users. So IIS 8 tries its best to configure all these settings automatically.

Automatic configuration is convenient, but it can't beat optimally tuned hardware performance. To enable best performance, advanced users can affinitize an IIS worker process to most optimal NUMA core(s). This can be done by manually configuring the *smpProcessorAffinityMask* attribute in the IIS configuration. This provides something called "hard affinity." When this configuration is used, the application pools are hard-affinitized, meaning that there is no spillover to other NUMA nodes. More explicitly, the threads cannot be executed by other cores on the system, regardless of whether other cores have extra CPU cycles or not.

For average users, Windows and IIS make the best attempt at offering automatic configurations that should yield the best performance. For automatic configuration, IIS uses something called "soft affinity." In soft affinity, when a process is affinitized to a core, the affinitized core is identified as the "preferred core." When a thread is about to be scheduled to be executed, the preferred core is considered first. However, depending on the load and the availability of other cores on the system, the thread may be scheduled on other cores on the system. In lab tests, it was observed that soft affinity is more forgiving in the case of misconfiguration compared to hard affinity.

When a system has multiple NUMA nodes, Windows uses a simple round-robin algorithm to assign processes between NUMA nodes to make sure that loads get distributed equally across nodes. This does not work best for IIS workloads because they are usually memory-constrained. IIS is aware of the memory consumption by each NUMA, so IIS 8.0 will enable another scheduling algorithm for worker processes started by the Windows Process Activation Service (WAS), which will schedule the processes on the node with the most available memory. This helps in minimizing access to memory on remote NUMA node. This capability is called Most Available Memory, and is the default process scheduling algorithm on NUMA hardware for automatically picking optimal NUMA node for the process.

Process scheduling and performance also depends on how IIS workload has been partitioned. As explained next, IIS supports two ways of partitioning the workload.

Run multiple worker processes in one application pool (that is, a web garden)

If you are using this mode, by default, the application pool is configured to run one worker process. For maximum performance, you should consider running the same number of worker processes as there are NUMA nodes, so that there is 1:1 affinity between the worker processes and NUMA nodes. This can be done by setting the Maximum Worker Processes application pool setting to 0. In this setting, IIS determines how many NUMA nodes are available on the hardware and starts the same number of worker processes.

Run multiple applications pools in single workload/site

In this configuration, the workload/site is divided into multiple application pools. For example, the site may contain several applications that are configured to run in separate application pools. This configuration effectively results in running multiple IIS worker processes for the workload/site, and IIS intelligently distributes and affinitizes the processes for maximum performance.

Harsh Mittal, Senior Program Manager
Eok Kim, Software Design Engineer
Aniello Scotto Di Marco, Software Design Engineer in Test
Microsoft Internet Information Services Team

How NUMA-aware scalability works

NUMA-aware scalability works by intelligently affinitizing worker processes to NUMA nodes. For example, let's say that you have a large enterprise web application that you want to deploy on an IIS 8 web garden. A *web garden* is an application pool that uses more than one worker process. The number of worker processes used by an application pool can be configured in the Advanced Settings dialog box of an application pool, and as Figure 4-1 shows, the out-of-the-box configuration for IIS is to assign one worker process to each application pool.

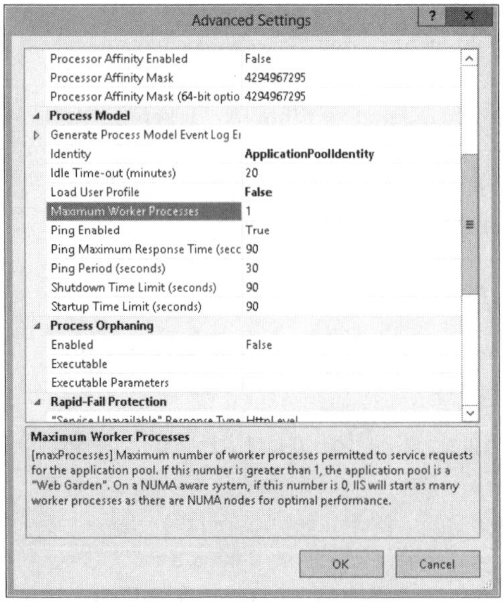

FIGURE 4-1 Configuring a web garden on IIS 8.

By increasing the Maximum Worker Processes setting over its default value of 1, you change the website associated with your application into a web garden. On NUMA-aware hardware, the result is that IIS will try to assign each worker process in the web garden to a different NUMA node. This manual affinity approach allows IIS 8 to support NUMA-capable systems with more than 64 logical cores. You can also use this approach on NUMA-capable systems with fewer than 64 logical cores if you want to try and custom-tune your workload.

On NUMA-capable systems with fewer than 64 logical cores, however, you can simply set Maximum Worker Processes to 0, in which case IIS will start as many worker processes as there are NUMA nodes on the system to achieve optimal performance. You might use this approach, for example, if you are a multi-tenant cloud hosting provider.

Benefits of NUMA-aware scalability

Internal testing by Microsoft has demonstrated the benefits that enterprises and cloud hosting providers can gain from implementing IIS 8 in their datacenters. For example, in a series of tests using the default IIS configuration of one worker process per application pool, the number of requests per second that could be handled by a web application actually decreased by about 20 percent as one goes from 32 to 64 cores on systems that are not NUMA-capable because of increased contention for the shared memory bus on such systems. In similar tests on NUMA-capable systems, however, the number of requests per second that could be handled increased by more than 50 percent as one goes from 32 to 64 cores. Such testing confirms the increased scalability that IIS 8 provides through its NUMA-aware capabilities.

Learn more

For more information on NUMA-aware scalability in IIS 8 on Windows Server 2012, see the topic "Web Server (IIS) overview" in the TechNet library at *http://technet.microsoft.com/en-us/library/hh831725.aspx*.

For instructions on how to implement NUMA-aware scalability on IIS 8, see the article titled "IIS 8.0 Multicore Scaling on NUMA Hardware" on IIS.NET at *http://learn.iis.net/page .aspx/1095/iis-80-multicore-scaling-on-numa-hardware/*.

Server Name Indication

In previous versions of IIS, you could use host headers to support hosting multiple HTTP websites using only a single shared IP address. But if you wanted these websites to use Hypertext Transfer Protocol Secure (HTTPS), then you had a problem because you couldn't use host headers. The reason is that host headers are defined at the application level of the networking stack, so when an incoming HTTPS request containing a host header comes to a web server hosting multiple SSL-encrypted websites, the server can't read the host header unless it decrypts the request header first. To decrypt the request header, the server needs to use one of the SSL certificates assigned to the server. Now, typically you have one certificate for each HTTPS site on the server, but which certificate should the server use to decrypt the header? The one specified by the host header in the incoming request. But the request is encrypted, so you basically have a chicken-and-egg problem.

The recommended solution in previous versions of IIS was to assign multiple IP addresses to your web server and bind a different IP address to each HTTPS site. By doing this, host headers are no longer needed, and IIS can determine which SSL certificate to use to decrypt an incoming HTTPS request. If your web server hosts hundreds (or even thousands) of different HTTPS websites, however, this means that you'll need hundreds or thousands of different IP addresses assigned to the network adapter of your server. That's a lot of management overhead—plus you may not have that many IP addresses available.

IIS 8 in Windows Server 2012 solves this problem by providing support for Server Name Indication (SNI), which allows a virtual domain name (another name for a host name) to be used to identify the network end point of an SSL/TSL connection. The result is that IIS can now host multiple HTTPS websites, each with their own SSL certificate, bound to the same shared IP address. SNI therefore provides the key benefit of increased scalability for web servers hosting multiple SSL sites, and it can help cloud hosting providers better conserve the dwindling resources of their pool of available IP addresses.

Both the server and client need to support SNI, and most newer browsers support SNI as well. Note, however, that Microsoft Internet Explorer 6 doesn't support it.

Configuring SNI

SNI can be configured on a per-site basis by editing the bindings for each HTTPS site from the IIS Manager console. Simply select the Require Server Name Indication check box as shown in Figure 4-2 and type a host name for the site, while leaving the IP Address setting as All Unassigned to use the single shared IP address on the server.

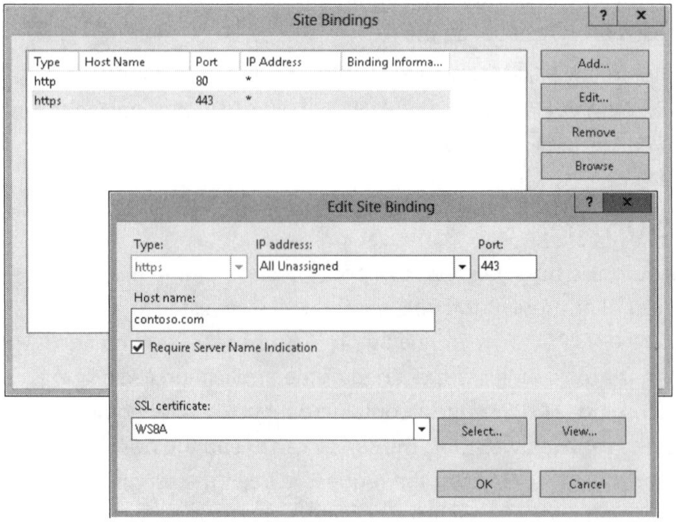

FIGURE 4-2 Configuring SNI on an SSL site.

SSL configuration and its order of applicability

SSL configuration and IIS network binding configuration are actually two separate and completely disconnected configurations on Windows. So when working on SNI, as well as Centralized SSL Certificate Support, new SSL configurations have been introduced.

At a high level, there are four SSL binding types, and they are applied in the following order:

Order	Syntax	Description
1	IP:Port	<ul><li>An exact *IP:port* SSL configuration is found.</li><li>MY/LM or MY/Web Hosting certificate stores are used.</li></ul>
2	Hostname:Port	<ul><li>An exact *hostname:port* SSL configuration is found.</li><li>This is the SNI configuration and is applied only if SSL connection is initiated by an SNI-capable client.</li><li>MY/LM or MY/Web Hosting certificate stores are used.</li></ul>
3	CCS:Port	<ul><li>This is the Centralized SSL Certificate Support (CCS) configuration.</li><li>In this configuration, a CCS provider is used to locate the SSL certificate. By default, IIS provides a file-based CCS provider.</li></ul>
4	[::]:Port	<ul><li>IPv6 wildcard match and the connection must be IPv6.</li></ul>
5	0.0.0.0:Port	<ul><li>IPv4 wildcard match and the connection can be either IPv4 or IPv6.</li></ul>

For example, consider the following configuration in IIS:

```
<site name="mySNIsite" id="1" serverAutoStart="true">
<application path="/" applicationPool="snidemocert0">
    <virtualDirectory path="/" physicalPath="C:\inetpub\wwwroot" />
</application>
<bindings>
    <binding protocol="https" bindingInformation="192.168.0.1:443:w
ww.mycontoso.com" />
    </bindings>
  </site>
```

With the following SSL configuration, this code is used:

```
    IP:port                : 192.168.0.1:443
Certificate Hash           : 2114e944c1e63dcdcd033e5d3fdb832ba423a52e


    Hostname:port          : www.mycontoso.com:443
Certificate Hash           : 0e62ac0f4deb8d6d78ac93a3088157e624ee540b
```

In this example, the first SSL certificate (as referenced by *2114e944c1e63dcdcd-033e5d3fdb832ba423a52e*) would be used because the IP:Port (192.168.0.1:443) configuration precedes Hostname:Port (*www.mycontoso.com:443*).

Won Yoo, Principal Program Manager
Jenny Lawrance, Software Design Engineer II
Eok Kim, Software Design Engineer II
Aniello Scotto Di Marco, Software Design Engineer in Test II
Microsoft Internet Information Services Team

Learn more

For more information on SNI in IIS 8 on Windows Server 2012, see the following topics in the TechNet library:

- "Web Server (IIS) Overview" at *http://technet.microsoft.com/en-us/library/hh831725.aspx.*

- "What's new in TLS/SSL (Schannel SSP)" at *http://technet.microsoft.com/en-us/library/hh831771.aspx.*

For instructions on how to configure SNI in IIS 8, see the article titled "IIS 8.0 Server Name Indication (SNI): SSL Scalability" on IIS.NET at *http://learn.iis.net/page.aspx/1096/iis-80-server-name-indication-sni-ssl-scalability/.*

Centralized SSL certificate support

Cloud hosting providers that need to host multiple HTTPS websites on each server in their web farms can also benefit from other SSL-related improvements in IIS 8. These improvements help make the IIS platform more scalable and manageable for hosting secure websites.

Managing SSL certificates on servers in web farms running earlier versions of IIS was time-consuming because the certificates had to be imported into every server in the farm. This made scaling out your farm by deploying additional servers a difficult chore. In addition, replicating certificates across servers in a farm was complicated by the need to ensure manually that certificate versions were in sync.

IIS 8 now makes managing SSL certificates on servers in web farms much easier by introducing a new central certificate store that lets you store all the certificates for your web servers in a file share on the network instead of in the certificate store of each server.

In addition to enhanced SSL manageability, IIS 8 includes significant improvements in the area of SSL scalability. For example, in previous versions of IIS, the certificate for an HTTPS website is loaded into memory (a process that could take considerable time) upon the first client accessing the site, and the certificate then remains in memory indefinitely. Hosting only a few SSL sites on an IIS server, therefore, could lead to large amounts of memory being wasted for secure sites that were rarely accessed.

In IIS 8, however, once a certificate is loaded into memory, it can now be unloaded automatically after the secure site has been idle for a configurable amount of time. In addition, certificates now load into memory almost instantaneously, which eliminates the delay often experienced by clients accessing secure sites for the first time in earlier versions of IIS. (Only the certificates for HTTPS requests are loaded, instead of all the certificates.) This change means that fewer certificates are kept in memory, which means that more memory is available on the server for other uses, such as running worker processes.

These scalability and manageability improvements mean that instead of hosting fewer than 500 secure sites on a single server, you can now host more than 10,000 SSL sites on one IIS 8 server. And as the next section discusses, configuring a central store for SSL certificates also increases the elasticity of your web farms.

Configuring a central store

To configure IIS to use a central store for storing SSL certificates, you first need to add the Centralized SSL Certificate Support feature. You can do this by starting the Add Roles And Features Wizard from Server Manager:

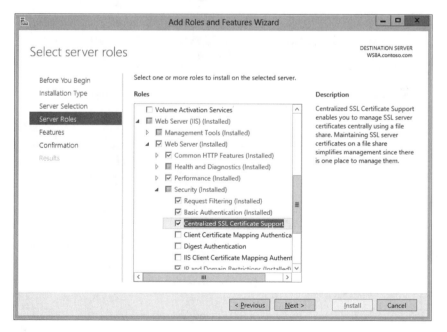

Once this feature has been enabled on your server, opening IIS Manager will show a Centralized Certificates node in the Management section of your server's configuration settings:

Selecting the Centralized Certificates node displays a message saying that a central certificates location has not yet been set:

Clicking Edit Feature Settings opens a dialog box that lets you enable this feature and configure the path and credentials for the shared folder on the network where SSL certificates should be stored:

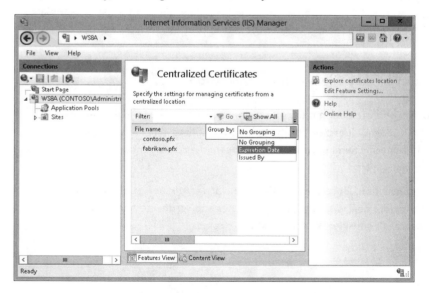

Note that the certificate password is necessary when you have created PFX files with a password that protects the private key. In addition, all your PFX files in the shared certificate store must use the same password. You cannot have a different password for each PFX file.

You can then group your SSL certificates in the Centralized Certificates pane by Expiration Date, or Issued By, to manage them more easily:

Once you've copied your SSL certificates to the central store, you can configure SSL websites to use the central store when you add them in IIS Manager:

Note that you don't need to select your certificate by name when you add a new SSL site in IIS Manager. If you had to do this for each new secure site and you had hundreds or thousands of certificates in your store, this would make configuring SSL sites too difficult. Instead, you simply make sure that the name of the certificate matches the host header name for the secure site that uses it. This dynamic configuration of certificates for SSL sites means that adding an SSL central store to your web farms makes your farms more elastic.

CCS and private key file naming convention

CCS is based on a provider model, so it is definitely possible to use this feature with other CCS providers. Out of the box, IIS is shipping a file-server-based provider with a specific naming convention to locate the corresponding SSL certificate on a file system.

The naming convention, loosely, is "<*subject name of a certificate*>.pfx," but how does the IIS provider deal with wildcard certificates and certificates with multiple subject names? Let's consider the following three cases.

Case 1: Certificate with one subject name

This is simple. If the subject name is www.contoso.com, then the IIS provider will simply look for *www.contoso.com.pfx*.

Case 2: Wildcard certificate

The IIS provider uses the underscore character (_) as a special character to indicate that it is a wildcard certificate. So, if the subject name in the SSL certificate is *.contoso.com, the administrator should name the file _.contoso.com.

It should be noted that the IIS provider will first try to look for a SSL certificate with the file name that exactly matches the domain name of the destination site. For example, if the destination site is www.contoso.com, the IIS provider first tries to locate *www.consoto.com.pfx*. If that is unsuccessful, then it tries to locate _.contoso.com.

Case 3: Certificate with multiple subject names

In this case, the administrator should name the file as many times as there are subject names. For example, separate SSL certificates may have been issued for both *www.contoso.com* and *www.example.com*. Although the files are exactly the same, there should be two *.pfx* files: *www.contoso.com.pfx* and *www.example.com.pfx*.

Finally, it is easy enough to see the relationship between SNI and CCS, especially when it comes to how CCS uses the naming convention based on the host name. However, it is important to note that CCS does not have a hard dependency on SNI. If the administrator wishes to use CCS without relying on SNI, the secure site must be configured using a dedicated IP address, but the same naming convention can be used.

For example, consider the following configuration in IIS:

```
    <site name="mySNIsite" id="1" serverAutoStart="true">
    <application path="/" applicationPool="snidemocert0">
      <virtualDirectory path="/" physicalPath="C:\inetpub\wwwroot" />
    </application>
    <bindings>
      <binding protocol="https" bindingInformation="192.168.0.1:443:w
ww.mycontoso.com" />
    </bindings>
  </site>
```

With the following SSL configuration, this code is used:

```
  Central Certificate Store        : 443

  Certificate Hash          : (null)
```

> In this case, if the client is SNI-capable, then the host name comes from the client as a part of SSL connection initiation. If the client is not SNI-capable, then IIS will look up the corresponding host name based on the IP address that the client has used to connect to the server. This is why the IIS configuration has both the IP address and the host name in this example (192.168.0.1:443:www.mycontoso.com).
>
> Won Yoo, Principal Program Manager
>
> Eok Kim, Software Design Engineer II
>
> Aniello Scotto Di Marco, Software Design Engineer in Test II
>
> *Microsoft Internet Information Services Team*

Learn more

For more information on centralized SSL certificate support in IIS 8 on Windows Server 2012, see the topic "Centralized Certificates" in the TechNet library at *http://technet.microsoft.com/en-us/library/hh831636.aspx*.

For instructions on how to configure centralized SSL certificate support in IIS 8, see the article titled "IIS 8.0 Centralized SSL Certificate Support: SSL Scalability and Manageability" on IIS.NET at *http://learn.iis.net/page.aspx/1091/iis-80-centralized-ssl-certificate-support-ssl-scalability-and-manageability/*.

IIS CPU throttling

Managing CPU resources on farms of web servers in a multi-tenant shared hosting environment can be challenging. When you are hosting websites and applications from many different customers, each of them wants to get its fair share of resources. It's clearly undesirable when one customer's site consumes so much CPU resources that other customers' sites are starved of the resources they need to process client requests.

IIS CPU throttling is designed to prevent one website from hogging all the processing resources on the web server. Previous versions of IIS included a rudimentary form of CPU throttling that basically just turned off a site once the CPU resources being consumed by the site reached a certain threshold by killing the worker processes associated with the site. Of course, this had the undesirable effect of temporarily preventing clients from accessing the site. As a result, web administrators sometimes used Windows System Resource Manager (WSRM) with IIS to control the allocation of processor and memory resources among multiple sites based on business priorities.

CPU throttling has been completely redesigned in IIS 8 to provide real CPU throttling instead of just on/off switching. Now you can configure an application pool to throttle the CPU usage so that it cannot consume more CPU processing than a user-specified threshold, and the Windows kernel will make sure that the worker process and all child processes stay below that level. Alternatively, you can configure IIS to throttle an application pool when the system is under load, which allows your application pool to consume more resources than your specified level when the system is idle because the Windows kernel will throttle the worker process and all child processes only when the system comes under load.

Configuring CPU throttling

CPU throttling can be configured in IIS 8 at the application pool level. To do this, open the Advanced Settings dialog box for your application pool in IIS Manager and configure the settings in the CPU section (see Figure 4-3).

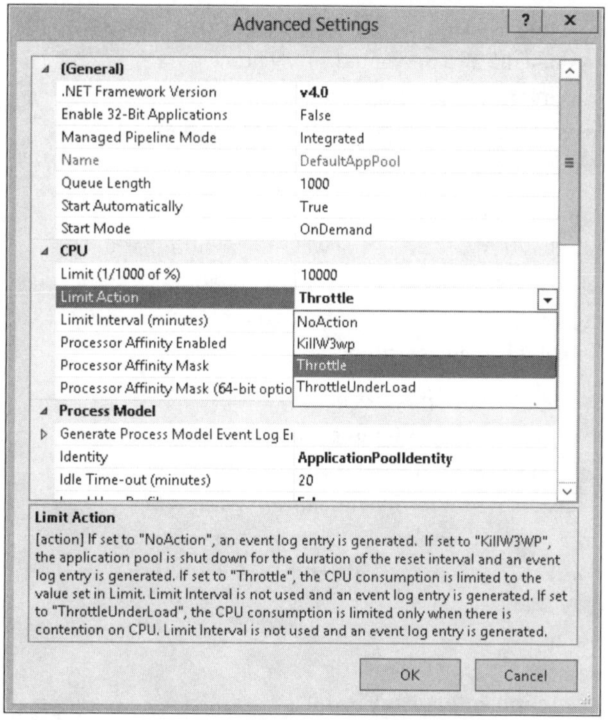

FIGURE 4-3 Configuring CPU throttling for an application pool.

You can also configure a default CPU throttling value for all application pools on the server by clicking Set Application Pool Defaults in the Actions pane when the Application Pools node is selected in IIS Manager.

CPU throttling configuration

CPU throttling has been included in prior versions of IIS, but for IIS 8.0, it has received a major reworking under the hood.

In earlier versions of IIS, a polling mechanism was used to check the CPU usage periodically and take action if it was above the configured threshold for a long enough time. The problem with this approach is that CPU usage wasn't truly limited—it could increase far beyond the configured limit and remain high for a period of time before the polling mechanism noticed. When the CPU was determined to be above the threshold, the only "corrective" action available was to kill the IIS worker process (W3pw.exe). When the process was killed, IIS also prevented a new process from being started for the offending application for a period of time so that it would not immediately come back and take over the CPU again. Any requests to the application during that time would fail, resulting in a poor user experience.

For IIS 8.0, we worked with the Windows Kernel team to implement true throttling of CPU usage. In place of the old polling design, the kernel will now ensure that CPU usage stays at the configured level. With this change, we no longer need to kill the W3WP process to halt an offending application, so the application stays active and responsive to user requests even when it is being throttled.

There are two new options for how CPU throttling works in IIS 8.0. The *Throttle* configuration option will keep the CPU near the configured limit at all times. The *ThrottleUnderLoad* configuration option will keep the CPU near the configured limit when there is contention for CPU resources, but it will let it consume more CPU if the server would otherwise be idle. In this model, once other processes need additional CPU resources, the IIS worker process are throttled to ensure that the other processes get the resources they need.

Shaun Eagan, Senior Program Manager
Eok Kim, Software Design Engineer II
Aniello Scotto Di Marco, Software Design Engineer in Test II
Ruslan Yakushev, Software Design Engineer II
Microsoft Internet Information Services Team

Learn more

For more information on CPU throttling in IIS 8, see the topic "CPU Throttling: IIS 7 vs IIS 8" in Sean Eagan's Blog on IIS.NET at *http://blogs.iis.net/shauneagan/archive/2012/03/15/cpu-throttling-iis-7-vs-iis-8.aspx.*

For instructions on how to configure CPU throttling in IIS 8, see the article titled "IIS 8.0 CPU Throttling: Sand-boxing Sites and Applications" on IIS.NET at *http://learn.iis.net/page.aspx/1092/iis-80-cpu-throttling-sand-boxing-sites-and-applications/.*

Application Initialization

Nothing frustrates users more than trying to open a website in their web browser and then waiting for the site to respond. With previous versions of IIS, the delay that occurred when a web application was first accessed was because the application needed to be loaded into memory before IIS could process the user's request and return a response. With complex Microsoft ASP.NET web applications often needing to perform lengthy startup tasks, such as generating and caching content, such delays could sometimes reach up to a minute or more in some cases.

Such delays are now a thing of the past with the new Application Initialization feature of IIS 8, which lets you configure IIS to spin up web applications so they are ready to respond to the first request received. Application pools can be prestarted instead of waiting for a first request, and application are initialized when their worker processes start. Administrators can decide which applications should be preloaded on the server.

In addition, IIS 8 can be configured to return a static "splash page" or other static content while an application is being initialized so the user feels the website being accessed is responding instead of failing to respond. This functionality can be combined with the URL Rewrite module to create more complex types of pregenerated static content.

Application Initialization can be configured at two levels:

- Machine-wide, in the ApplicationHost.config file for the server
- Per application, in the Web.config file for the application

The Application Initialization role service of the Web Server role must also be added to the server to use this feature. For more information on configuring Application Initialization, see the section "Generating Windows PowerShell scripts Using IIS Configuration Editor," later in this chapter.

Identifying "fake" requests used by Application Initialization

The Application Initialization feature introduces the concept of a warm-up period to IIS. When this feature is configured, the set of URLs specified by the application developer will be sent a "fake" request as part of warming up the application. Once all the fake requests return, the application is considered initialized, and the warm-up period ends.

Depending on your application, you may decide to handle these fake requests differently than normal requests coming from the wire. If you choose to do this, using the URL Rewrite module allows you to look at the request headers and identify the fake requests.

Identifying fake requests is easy if you know what to look for. A fake request sent to a URL as part of application-level initialization has the following properties.

- User Agent = IIS Application Initialization Warm-up

- Server Variables = the WARMUP_REQUEST server variable is set

In addition to application-level initialization, the Application Initialization feature also allows server administrators to "preload" important applications so that they will be initialized as soon as the worker process starts. Preload is also done using a fake request to the root of the application. The Preload fake request has the following properties:

- User Agent = IIS Application Initialization Preload

- Server Variables = the PRELOAD_REQUEST server variable is set

You may also want to perform special handling for normal requests that are received during the warm-up period. All normal requests received during warm-up have the *APP_WARMING_UP* server variable set, which you can use to identify these requests and handle them as desired.

Shaun Eagan, Senior Program Manager
Stefan Schackow, Principal Program Manager
Jeong Hwan Kim, Software Design Engineer in Test II
Ahmed ElSayed, Software Design Engineer in Test
Microsoft Internet Information Services Team

Learn more

For instructions on how to configure Application Initialization in IIS 8, see the article titled "IIS 8.0 Application Initialization" on IIS.NET at *http://learn.iis.net/page.aspx/1089/iis-80-application-initialization/.*

See also the article titled "(Re)introducing Application Initialization" in Wade Hilmo's blog on IIS.NET at *http://blogs.iis.net/wadeh/archive/2012/04/16/re-introducing-application-initialization.aspx.*

Dynamic IP Address Restrictions

When a web server receives unwanted activity from malicious clients, it can prevent legitimate users from accessing websites hosted by the server. One way of dealing with such situations in previous versions of IIS was to use static IP filtering to block requests from specific clients. Static filtering had two limitations, however:

- It required that you discover the IP address of the offending client and then manually configure IIS to block that address.

- There was no choice as to what action IIS would take when it blocked the client—an HTTP 403.6 status message was always returned to the offending client.

In IIS 8, however, blocking malicious IP addresses is now much simpler. Dynamic IP Address Restrictions now provides three kinds of filtering to deal with undesirable request traffic:

- Dynamic IP address filtering lets you configure your server to block access for any IP address that exceeds a specified number of concurrent requests or exceeds a specified number of requests within a given period of time.

- You can now configure how IIS responds when it blocks an IP address; for example, by aborting the request instead of returning HTTP 403.6 responses to the client.

- IP addresses can be blocked not only by client address, but also by addresses received in the X-Forwarded-For HTTP header used in proxy mode.

Configuring dynamic IP address filtering

To configure dynamic IP address filtering for your server, website, or folder path, select the corresponding IP Address And Domain Restrictions node in IIS Manager. This opens the Dynamic IP Restriction Settings dialog box shown in Figure 4-4, which lets you deny IP addresses based on the number of concurrent requests and/or the number of requests received over a specified period of time.

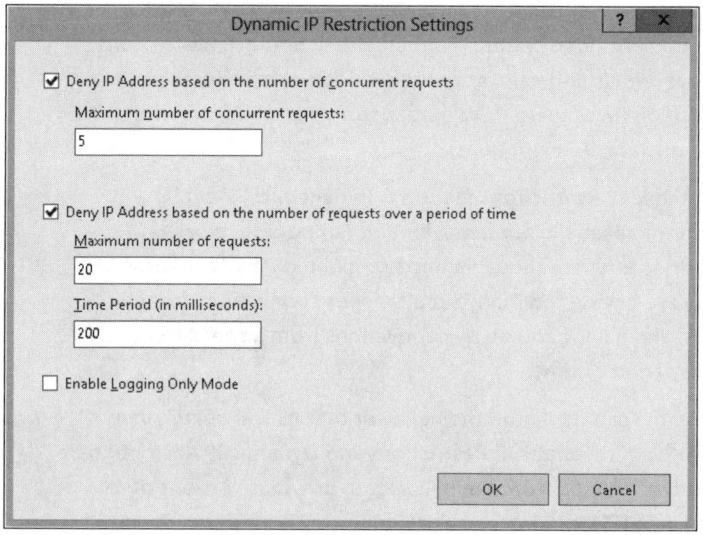

FIGURE 4-4 Configuring dynamic IP address filtering.

Once dynamic IP address filtering has been configured, you can configure how IIS responds to clients whose requests are dynamically filtered. To do this, select the appropriate IP Address And Domain Restrictions node in IIS Manager and click Edit Feature Settings in the Actions pane. Doing this opens the Edit IP And Domain Restriction Settings dialog box shown in Figure 4-5, which lets you specify the type of response and whether to enforce such responses when the incoming request passes through a proxy, such as a firewall or load balancer, that changes the source IP address of the request.

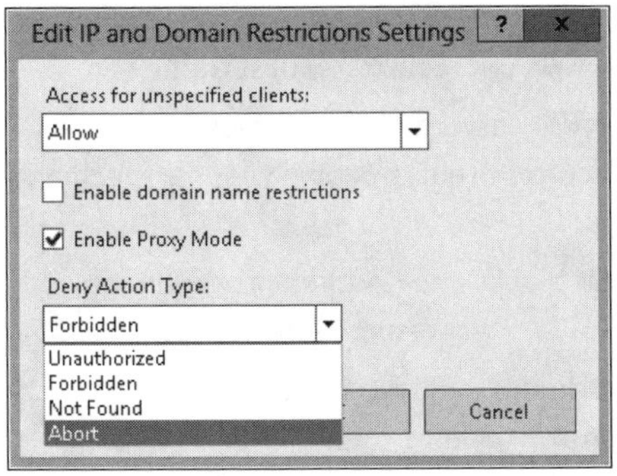

FIGURE 4-5 Configuring the response behavior to dynamically filtered requests, including when a proxy is encountered along the request path.

Dynamic IP restrictions

Previous versions of IIS have a Static IP Restrictions feature, which allows server administrators to block IP addresses that are exhibiting undesirable behavior. When an HTTP request is made from an IP address that had been blocked, IIS will return an HTTP 403 Access Forbidden status. That being said, Static IP Restrictions are a manual process—server administrators are required to perform forensic analysis of their IIS logs to discover these behavioral patterns and add the offending IP addresses to their list of static IP restrictions.

The goal behind the Dynamic IP Restrictions feature is to dynamically detect two specific forms of potentially malicious behavior and temporarily block HTTP requests from the IP addresses where those requests originated. The two forms of behavior that IIS detects are having too many simultaneous connections from a specific client IP address, and having too many connections from a specific client IP address within a specific period of time.

In IIS 8, server administrators can configure the behavior that IIS will use when it blocks HTTP requests for both the Static IP Restrictions and Dynamic IP Restrictions features; this is an important change from the behavior in previous versions of IIS, which always returned an HTTP 403 Access Forbidden status message. Server administrators can now configure IIS 8 to return HTTP 401 Access Denied, HTTP 403 Access Forbidden, HTTP 404 Not Found, or abort the request entirely. For each of these HTTP statuses, IIS will mark the requests with a substatus code that signifies why the request was blocked. IIS can also be configured to simply log the behavior, in which case the requests will succeed or fail based on the nature of an HTTP request, but IIS will still mark these requests with a substatus code that indicates that the request would have been blocked. These substatus codes make it easier for server administrators to forensically examine their IIS activity logs to identify potentially malicious activity from specific IP addresses and then add those IP addresses to the list of denied static IP addresses.

The following table lists the substatuses that IIS 8 adds:

Dynamic IP Restrictions	
501	Deny by concurrent requests limit
502	Deny by requests over time limit
Static IP Restrictions	
503	Deny by IP address match
504	Deny by hostname match

For example, if you configured IIS to return an HTTP 404 Not Found status for the Dynamic IP Restrictions feature and IIS blocks an HTTP request because of too many concurrent connections, IIS will write an HTTP 404.501 status message in the IIS activity logs. Alternatively, if you configured the Dynamic IP Restrictions feature to only log the activity, IIS would write an HTTP 200.501 status in the IIS activity logs.

When a server that is running IIS is located behind a firewall or load-balancing server, the client IP addresses for all the HTTP requests may appear to be from the firewall or load-balancing server. Because of this scenario, the IP Restrictions features in IIS 8 can be configured to operate in Proxy mode. In this mode, IIS will examine the values in the X-Forwarded-For HTTP header, and determine the client IP from the list of IP addresses for which the HTTP request was forwarded. By way of explanation, the X-Forwarded-For HTTP header is an accepted standard within the Internet community, whereby each server in the chain between an Internet client and server will append its IP address to the end of the header and separated by a comma. For example, if an HTTP request from an Internet client must travel through two firewall servers to reach the server, there should be three IP addresses in the X-Forwarded-For header: the client's IP address, followed by the two IP addresses of the firewall servers, as illustrated in the following example HTTP request:

```
GET / HTTP/1.1
Host: example.com
Accept: */*
X-Forwarded-For: 10.0.51.50, 192.168.21.12, 172.16. 19.84
```

When IIS examines the X-Forwarded-For HTTP header in an HTTP request like the preceding example, IIS will block the originating client's IP address (10.0.51.50) instead of the IP address of the firewall server (172.16. 19.84).

Robert McMurray, Program Manager
Jenny Lawrance, Software Design Engineer
Wade Hilmo, Principal Development Lead
Ahmed ElSayed, Software Design Engineer in Test
Microsoft Internet Information Services Team

Learn more

For more information on Dynamic IP Address Restrictions in IIS 8, see the topic "IP Address and Domain Restrictions" in the TechNet library at *http://technet.microsoft.com/en-us/library/hh831785.aspx*.

For instructions on how to configure Dynamic IP Address Restrictions in IIS 8, see the article titled "IIS 8.0 Dynamic IP Address Restrictions" on IIS.NET at *http://learn.iis.net/page.aspx/1093/iis-80-dynamic-ip-address-restrictions/*.

FTP Logon Attempt Restrictions

Brute-force attacks can create a Denial-of-Service (DoS) condition that can prevent legitimate users from accessing an FTP server. To prevent this from happening, IIS 8 includes a new feature called FTP Logon Attempt Restrictions that lets you block offending users from logging on to an IIS FTP server for a specified period of time. Unlike the Dynamic IP Address Restrictions described in the previous section, which blacklists any client whose IP address violates the configured dynamic IP address filtering settings, FTP Logon Attempt Restrictions uses a "graylisting" approach that denies only the offending user for a certain period of time. However, by configuring this time period to be slightly more than that specified by your domain account lockout policy, you can prevent malicious users from locking legitimate users out of accessing your FTP server.

Understanding FTP logon attempt restrictions

Running an FTP service on an Internet-facing server has unfortunately yielded an additional surface area for attack for server administrators to manage. Because hackers can connect to an FTP service with a wide array of publicly available or special-purpose FTP clients, an FTP server offers a way for hackers to continuously send requests to guess a username/password combination and gain access to an account on a server.

This situation has required server administrators to implement additional security measures to counter this behavior; for example, server administrators should always disable or rename well-known accounts like the Administrator or Guest accounts. Administrators should also implement policies that enforce strong passwords, password expiration, and password lockouts. An unfortunate downside to password lockouts is that a valid account can be locked out by a hacker who is attempting to gain access to the account; this may require the server administrator to re-enable accounts that have been locked out as a result of good password management practices.

From an FTP 7 perspective, there are additional measures that server administrators can implement; for example, administrators can deny well-known accounts at the global level for their FTP server. In addition, administrators can use one of the alternate built-in authentication providers instead of FTP's Basic Authentication provider. For example, you can use the ASP.NET Membership Authentication provider;

by using this provider, if an account was successfully hacked, that account will have no access to the actual server because it exists only in the ASP.NET Membership database.

In FTP 8, an extra layer of security was added that is called FTP Logon Attempt Restrictions; this feature provides an additional password lockout policy that is specific to the FTP service. Server administrators can use this feature of the FTP server to configure the maximum number of logon attempts that are allowed within a specific time period; once the number of logon attempts has been reached, the FTP service will disconnect the FTP session, and it will block the IP address of the client from connecting until the time period has passed.

Server administrators can configure the FTP Logon Attempt Restrictions feature in combination with their password lockout policies to configure a secure environment for their network, which allows uninterrupted functionality for valid users. For example, if you configured your FTP 8 server for a maximum of four failed logon attempts, you could configure your password lockout policy for a maximum of five failed logon attempts. In this way, a malicious FTP client would be blocked once it reached four failed logon attempts, and yet the valid user would still be able to access the account if he or she attempted to log on during the time period where the attacker was blocked.

Robert McMurray, Program Manager
Eok Kim, Software Design Engineer
Aniello Scotto Di Marco, Software Design Engineer in Test
Microsoft Internet Information Services Team

Configuring FTP Logon Attempt Restrictions

To configure FTP Logon Attempt Restrictions for FTP sites on your server, select the FTP Logon Attempt Restrictions node for your server in IIS Manager. This displays the settings shown in Figure 4-6, which let you enable the feature and specify a maximum number of failed logon attempts within a given amount of time. Alternatively, you can enable this feature in logging-only mode to collect data concerning possible brute-force password attacks being conducted against your server.

Library Cards and FTP Servers

I t's true. I have a library card. I know there are a million other ways to get information—that Internet thingy, book downloads, having Amazon deliver stuff in boxes to my door.

But the library is pretty reliable and generally easy to use—even if it's not cutting-edge. The main drawback is I have to GO there, on THEIR hours.

Think of FTP like a library.

Sure, maybe it's not the most exciting protocol in the world. But FTP has been around since the 1970s, and it is still found in a large number of environments simply because it is reliable and generally easy to use.

However, like the library, FTP has some drawbacks. Like Simple Mail Transfer Protocol (SMTP) and other older protocols, FTP was never designed to be a highly secure protocol. In its default configuration, FTP users authenticate using a user-name/password combination that is typically sent in clear text. The server can be set up to allow users to connect anonymously as well.

This has often made FTP servers the target of brute-force attacks, where attackers simply try different user name and password combinations over and over until they find a valid combination. To mitigate this, there are several things you might do:

1. **Block the "bad guy's" IP address.** This generally involves combing through your FTP log files to figure out the bad guy's addresses, which can be very time-consuming and, frankly, a little boring.

2. **Create password lockout policies for user accounts.** This was less of a manual process to institute, but it created a different problem. If the bad guy managed to find a valid user name, after a few failed attempts at authentication, the password policy would lock the user account—which then means you have to spend time unlocking user accounts.

Enter Windows Server 2012 and FTP Logon Attempt Restrictions. This feature takes the best of both of these capabilities and combines them into one. The idea is this:

You define the maximum number of failed logon attempts that you want to allow, and the time frame within which those attempts can take place. If the user fails to log on correctly during that time frame, you can either tell the FTP server to write an entry to the log file or you can have the FTP server automatically deny access from the requesting IP address. If you choose to deny the access, the FTP server will drop the connection, and the IP address of the bad guy will be blocked.

Two "gotchas" to keep in mind when configuring this feature:

1. Writing the entry to the log file does *not* block further logon attempts. It does exactly what it says—it simply writes an entry to the log file.

2. The FTP Logon Attempt Restriction setting is defined for the server itself. It cannot be defined on a per-site basis.

So, using FTP Logon Attempt Restrictions will allow you to add a layer of security to your humble, yet functional FTP service.

David Branscome
Senior Premier Field Engineer

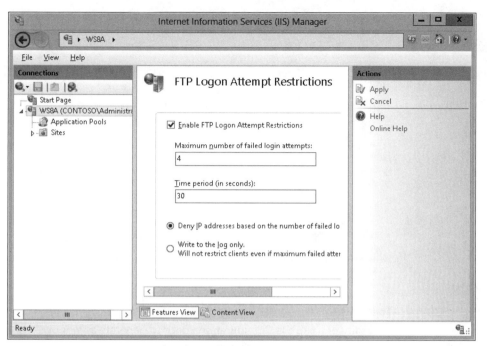

FIGURE 4-6 Configuring FTP Logon Attempt Restrictions.

Learn more

For instructions on how to configure FTP Logon Attempt Restrictions in IIS 8, see the article titled "IIS 8.0 FTP Logon Attempt Restrictions" on IIS.NET at *http://learn.iis.net/page.aspx/1094/iis-80-ftp-logon-attempt-restrictions/.*

See also the article titled "FTP Logon Restrictions in IIS 8" in Robert McMurray's blog on IIS.NET at *http://blogs.iis.net/robert_mcmurray/archive/2012/03/19/ftp-logon-restrictions-in-iis-8.aspx.*

Generating Windows PowerShell scripts using IIS Configuration Editor

Although IIS Manager lets you configure many aspects of IIS, there are a number of configuration settings that are not exposed in the user interface. To configure these settings, you need to drill down and edit configuration files like ApplicationHost.config, the root configuration file that includes detailed definitions of all sites, applications, virtual directories, and application pools on the server, as well as global defaults for all web server settings. These configuration files are schematized XML files, and you can either edit them in Notepad (yikes!) or use the Configuration Editor, one of the management features in IIS Manager.

New in IIS 8 is the capability of using the Configuration Editor to generate a Windows PowerShell script for any configuration changes that you make to your server using the Configuration Editor. This capability can be particularly useful for cloud hosting providers who need to automate the configuration of large numbers of web servers because you can use such a generated script as a template for creating a finished script that can perform the task that you need to automate.

Let's see how this works. The section "Application Initialization," earlier in this chapter, discussed how you can globally configure application pools on your server so that web applications on the server are initialized before the first request comes in to access them. To enable Application Initialization globally like this, you can edit the ApplicationHost.config file so that the following line in the <applicationPools> section:

```
<add name=".NET v4.5" managedRuntimeVersion="v4.0" />
```

changes to this:

```
<add name=".NET v4.5" startMode="AlwaysRunning" managedRuntimeVersion="v4.0" />
```

To do this using IIS Manager, open the Configuration Editor and select applicationPools in the system.applicationHost/applicationPools section as shown here:

Then you expand applicationPoolDefaults and change startMode from OnDemand to AlwaysRunning:

Once you've applied this change, you can click Generate Script in the Actions pane. Doing this opens the Script Dialog dialog box, and on the PowerShell tab is a PowerShell script that you can customize to automate this configuration change on other servers in your farm:

```
Script Dialog                                    _  □  X

Managed Code (C#) | Scripting (JavaScript) | Command Line (AppCmd) | PowerShell

Set-WebConfigurationProperty -pspath 'MACHINE/WEBROOT/APPHOST'   -filter "system.appl



                                                              Close
```

Note that configuration Application Initialization requires additional steps. For more information, see the article titled "IIS 8.0 Application Initialization" on IIS.NET at *http://learn.iis.net/page.aspx/1089/iis-80-application-initialization/*.

Learn more

For more information on generating PowerShell scripts using IIS Configuration Editor, see the article titled "PowerShell script generation in IIS Configuration Editor" in Won Yoo's blog on IIS.NET at *http://blogs.iis.net/wonyoo/archive/2012/03/05/powershell-script-generation-in-iis-configuration-editor.aspx*.

Support for open standards

Support for open industry standards is important in a heterogeneous world. Platforms need to interoperate seamlessly so that companies can focus on doing business instead of solving technical problems. Hybrid solutions are becoming the norm, and web hosting platforms need to support a wide variety of different development paradigms and communication protocols so that innovation can continue to drive business forward.

IIS 8 in Windows Server 2012 includes support for all the latest web standards and protocols, such as the WebSocket protocol, HTML 5, Asynchronous JavaScript And XML (AJAX), and for both ASP.NET 3.5 and ASP.NET 4.5. Together with Windows Internet Explorer 10 on the client running Windows Server 2012, and with the next version of the Microsoft Visual Studio development platform, organizations will have everything they need to build tomorrow's web.

WebSocket

Interactive web applications developed using HTML 5 and AJAX need secure real-time bidirectional communications between the web browser client and the web server. Support for WebSocket in IIS 8 brings just that. And although it's designed to be implemented in web browsers and web servers, it can be used by any client or server application.

How WebSocket works

WebSocket is a stable, open industry-standard protocol that is defined by the Internet Engineering Task Force (IETF) in RFC 6455 that lets web servers push messages from the server to the client instead of just letting the client pull messages from the server. It works by establishing a bidirectional, full-duplex Transmission Control Protocol (TCP) socket that is initiated by HTTP, which makes it easy for tunneling through proxies and firewalls. It also works well with Layer 4 TCP load balancers. The protocol has low latency and low bandwidth overhead, and it uses SSL for secure communications. For further details concerning how WebSocket communications are established, see the following sidebar.

WebSocket handshake

To establish a WebSocket connection, the client and server perform a "handshake" where they agree that they both understand the same version of WebSocket and the requested server resource supports WebSocket. The following client request and server response make up the handshake performed to establish a WebSocket connection.

The following is a sample WebSocket request from a client:

```
    GET /sampleapp HTTP/1.1
Host: contoso.com
Upgrade: websocket
Connection: Upgrade
Origin: http://contoso.com
Sec-WebSocket-Key: dGhlIHNhbXBsZSBub25jZQ==
Sec-WebSocket-Version: 13
```

IIS handling of WebSocket request

When the server evaluates this request, it notices that the Upgrade header is requesting that the connection be upgraded to a WebSocket connection. The server responds with an HTTP 101 response indicating that the protocol is being changed to use WebSocket.

IIS implements a native WebSocket module on the IIS request pipeline architecture, which applications can use to communicate over WebSocket. The IIS WebSocket module listens on the RQ_SEND_RESPONSE notification of the request pipeline.

On send response notification (before the response is returned to the client), if the HTTP status code of the response is 101, IIS calls into the Websocket.dll (the Win32 library in Windows Server 2012, which implements WebSocket framing). The WebSocket dll then computes a value for the Sec-WebSocket-Accept header based on the value of the Sec-WebSocket-Key from the request header.

These values are then set into the response headers. On the send call to HTTP, IIS also sets the HTTP_SEND_RESPONSE_FLAG_OPAQUE flag, which indicates that HTTP should go into opaque mode. This flag tells HTTP that the request and response from that point on will not be HTTP-compliant, and all subsequent bytes should be treated as an entity-body and appends the Sec-WebSocket-Accept header to the response.

The following is a sample response from a server:

```
HTTP/1.1 101 Switching Protocols
Upgrade: websocket
Connection: Upgrade
Sec-WebSocket-Accept: s3pPLMBiTxaQ9kYGzzhZRbK+xOo=
```

The server response indicates to the client that it is switching to WebSocket and returns the result of the operation that it performed on the Sec-WebSocket-Key in the Sec-WebSocket-Accept header. The client uses this to confirm that the server properly understands WebSocket. This concludes the handshake.

Using the WebSocket connection

If the handshake is successful, applications can get a pointer to the *IWebSocketContext* interface from the *IHttpContext* of the request. The *IWebSocketContext* interface is stored in the Named Context containers of *IHttpContext*. Applications can query the named context container with the query key "websockets" to get the pointer to this interface.

Applications can then do WebSocket I/O through the APIs exposed by this interface. WriteFragment, ReadFragment, SendConnectionClose, GetCloseStatus, and CloseTcpConnection are the APIs implemented for Windows Server 2012.
Shaun Eagan, Senior Program Manager
Jenny Lawrance, Software Design Engineer II
Wade Hilmo, Principal Development Lead
Aspaan Kamboj, Software Design Engineer in Test
Pandian Ramakrishnan, Software Design Engineer in Test
Microsoft Internet Information Services Team

Learn more

For more information on WebSocket, see the following resources:

- The article "WebSockets in ASP.NET" in the TechNet Wiki at *http://social.technet.microsoft.com/wiki/contents/articles/7148.websockets-in-asp-net.aspx*.

- The article "WebSockets" in the Internet Explorer Developer Center on MSDN at *http://msdn.microsoft.com/en-us/library/ie/hh673567(v=vs.85).aspx*.

- RFC 6455 on the RFC Editor site at *http://www.rfc-editor.org/rfc/rfc6455.txt*.

Support for HTML 5

HTML 5 is an open, industry-standard markup language being developed by the World Wide Web Consortium (W3C) and the Web Hypertext Application Technology Working Group (WHATWG). At present, it consists of more than 100 different specifications that define the next generation of web application technologies. The actual name "HTML 5" can be thought of as a kind of umbrella term that defines a collection of different HTML, Cascading Style Sheets (CSS), and JavaScript specifications that allow developers to create rich, interactive web applications using asynchronous script execution, drag-and-drop APIs, sandboxing, channel messaging, and other advanced capabilities.

IIS 8 in Windows Server 2012 includes built-in support for the latest HTML5 standards. Together with Internet Explorer 10 running on Windows Server 2012 and with the upcoming release of Visual Studio 11, businesses will have all the tools and platforms needed to build the modern, interactive web.

Learn more

For more information on HTML 5 support in upcoming Microsoft products, see the following resources:

- The article "Building Apps with HTML5: What You Need to Know" in MSDN Magazine at *http://msdn.microsoft.com/en-us/magazine/hh335062.aspx*.

- The article "HTML5" in the Internet Explorer Developer Center on MSDN at *http://msdn.microsoft.com/en-us/library/ie/hh673546(v=vs.85).aspx*.

- The article "How to build your first HTML5 Metro Style Smooth Streaming Player" in Cenk Dingiloglu's Blog on IIS.NET at *http://blogs.iis.net/cenkd/archive/2012/03/28/How-to-build-your-first-html5-metro-style-smooth-streaming-player.aspx*.

- HTML5Labs (*http://html5labs.com*), where Microsoft prototypes early and unstable specifications from web standards bodies such as W3C.

- Visual Studio 11 Beta, which can be downloaded from *http://www.microsoft.com/visualstudio/11/*.

Up next

The next and final chapter describes how Windows Server 2012 helps enable the modern work environment by enabling secure access virtually anywhere, from any device, with the full Windows experience.

CHAPTER 5

Enabling the modern workstyle

The final chapter of this book deals with how Windows Server 2012 can enhance the modern workplace. Today's business users want things simple. They want to be able to access their desktop, applications, and data virtually anywhere, from any device, and have the full Windows experience. And from an IT perspective, this must be done securely and in ways that can ensure compliance at all times. New features and enhancements in Windows Server 2012 make this possible.

Access virtually anywhere, from any device

If you are an office worker in today's accelerated business world, you need to be able to access your applications and data from any device—your personal computer, mobile computer, tablet computer, or other mobile device. And if you are an IT person involved in supporting such an environment, you want to be able to implement such capabilities easily and without hassles or additional costs.

Improvements in several Windows Server 2012 features now make it simple to deploy, configure, and maintain an IT infrastructure that can meet the needs of the modern workstyle. Remote access is now an integrated solution that you can use to deploy DirectAccess and traditional virtual private network (VPN) solutions quickly. Enhancements to Remote Desktop Services now make it easier than ever to deploy both session-based desktops and virtual desktops and to manage your RemoteApp programs centrally. User-Device Affinity now makes it possible for you to map roaming users to specific computers and devices. BranchCache has been enhanced to improve performance and make better use of expensive wide area network (WAN) bandwidth. And Branch Office Direct Printing enables branch office users to get their print jobs done faster while putting less strain on the WAN.

Unified remote access

Today's enterprises face an increasingly porous perimeter for their IT infrastructures. With a larger portion of their workforce being mobile and needing access to mobile data, enterprises are presented with new security challenges to address. Cloud computing promises to help resolve some of these issues, but the reality is that most organizations will deploy a hybrid cloud model that combines traditional datacenter computing with hosted cloud services.

Providing remote access to corporate network resources in a secure, efficient, and cost-effective way is essential for today's businesses. The previous version of Windows Server supported a number of different options for implementing remote access, including:

- Point-to-Point Tunneling Protocol (PPTP) VPN connections
- Layer 2 Transport Protocol over IPsec (L2TP/IPsec) VPN connections
- Secure Sockets Layer (SSL) encrypted Hypertext Transfer Protocol (HTTP) VPN connections using the Secure Socket Tunneling Protocol (SSTP)
- VPN Reconnect, which uses Internet Protocol Security (IPsec) Tunnel Mode with Internet Key Exchange version 2 (IKEv2)
- DirectAccess, which uses a combination of Public Key Infrastructure (PKI), IPsec, SSL, and Internet Protocol version 6 (IPv6)

Implementing remote access could be complex in the previous version of Windows Server because different tools were often needed to deploy and manage these different solutions. For example, the Remote Access and Routing (RRAS) component was used for implementing VPN solutions, whereas DirectAccess was configured separately using other tools.

Beginning with Windows Server 2012, however, the process of deploying a remote access solution has been greatly simplified by integrating both DirectAccess and VPN functionality into a single Remote Access server role. In addition, functionality for managing remote access solutions based on both DirectAccess and VPN has now been unified and integrated into the new Server Manager. The result is that Windows Server 2012 now provides you with an integrated remote access solution that is easy to deploy and manage. Note that some advanced RRAS features, such as routing, are configured using the legacy Routing and Remote Management console.

Simplified DirectAccess

If remote client devices can be always connected, users can work more productively. Devices that are always connected are also more easily managed, which helps improve compliance and reduce support costs. DirectAccess, first introduced in Windows Server 2008 R2 and supported by client devices running Windows 7, helps address these needs by giving users the experience of being seamlessly connected to their corporate network whenever they have Internet access. DirectAccess does this by allowing users to access corpnet resources such as shared folders, websites, and applications remotely, in a secure manner, without the need of first establishing a VPN connection. DirectAccess does this by automatically establishing bidirectional connectivity between the user's device and the corporate network every time the user's device connects to the Internet.

DirectAccess alleviates the frustration that remote users often experience when using traditional VPNs. For example, connecting to a VPN usually takes several steps, during which the user needs to wait for authentication to occur. And if the corporate network has Network Access Protection (NAP) implemented for checking the health of computers before allowing them to connect to the corporate network, establishing a VPN connection could sometimes take several minutes or longer depending on the remediation require, or the length of time of the user's last established the VPN connection. VPN connections can also be problematic for environments that filter out VPN traffic, and Internet performance can be slow for the user if both intranet and Internet traffic route through the VPN connection. Finally, any time users lose their Internet connection, they have to reestablish the connection from scratch.

DirectAccess solves all these problems. For example, unlike a traditional VPN connection, DirectAccess connectivity is established even before users log on so that they never have to think about connecting resources on the corporate network or waiting for a health check to complete. DirectAccess can also separate intranet traffic from Internet traffic to reduce unnecessary traffic on the corporate network. Because communications to the Internet do not have to travel to the corporate network and back to the Internet, as they typically do when using a traditional VPN connection, DirectAccess does not slow down Internet access for users.

Finally, DirectAccess allows administrators to manage remote computers outside the office even when the computers are not connected via a VPN. This also means that remote computers are always fully managed by Group Policy, which helps ensure that they are secure at all times.

In Windows Server 2008 R2, implementing DirectAccess was a fairly complex task and required performing a large number of steps, including some command-line tasks that needed to be performed both on the server and on the clients. With Windows Server 2012, however, deploying and configuring DirectAccess servers and clients is greatly simplified. In addition, DirectAccess and traditional VPN remote access can coexist on the same server, making it possible to deploy hybrid remote access solutions that meet any business need. Finally, the Remote Access role can be installed and configured on a Server Core installation.

DirectAccess—Making "easy" easier

DirectAccess with Windows 7 and Windows Server 2008 R2 was a tremendous improvement in remote access technologies. In my role, I work remotely almost 100 percent of the time—either at a customer site or from home—so my laptop is rarely physically connected to Microsoft's internal network.

However, I often need to access internal resources for my work. Now, I could connect over the Microsoft VPN, which in my case requires plugging in a smart-card reader, inserting the smart card, and entering a PIN. Certainly not a terrible experience, but we all prefer "EASY."

DirectAccess is easy. If I have Internet connectivity, the odds are pretty good that I have DirectAccess connectivity. I say "pretty good" because like many technologies, there are times when something prevents it from working. The question is "What is that something?" Troubleshooting DirectAccess connectivity can be difficult in Windows 7.

With Windows 8, the client experience is much better. The properties of your DirectAccess connection are easily accessible through the network's user interface. This interface will show you what your current DirectAccess status is and will offer remediation options if you are not currently connected. Additionally, in scenarios where there may be multiple network entry points for DirectAccess users, the interface will display the current site you are connected to and allow you to connect to a different site entry point if necessary.

If all else fails, though, the properties page also allows the client to collect DirectAccess logs (stored in a very readable HTML format) and email them to your support staff to assist in the troubleshooting process.

Of course, it wouldn't qualify as a "cool technology" unless you could shut it off and prevent people from using it! So naturally, being able to configure the support staff email address, providing users with the ability to switch to a different entry point and even the ability to disconnect from DirectAccess temporarily can be controlled through a Group Policy Object (GPO).

DirectAccess deployment scenarios

When deploying DirectAccess on Windows Server 2012, keep in mind that there are two types of deployment scenarios: Express Setup and Advanced Configuration. At a high level, the differences between the two are given in this table:

Express Setup	Advanced Configuration
PKI is optional	PKI and CA required
Uses a single IPSec tunnel configuration	Uses double IPSec tunnel configuration
Requires Windows 8 clients	Can use single factor, dual factor, and certificate authentication
	Supports clients running both Windows 8 and Windows 7
	Required when designing a multisite configuration

David Branscome
Senior Premier Field Engineer

DirectAccess enhancements

Besides simplified deployment and unified management, DirectAccess has been enhanced in other ways in Windows Server 2012. For example:

- You can implement DirectAccess on a server that has only one network adapter. If you do this, IP-HTTPS will be used for client connections because it enables

DirectAccess clients to connect to internal IPv4 resources when other IPv4 transition technologies such as Teredo cannot be used. IP-HTTPS is implemented in Windows Server 2012 using NULL encryption, which removes redundant SSL encryption during client communications to improve performance.

- You can access a DirectAccess server running behind an edge device such as a firewall or network address translation (NAT) router, which eliminates the need to have dedicated public IPv4 addresses for DirectAccess. Note that deploying DirectAccess in an edge configuration still requires two network adapters, one connected directly to the Internet and the other to your internal network. Note also that the NAT device must be configured to allow traffic to and from the Remote Access server.

- DirectAccess clients and servers no longer need to belong to the same domain but can belong to any domains that trust each other.

- In Windows Server 2008 R2, clients had to be connected to the corporate network in order to join a domain or receive domain settings. With Windows Server 2012 however, clients can join a domain and receive domain settings remotely from the Internet.

- In Windows Server 2008 R2, DirectAccess always required establishing two IPsec connections between the client and the server; in Windows Server 2012 only one IPsec connection is required.

- In Windows Server 2008 R2, DirectAccess supported both IPsec authentication and two-factor authentication by using smart cards; Windows Server 2012 adds support for two-factor authentication using a one-time password (OTP) in order to provide interoperability with OTP solutions from third-party vendors. In addition, DirectAccess can now use the Trusted Platform Module (TPM)–based virtual smart card capabilities available in Windows Server 2012, whereby the TPM of clients functions as a virtual smart card for two-factor authentication. This new approach eliminates the overhead and costs incurred by smart card deployment.

Deploying remote access

To see unified remote access at work, let's walk through the initial steps of deploying a DirectAccess solution. Although we've used the UI for performing the steps described below, you can also use Windows PowerShell. You can also deploy the Remote Access role on a Windows Server Core installation of Windows Server 2012.

After making sure that all the requirements have been met for deploying a DirectAccess solution (for example, by making sure your server is domain-joined and has at least one network adapter), you can start the Add Roles And Features Wizard from Server Manager. Then, on the Select Installation Type page, begin by selecting the Role-based Or Feature-based Installation option, as shown here:

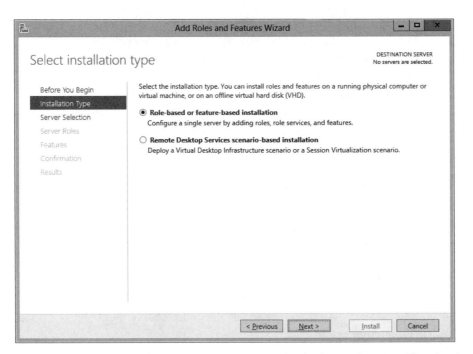

After choosing the server(s) you want to install remote access functionality on, select the Remote Access role on the Select Server Roles page:

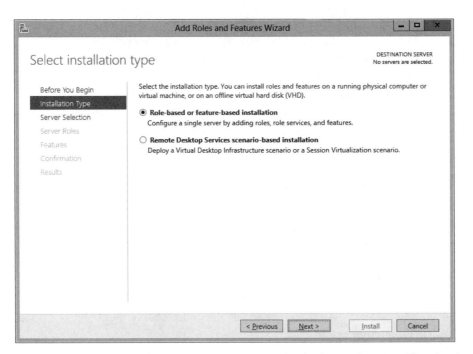

On the Select Role Services page, select the DirectAccess And VPN (RAS) option, as shown here:

Continue through the wizard to install the Remote Access server role. Once this is finished, click the Open The Getting Started Wizard link on the Installation Progress page shown here to begin configuring remote access:

Windows Server 2012 presents you with three options for configuring remote access:

- Deploying both DirectAccess and VPN server functionality so that DirectAccess can be used for clients running Windows 7 or later while the VPN server can be used so that clients that don't support DirectAccess can connect to your corporate network via VPN

- Deploying only DirectAccess, which you might choose if all your clients are running Windows 7 or later

- Deploying only a VPN server, which you might use if you've invested heavily in third-party VPN client software and you want to continue using these investments

Let's choose the recommended option by selecting the Deploy Both DirectAccess And VPN option:

On the Remote Access Server Setup page of the Configure Remote Access wizard, you now choose the network topology that best describes where your DirectAccess server is located. The three options available are:

- Edge, which requires that the server have two network interfaces, one connected to the public Internet and one to the internal network

- Behind An Edge Device (With Two Network Adapters), which again requires that a server has two network interfaces with the DirectAccess server being located behind a NAT device

- Behind An Edge Device (Single Network Adapter), which only requires the server (located behind a NAT device) to have one network interface connected to the internal network

Because the server used in this walkthrough has only one network adapter and is located behind a NAT inside, we'll choose the third option listed here. We'll also specify Corpnet. contoso.com as the Domain Name System (DNS) name to which the DirectAccess clients will connect:

Note that if the server has two network interfaces, with one connected to the Internet, the Configure Remote Access wizard will detect this and configure the two interfaces as needed.

When you are ready to finish running the Configure Remote Access wizard, you will be presented with a web-based report of the configuration changes that the wizard will make before you apply them to your environment. For example, performing the steps previously described in this walkthrough will result in the following changes:

- A new GPO called DirectAccess Server Settings will be created for your DirectAccess server.
- A new GPO called DirectAccess Client Settings will be created for your DirectAccess clients.
- DirectAccess settings will be applied to all mobile computers in the CONTOSO\Domain Computers security group.
- A default web probe will be created to verify internal network connectivity.
- A connection name called Workplace Connection will be created on DirectAccess clients.
- The remote access server has DirectAccess configured to use Corpnet.contoso.com as the public name to which remote clients connect.
- The network adapter connected to the Internet (via the NAT device) will be identified by name.

- Configuration settings for your VPN server will also be summarized; for example, how VPN client address assignment will occur (via DHCP server) and how VPN clients will be authenticated (using Windows authentication).

- The certificate used to authenticate the network location server deployed on the Remote Access server, which in the above walkthrough was CN=DirectAccess-NLS. contoso.com, is identified.

Configuring and managing remote access

Deploying the Remote Access server role also installs some tools for configuring and managing remote access in your environment. These tools include:

- The Remote Access Management Console (see Figure 5-1), which can be started from Server Manager

- The Remote Access module for Windows PowerShell

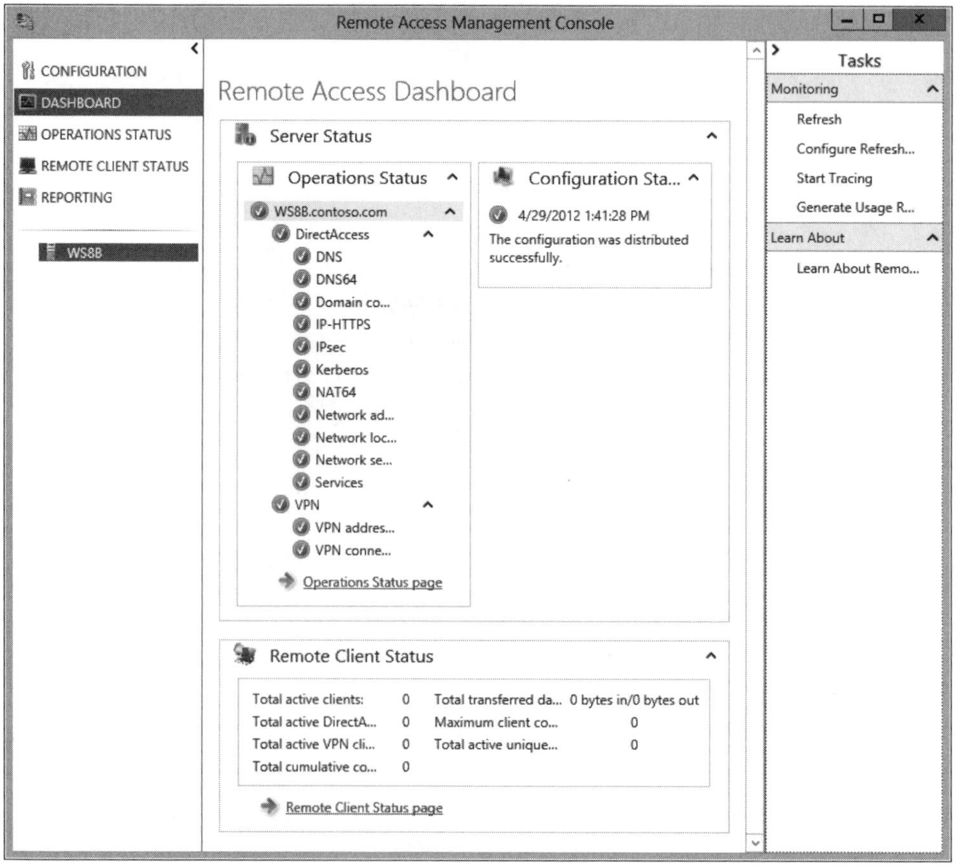

FIGURE 5-1 The Remote Access Management Console is integrated into Server Manager.

In addition to allowing you to monitor the operational status of your remote access servers and clients, the Remote Access Management Console enables you to perform an additional configuration of your remote access environment (see Figure 5-2).

FIGURE 5-2 Using the Remote Access Management Console to perform additional configuration of a remote access environment.

The Configuration page of the Remote Access Management Console lets you perform additional configuration if needed (or initial configuration if desired) in four areas:

- **Step 1: Remote Clients**   Lets you select between two DirectAccess scenarios:
    - Deploying full DirectAccess for client access and remote management so that remote users can access resources on the internal network and their computers can be managed by policy
    - Deploying DirectAccess for remote management only so that the computers of remote users can be managed by policy but the users cannot access resources on the internal network

You can also select which group or groups of computers will be enabled for DirectAccess (by default, the Domain Computers group), choose whether to enable DirectAccess for mobile computers only (enabled by default), and choose whether to use force tunneling so that DirectAccess clients connect to both the internal network and the Internet via the Remote Access server (disabled by default).

- **Step 2: Remote Access Server**   Lets you configure the network topology of the Remote Access server (but only if not previously configured), the public name or IPv4 address used by clients to connect to the server, which network adapter is for the internal network, which certificate to use to authenticate IP-HTTPS connections, how user authentication is performed, whether to enable clients running Windows 7 to connect via DirectAccess, and how your VPN server assigns IP addresses and performs authentication

- **Step 3: Infrastructure Servers**   Lets you configure the name of your network location server for DirectAccess clients, DNS settings for remote access, and other settings

- **Step 4: Application Servers**   Lets you specify whether to extend IPsec authentication and encryption to selected application servers on your internal network

DirectAccess advantages over traditional VPNs

DirectAccess was originally released with Windows 7 and Windows Server 2008 R2. Many people think of it as another VPN solution. However, it is more than just a VPN. A traditional VPN is initiated by the user after he or she logs on to the computer. DirectAccess creates the connection to the corporate network in the operating system before the user even sees the logon screen. DirectAccess connection is a virtual extension of the corporate network. No matter where the computer physically resides, so long as it has Internet access, it is a part of the corporate network and the user has access to available corporate resources.

The fact that a computer is now always a part of the corporate network, even when it is on the Internet, provides advantages to a company—especially for a company with many people that travel frequently (that is, the road warriors). Without DirectAccess, once a computer leaves the corporate doors, it becomes increasingly difficult to manage. The only time that IT will "see" the computer is when the user VPNs into the corporate network to access needed resources. For many, the only resource that they need is their email or instant messages. Advances such as Remote Procedure Calls (RPCs) over HTTP in Microsoft Exchange Server, Microsoft Outlook, and Microsoft Lync further limit the number of times a user would need to create a connection to corporate. If this is all the user needs, it's possible that he or she might never VPN back into the corporate network.

By introducing DirectAccess to the corporate environment, IT now has the advantage of treating the remote computers just as they would if the machine were still inside the corporate walls. The computers can now be managed, patched, and inventoried just as every asset inside the corporation is. IT is no longer hoping that the user keeps up to date with operating system patches and antivirus signatures. IT now can push these updates to the remote computers, using the tools they already use in-house, and report on the status of all remote computers.

The ability to be able to report on asset status and maintain accurate asset inventory could also be a potential financial advantage for a company. Frequently, IT groups that I work with report that when an asset leaves the corporation, they do not know if they will ever see the asset again. Machines can move from person to person. The computers are used in a fashion that does not require the user to connect back into the corporate network, so no accurate inventory can be kept. (One customer of mine reported that at any given time, they could have over 1,000 machines that they would not be able to track down, and they are written off as a loss.) DirectAccess gives IT the ability to keep track of these assets because the machines "stay" on the corporate network now.

DirectAccess is one of the first applications that require IPv6. The client, as well as the internal corporate resource, must both be running IPv6 in order for the client machine to be able to successfully access the resource. Although IPv6 is beginning to be adopted by Internet sites, corporations have been slower to pick up the technology. This is one reason that a company may not consider adopting DirectAccess.

Lack of IPv6 in the corporate network does not need to be a roadblock to implementing DirectAccess. As part of the Forefront family of products, Microsoft has a product called Unified Access Gateway, or UAG (*http://www.microsoft.com/en-us/server-cloud/forefront/unified-access-gateway.aspx*). One of the functions of UAG is that it can act as an IPv6-to-IPv4 gateway. This gateway functionality can allow the client on DirectAccess to access internal resources that are not yet on IPv6.

UAG can be implemented in two ways. First, the software can be acquired and implemented on hardware in the customer site in a similar fashion to most Microsoft products. Second, the product can also be acquired on a hardware appliance from a third-party partner.
Ian S. Lindsay
Sr. Account Technology Strategist, Microsoft Mid-Atlantic District

Learn more

For more information about remote access in Windows Server 2012, see the following topics in the TechNet Library:

- "Remote Access Overview" at
  http://technet.microsoft.com/en-us/library/hh831416.aspx.
- "Remote Access Technical Preview" at
  http://technet.microsoft.com/en-us/library/hh831519.aspx.
- "Simplified Remote Access with DirectAccess: scenario overview" at
  http://technet.microsoft.com/en-us/library/hh831819.aspx.

See also "Understand and Troubleshoot Remote Access in Windows Server '8' Beta," which you can download from *http://www.microsoft.com/en-us/download/details.aspx?id=29004.*

Simplified VDI deployment

Virtual desktop infrastructure (VDI) is an emerging alternative to the traditional PC-based desktop computing paradigm. With the VDI approach, users access secure, centrally managed virtual desktops running on virtualization hosts located in the datacenter. Instead of having a standard PC to work with, VDI users typically have less costly thin clients that have no hard drive and only minimal processing power.

A typical environment where the VDI approach can provide benefits might be a call center where users work in shifts using a shared pool of client devices. In such a scenario, VDI can provide greater flexibility, more security, and lower hardware costs than providing each user with his or her own PC. The VDI approach can also bring benefits to organizations that frequently work with contractors because it eliminates the need to provide contractors with PCs and helps ensure that corporate intellectual property remains safely in the datacenter. A help desk also benefits from the VDI approach because it's easier to re-initialize failed virtual machines remotely than with standard PCs.

Although implementing a VDI solution may be less expensive than provisioning PCs to users, VDI can have some drawbacks. The server hardware for virtualization hosts running virtual desktops must be powerful enough to provide the level of performance that users have come to expect from using desktop PCs. Networking hardware must also be fast enough to ensure that it doesn't become a performance bottleneck. And in the past, deploying and managing virtual desktops using previous Windows Server versions has been more complex than deploying and managing PCs because it requires deploying RDS with Hyper-V in your environment.

Windows Server 2012, however, eliminates the last of these drawbacks by simplifying the process by which virtual desktops are deployed and managed. The result is that VDI can now be a viable option to consider even for smaller companies who are looking for efficiencies that can lead to cost savings for their organization.

Deployment types and scenarios

Windows Server 2012 introduces a new approach to deploying the Remote Desktop Services server role based on the type of scenario you want to set up in your environment:

- **Session virtualization** Lets remote users connect to sessions running on a Remote Desktop Session Host to access session-based desktop and RemoteApp programs

- **VDI** Lets remote users connect to virtual desktops running on a Remote Desktop Virtualization Host to access applications installed on these virtual desktops (and also RemoteApp programs if session virtualization is also deployed)

Whichever RDS scenario you choose to deploy, Windows Server 2012 gives you two options for how you can deploy it:

- **Quick Start** This option deploys all the RDS role services required on a single computer using mostly the default options and is intended mainly for test environments.

- **Standard deployment** This option provides you with more flexibility concerning how you deploy different RDS role services to different servers and is intended for production environments.

RDS enhancements

Besides enabling scenario-based deployment of RDS role services like Remote Desktop Session Host, Remote Desktop Virtualization Host, Remote Desktop Connection Broker, and Remote Desktop Web Access, RDS in Windows Server 2012 includes other enhancements such as:

- A unified administration experience that allows you to manage your RDS-based infrastructure directly from Server Manager

- Centralized resource publishing that makes it easier to deploy and manage RemoteApp programs for both session virtualization and VDI environments

- A rich user experience using the latest version of Remote Desktop Protocol (RDP), including support for RemoteFX over WAN

- USB Redirection, for enhanced device remoting for both session virtualization and VDI environments

- User profile disks that let you preserve user personalization settings across collections of sessions or pooled virtual desktops

- The ability to automate deployment of pooled virtual desktops by using a virtual desktop template

- Support for using network shares for storing personal virtual desktops

- Support for Storage Migration between host machines when using pooled virtual desktops

Some of these enhancements are described in more detail later in this chapter in the section titled "Full Windows experience." Because session virtualization has been around much longer on the Windows Server platform, the remainder of this section will focus on VDI.

Virtual desktops and collections

A virtual desktop is a virtual machine running on a Hyper-V host that users can connect to remotely using RDS. A collection consists of one or more virtual desktops used in a VDI deployment scenario. Virtual desktops can either be managed or unmanaged:

- **Managed collections**   These can be created from an existing virtual machine that has been sysprepped so it can be used as a template for creating other virtual desktops in the collection.

- **Unmanaged collections**   These can be created from an existing set of virtual desktops, which you then add to the collection.

Virtual desktops can also be pooled or personal:

- **Pooled virtual desktops**   This type allows the user to log on to any virtual desktop in the pool and get the same experience. Any customizations performed by the user on the virtual desktop are saved in a dedicated user profile disk. (See the section titled "User Profile Disks" later in this chapter for more information.)

- **Personal virtual desktops**   This type permanently assigns a separate virtual desktop to each user account. Each time the user logs on, he or she gets the same virtual desktop, which can be customized as desired, with customizations being saved within the virtual desktop itself.

Table 5-1 summarizes some of the differences between pooled and personal virtual desktops when they are configured as managed virtual desktops, whereas Table 5-2 lists similar kinds of differences between them when they are configured as unmanaged virtual desktops.

TABLE 5-1 Comparison of pooled and personal managed virtual desktops

Capability	Pooled?	Personal?
New virtual desktop creation based on virtual desktop template	✓	✓
Re-create virtual desktop based on virtual desktop template	✓	
Store user settings on a user profile disk	✓	
Permanent user assignment to the virtual desktop		✓
Administrative access on the virtual desktop		✓

TABLE 5-2 Comparison of pooled and personal unmanaged virtual desktops

Capability	Pooled?	Personal?
New virtual desktop creation based on virtual desktop template		
Re-create virtual desktop based on virtual desktop template		
Store user settings on a user profile disk	✓	
Permanent user assignment to the virtual desktop		✓
Administrative access on the virtual desktop		✓

Deploying VDI

To see simplified VDI deployment at work, let's walk through the initial steps of deploying a Quick Start VDI deployment. Begin by starting the Add Roles And Features Wizard from Server Manager. Then on the Select Installation Type page, begin by selecting the Remote Desktop Services Scenario-based Installation option, as shown here:

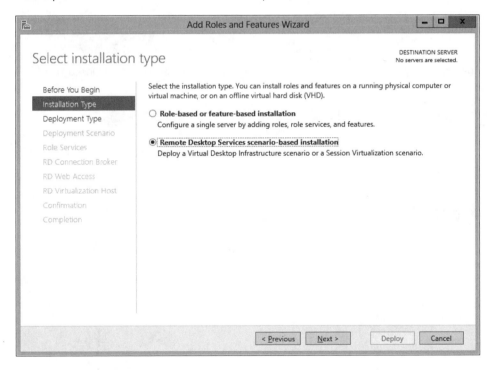

Select the Quick Start option on the Select Deployment Type page:

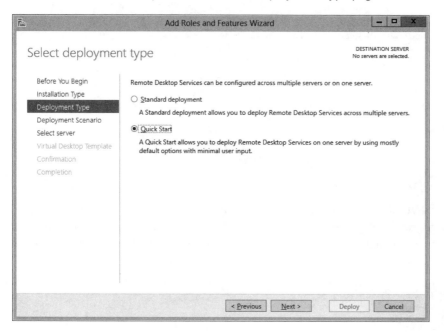

On the Select Deployment Scenario page of the wizard, choose the Virtual Desktop Infrastructure option:

Select a server from your server pool for deploying RDS role services onto:

On the next page, browse to select a virtual hard disk (VHD) file on which a VDI-capable client operating system like Windows 8 or Windows 7 has been installed together with any locally installed applications needed on the virtual desktop. The Windows installation on this VHD must have been prepared by running *sysprep /generalize* on it so that it can function as a reference image for adding new virtual desktops to your collection.

Completing the wizard and clicking Deploy begins the process of deploying your VDI environment. Three RDS role services (Connection Broker, RD Virtualization Host, and RD Web Access) are first installed on the selected server, which is then restarted to complete installation of these role services. A virtual desktop template is then created from the previously specified VHD file, and a new pooled virtual desktop collection named QuickVMCollection is created with two pooled virtual desktops based on the virtual desktop template:

The VDI deployment process also creates a new Hyper-V network switch named RDS Virtual and assigns the pooled virtual desktops to that switch.

Managing VDI

Once the Quick Start VDI deployment process is finished, you can manage your VDI environment by using the Remote Desktop Services option that now appears in Server Manager. For example, the Overview page of the Remote Desktop Services option provides you with visual information concerning your RDS infrastructure, virtualization hosts, and collections (see Figure 5-3). You can use the Remote Desktop Services option in Server Manager to configure your RDS role services, manage your virtualization hosts, create new collections, and perform other VDI-related tasks.

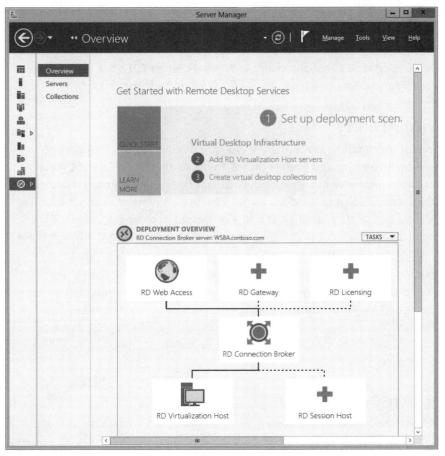

FIGURE 5-3 The Remote Desktop Services option in Server Manager.

Learn more

For more information about simplified VDI deployment in Windows Server 2012, see the following topics in the TechNet Library:

- "Remote Desktop Services Technical Preview" at *http://technet.microsoft.com/en-us/library/hh831616.aspx*.

- "Remote Desktop Services overview" at *http://technet.microsoft.com/en-us/library/hh831447.aspx*.

Also see the following Understand and Troubleshoot Guides (UTGs):

- "Understand and Troubleshoot Remote Desktop Services in Windows Server '8' Beta," which can be downloaded from *http://www.microsoft.com/en-us/download/details.aspx?id=29006*.

- "Understand and Troubleshoot Remote Desktop Services Desktop Virtualization in Windows Server '8' Beta," which can be downloaded from *http://www.microsoft.com/en-us/download/details.aspx?id=29022*.

For more information on RDS enhancements in Windows Server 2012, see the Remote Desktop Services (Terminal Services) Team Blog at *http://blogs.msdn.com/b/rds/*.

User-Device Affinity

Previous versions of the Windows platform have included three features for supporting roaming users, namely roaming user profiles (RUPs), Folder Redirection (FR), and Offline Files. What was missing was a way of associating each user profile with specific computers or devices. Windows Server 2012 and Windows 8 now provide such functionality in the form of User-Device Affinity, which lets you map a user to a limited set of computers where RUP or FR is used. As a result, administrators can control on which computers RUPs and offline files are stored.

User-Device Affinity benefits organizations by enabling new types of scenarios. For example, you could configure the environment so the user's data and settings can be roamed between the user's desktop PC and his or her laptop but cannot be roamed to any other computers. That way, for example, when the user logs on to a shared computer in the public foyer of the building, there is no danger that the user's personal or corporate data will be left behind on the computer.

Configuring User-Device Affinity

User-Device Affinity can be implemented using Group Policy by configuring the Evaluate User Device Affinity Configuration For Roaming Profiles And Folder Redirection policy setting found under System\User State Technologies. When you enable this policy setting, you can select from three possible configuration options:

- **Apply To Neither Roaming Profiles Nor Folder Redirection**   Disables the primary computer check when logging on
- **Apply To Roaming Profiles And Folder Redirection Only**   Roams the user profile and applies FR only when logging on to primary computers
- **Apply To Roaming Profiles Only Only**   Roams the user profile when logging on to primary computers, and always applies FR

Learn more

For more information about User-Device Affinity in Windows Server 2012 and Windows 8, see the topic "User-Device Affinity Technical Preview" in the TechNet Library at *http://technet.microsoft.com/en-us/library/hh831401.aspx*.

Enhanced BranchCache

BranchCache was first introduced in Windows Server 2008 R2 and Windows 7 as a way of caching content from file and web servers on a WAN locally at branch offices. When another client at the branch office requests the same content, the client downloads it from the local cache instead of downloading it across the WAN. By deploying BranchCache, you can increase the network responsiveness of centralized applications that are being accessed from remote offices, with the result that branch office users have an experience similar to being directly connected to the central office.

BranchCache has been enhanced in Windows Server 2012 and Windows 8 in a number of different ways. For example:

- The requirement of having a GPO for each branch office has been removed to simplify the deployment of BranchCache.

- BranchCache is tightly integrated with the File Server role and can use the new Data Deduplication capabilities of Windows Server 2012 to provide faster download times and reduced bandwidth consumption over the WAN.

- When identical content exists in a file or multiple files on either the content server or hosted cache server, BranchCache stores only a single instance of the content and clients at branch offices download only a single instance of duplicated content. The results are more efficient use of disk storage and savings in WAN bandwidth.

- BranchOffice provides improved performance and reduced bandwidth usage by performing offline calculations that ensure content information is ready for the first client that requests it.

- New tools are included in Windows Server 2012 that allow you to preload cachable content onto your hosted cache servers even before the content is first requested by clients.

- Cached content is encrypted by default to make it more secure.

- PowerShell can be used to manage your BranchCache environment, which enables automation that makes it simpler to deploy BranchCache in cloud computing environments.

Learn more

For more information about BranchCache and related technologies in Windows Server 2012, see the following topics in the TechNet Library:

- "BranchCache Overview" at *http://technet.microsoft.com/en-us/library/hh831696.aspx.*

- "Data Deduplication overview" at *http://technet.microsoft.com/en-us/library/hh831602 .aspx.*

Branch Office Direct Printing

Branch Office Direct Printing is a new feature of Windows Server 2012 that enables print jobs from a branch office to be redirected to local printers without the requirement of first having them sent to a print server on the network. As a result, when a print job is initiated from a branch office, the printer configuration and drivers are still accessed from the print server if needed, but the print job itself is sent directly to the local printer at the branch office.

Implementing this feature has several benefits, including reducing printing time at branch offices and making more efficient use of costly WAN bandwidth. In addition, cost can be reduced because you no longer need to deploy costly WAN optimization appliances at branch offices specifically for printing purposes.

Enabling Branch Office Direct Printing

Branch Office Direct Printing is a new feature in Windows Server 2012 designed to reduce network bandwidth in printing situations when your print server is centralized or located across a WAN link. When Branch Office Direct Printing is enabled, the print traffic from the client to the printer does not need to route through the server. Instead the client gets the port and driver information from the server and then prints directly to the printer, saving the traversal of data across a wide area connection. Branch Office Direct Printing can be enabled on an individual print queue and requires no interaction from the client to use. Once a print queue is established on a client, the information is cached in the event that the centralized printer server is unavailable. This is ideal in situations where local printing must be available during a WAN outage.

To enable Branch Office Direct Printing, open the Print Management Console, select the desired printer queue that you wish to designate as a branch printer, and select Enable Branch Office Direct Printing from the Actions menu:

John Yokim
Account Technology Strategist, Microsoft Mid-Atlantic District

Learn more

For more information about Branch Office Direct Printing, see the topic "Print and Document Services overview" in the TechNet Library at *http://technet.microsoft.com/en-us/library/hh831468.aspx*.

See also "Understand and Troubleshoot Printing in Windows Server '8' Beta," which can be downloaded from *http://www.microsoft.com/en-us/download/details.aspx?id=29003*.

Full Windows experience

Today's users expect and demand the full Windows experience, even when they work in virtual environments. Windows Server 2012 delivers this experience better than ever before with enhancements to RemoteFX, USB redirection, and the new User Profile Disks feature. This section introduces these new features and enhancements.

RemoteFX enhancements

RemoteFX was first introduced in Windows Server 2008 R2 as a way of delivering a full Windows experience over the RDP across a wide variety of client devices. RemoteFX is part of the Remote Desktop Services role service and is intended mainly for use in VDI environments to support applications that use rich media, including 3-D rendering. RemoteFX uses two capabilities for providing remote users with a rich desktop environment similar to the local desktop environment that PC users enjoy:

- **Host side rendering**   Allows graphics to be rendered on the host instead of the client by utilizing the capabilities of a RemoteFX-capable graphics processing unit (GPU) on the host. Once rendered on the host, graphics are delivered to the client over RDP in an adaptive manner as compressed bitmap images. In addition, multiple GPU cards are now supported on Windows Server 2012 as well as using a software GPU.

- **GPU Virtualization**   Exposes a virtual graphics device to a virtual machine running on a RemoteFX-capable host and allows multiple virtual desktops to share the single GPU on the host.

RemoteFX can benefit organizations by enabling flexible work scenarios like hot-desking and working from home. By making the virtual desktop experience similar to that of traditional PCs, RemoteFX can make VDI a more feasible solution for organizations who want increased data security and simplified management of the desktop environment.

RemoteFX has been enhanced in Windows Server 2012 in a number of different ways, including the following:

- RemoteFX is integrated throughout the RDS role services instead of being installed as its own separate role service and is installed automatically whenever the Remote Desktop Virtualization Host role service is installed.

- The performance when delivering streaming media content over RDP has been greatly improved.

- RemoteFX can dynamically adapt to changing network conditions by using multiple codecs to optimize how content is delivered.

- RemoteFX can choose between Transmission Control Protocol (TCP) and User Datagram Protocol (UDP) to optimize performance when sending RDP traffic over the WAN (this is called RemoteFX for WAN).

- Support for multi-touch gestures and manipulations in remote sessions is included.

- Improved multimonitor support over RDP, which allows a virtual machine to support up to four monitors regardless of their resolution, is available.

- There is now the ability to use VMConnect to manage virtual machines that have the RemoteFX 3D Video Adapter installed in them. (In the previous version of Windows Server, you had to use a Remote Desktop connection to manage the virtual machines.)

Configuring RemoteFX

To use RemoteFX, the host machine must:

- Support hardware-assisted virtualization and data execution prevention (DEP)

- Have at least one GPU listed as supporting RemoteFX in the Windows Server Catalog

- Have a CPU that supports Second Level Address Translation (SLAT). Note that Intel refers to SLAT as Extended Page Tables (EPT), whereas AMD refers to SLAT as Nested Page Tables (NPT)

To configure a Windows Server 2012 host to use RemoteFX, you can use the new GPU management interface in the Hyper-V settings of the host (see Figure 5-4). This interface lets you select from a list of available GPUs on the host that are RemoteFX-capable (if any) and then enable or disable RemoteFX functionality for the selected GPU. The interface also shows the details concerning each RemoteFX-capable GPU on the host.

Learn more

For more information about RemoteFX in Windows Server 2012, see the following topics in the TechNet Library:

- "Remote Desktop Services Technical Preview" at *http://technet.microsoft.com/en-us/library/hh831616.aspx.*

- "Microsoft RemoteFX" at *http://technet.microsoft.com/en-us/library/ff817578(v=WS.10).aspx.*

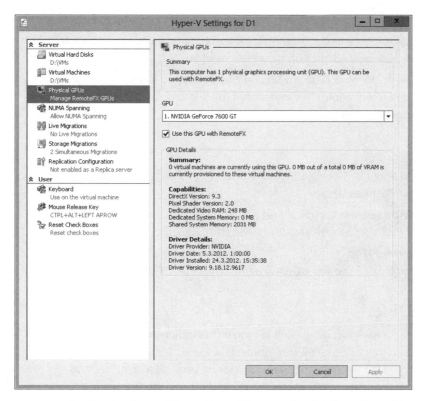

FIGURE 5-4 Configuring RemoteFX on a Hyper-V host running Windows Server 2012.

Enhanced USB redirection

USB redirection in RemoteFX is an important ingredient in establishing parity of experience between virtual desktops and traditional PCs. USB redirection was first introduced in Windows 7 Service Pack 1 and Windows Server 2008 R2 Service Pack 1 to support RemoteFX VDI scenarios. USB redirection occurs at the port protocol level and enables redirection of a wide variety of different types of universal serial bus (USB) devices, including printers, scanners, webcams, Voice over Internet Protocol (VoIP) headsets, and biometric devices. USB redirection does not require hardware drivers to be installed on the virtual machines. Instead, the necessary drivers are installed on the host.

In Windows 7 SP1 and Windows Server 2008 R2 SP1, RemoteFX USB redirection was supported only within virtual desktops running Remote Desktop Virtualization Host. New in Windows Server 2012 and Windows 8 is support for USB redirection for Remote Desktop Session Host. This enables new kinds of scenarios where RemoteFX can bring a richer desktop experience for businesses that implement session virtualization solutions.

Other enhancements to USB redirection in Windows Server 2012 include the following:

- USB redirection for Remote Desktop Virtualization Host no longer requires installing the RemoteFX 3D Video Adapter on the virtual machine.
- USB redirection for Remote Desktop Session Host is isolated to the session in which the device is being redirected. This means that users in one session will not be able to access USB devices redirected in a different session.

Learn more

For more information about RemoteFX USB redirection in Windows Server 2012, see the following topics in the TechNet Library:

- "Remote Desktop Services Technical Preview" at
  http://technet.microsoft.com/en-us/library/hh831616.aspx.
- "Microsoft RemoteFX" at
  http://technet.microsoft.com/en-us/library/ff817578(v=WS.10).aspx.

User Profile Disks

Preserving the user state is important in both session virtualization and VDI environments. Users who have worked in traditional PC environments are used to being able to personalize their desktop environment and applications by configuring settings such as desktop backgrounds, desktop shortcuts, application settings, and other customizations. When these same users encounter session virtualization or VDI environments, they expect the same personalization capabilities that traditional PCs provide.

In previous versions of Windows Server, preserving user state information for sessions and virtual desktops required using Windows roaming technologies like RUPs and FR. This approach had certain limitations, however. For one thing, implementing RUP and FR adds more complexity to deploying RDS for session virtualization or VDI. And for VDI deployments in particular, RUP/FR restricted the solution to using personal virtual desktops because pooled virtual desktops did not support preserving user state with RUP/FR.

Other problems could arise when using RUP/FR with RDS in previous versions of Windows Server. For example, if the user's RUP was accidentally used outside the RDS environment, data could be lost, making the profile unusable. RUP/FR could also increase the time it takes for a user to log on to a session or virtual desktop. Finally, applications that were poorly designed and didn't write user data and settings to the proper location might not function as expected when RUP/FR was used as a roaming solution.

Windows Server 2012 solves these problems with the introduction of User Profile Disks, which store user data and settings for sessions and virtual desktops in a separate VHD file that can be stored on a network share.

Configuring User Profile Disks

Configuring a user profile disk for a virtual desktop collection is done when you create the collection. Before you do this however, you need to create a server message block (SMB) file share where your user profile disk will be stored on the network and configure permissions on the file share so the computer account of your host has at least write access.

Begin by starting the Create Collection wizard by clicking Create Virtual Desktop Collections on the Overview page of the Remote Desktop Services section of Server Manager (see Figure 5-3 earlier in this chapter). Then on the Specify User Profile Disks page of the Create Collection wizard, make sure Enable User Profile Disks is selected and type the Universal Naming Convention (UNC) path to the file share where you'll store your user profile disks on the network:

Once your new collection has been created, you can further configure your user profile disk settings by selecting the collection on the Collections page of the Remote Desktop Services section of Server Manager, clicking the Tasks control in the Properties area, and clicking Edit Properties:

On the Virtual Desktop Collection page of the properties of your collection, you can customize how your user profile disk will be used. By default, all user profile data and settings are stored on the user profile disk, but you can configure these settings by selecting folders that should be excluded from being stored on your user profile disk. Alternatively, you can configure which specific types of items should be stored on your user profile disk; for example, only the user's Documents folder and user registry data:

Learn more

For more information about user profile disks, see the topic "Remote Desktop Services Technical Preview" in the TechNet Library at *http://technet.microsoft.com/en-us/library/hh831616.aspx.*

Also see "Understand and Troubleshoot Remote Desktop Services in Windows Server '8' Beta," which can be downloaded from *http://www.microsoft.com/en-us/download/details.aspx?id=29004.*

Enhanced security and compliance

Security and compliance are two areas that have been significantly extended in Windows Server 2012. Dynamic Access Control now allows centralized control of access and auditing functions. BitLocker Drive Encryption has been enhanced to make it easier to deploy, manage, and use. And implementing Domain Name System Security Extensions (DNSSEC) to safeguard name resolution traffic can now be performed using either user interface (UI) wizards or PowerShell. This concluding section covers these new features and enhancements.

Dynamic Access Control

Controlling access and ensuring compliance are essential components of IT systems in today's business environment. Windows Server 2012 includes enhancements that provide improved authorization for file servers to control and audit who is able to access data on them. These enhancements are described under the umbrella name of Dynamic Access Control and enable automatic and manual classification of files, central access policies for controlling access to files, central audit policies for identifying who accessed files, and the application of Rights Management Services (RMS) protection to safeguard sensitive information.

Dynamic Access Control is enabled in Windows Server 2012 through the following new features:

- A new authorization and audit engine that supports central policies and can process conditional expressions

- A redesigned Advanced Security Settings Editor that simplifies configuration of auditing and determination of effective access.

- Kerberos authentication support for user and device claims

- Enhancements to the File Classification Infrastructure (FCI) introduced previously in Windows Server 2008 R2

- RMS extensibility to allow partners to provide solutions for applying Windows Server–based RMS to non-Microsoft file types

Implementing Dynamic Access Control in your environment requires careful planning and the performing of a number of steps that include configuring Active Directory, setting up a file classification scheme, and more. For a full description of what's involved in deploying Dynamic Access Control, see the "Understanding and Troubleshooting Guide" referenced in the "Learn more" section at the end of this topic.

Just to give you a taste, however, let's look briefly at the redesigned Advanced Security Settings Editor that simplifies the configuration of auditing and determination of effective access. As in previous versions of Windows, the advanced permissions for a file or folder can be opened from the Security tab of the Properties dialog box for the file or folder. As you can see here, the Permissions tab of the Advanced Security Settings Editor in Windows Server 2012 and Windows 8 looks fairly similar to the one in previous versions of Windows:

However, the Effective Permissions tab of the Advanced Security Settings Editor in earlier versions of Windows has been replaced with a tab named Effective Access, which lets you choose not only the user or group being used for accessing the file or folder, but also the device:

The Auditing tab of the Advanced Security Settings Editor in earlier versions of Windows has been completely redesigned and now allows you to add auditing entries that can include conditions to limit their scope:

Auditing Entry for testshare

Principal: Everyone   Select a principal

Type: Success

Applies to: This folder, subfolders and files

Permissions: Show advanced permissions
- [ ] Full control
- [ ] Modify
- [x] Read & execute
- [x] List folder contents
- [x] Read
- [ ] Write
- [ ] Special permissions

[ ] Only apply these auditing settings to objects and/or containers within this container   Clear all

Add a condition to limit the scope of this auditing entry. Security events will be logged only if conditions are met.

Manage grouping   Group

[ ] Device | Group | Member of any | Value | 3 item(s) selected | Add items   Remove
     And
[ ] User | Group | Member of each | Value | Click Add items | Add items   Remove
Add a condition

OK   Cancel

For more information on these user interface improvements, see the following sidebar.

New Effective Access user interface

Windows Server 2012 provides an improved way for administrators to help resolve authorization problems. The new Advanced Security Settings Editor provides a new Effective Access tab that shows simulated access results of a user, computer, or group against targeted resources like a files or folder. The newly designed Effective Access tab provides substantial improvements over its predecessor, the Effective Permissions tab, in the following ways:

- Simulates access accurately, both locally and remotely
- Evaluates conditional permission entries, Share permissions, and Central Access Policies
- Enables administrators to insert user and device claims before evaluating access
- Enables administrators to delegate troubleshooting access issues

The Advanced Security Settings editor remotely tells a file server to simulate a logon of the user and device selected, inserts additional user and device claims in the evaluation, and gathers permissions from the file system, share, and Central Access Policies.

The Effective Access tab represents the easiest way to diagnose problems with users accessing files and folders on Windows Server 2012 file servers. Use the results from the Effective Access tab to determine which aspect of access control to troubleshoot next.

Typically, the Effective Access tab identifies possible problems with red X's in the Access Limited By column.

The Effective Access dialog box's Access Limited By column for file system resources can show Share, File Permissions, and the names of any Central Access Policy that applies to the file folder on the file server. The Access Limited By column indicates the point of access control that Windows perceives is responsible for limiting access to files or folders.

The Effective Access tab lists all points of access control that limits the specified permission for the designated security principal (and device, optionally). Therefore, each entry in the Access limited by column can show one or more limitations. Each limitation listed either specifically limits the security principal's access or does not provide access to the security principal.

For example, a security principal that is implicitly denied access occurs when none of the points of access control provides access. In this scenario, the Effective Access tab shows limitations for all points of access control (Share, File Permissions, and Central Access Policies applied to the folder). Each point of access control requires investigation to ensure that it allows the security principal the designated access.
Mike Stephens
Sr. Support Escalation Engineer, Windows Distributed Systems

Learn more

For more information about Dynamic Access Control in Windows Server 2012, see the following topics in the TechNet Library:

- "Dynamic Access Control Technical Preview" at *http://technet.microsoft.com/en-us/library/hh831573.aspx*.

- "Dynamic Access Control: scenario overview" at *http://technet.microsoft.com/en-us/library/hh831717.aspx*.

- "What's New in Security Auditing" at *http://technet.microsoft.com/en-us/library/hh849638.aspx*.

Also see "Understand and Troubleshoot Dynamic Access Control in Windows Server '8' Beta," which can be downloaded from *http://www.microsoft.com/en-us/download/details.aspx?id=29023*.

BitLocker enhancements

BitLocker Drive Encryption is a data protection feature first introduced in Windows Vista and Windows Server 2008. BitLocker encrypts entire disk volumes to help safeguard sensitive business data from theft, loss, or inappropriate decommissioning of computers.

BitLocker has been enhanced in several ways in Windows Server 2012 and Windows 8:

- It's now easy to provision BitLocker before deploying the operating system onto systems. This can be done either from the Windows Preinstallation Environment (WinPE) or by using Microsoft Deployment Toolkit (MDT) 2012 to deploy your Windows installation.

- The process of encrypting a volume with BitLocker can occur more rapidly in Windows Server 2012 and Windows 8 by choosing to encrypt only the used disk space instead of both used and unused disk space, as was the only option in previous versions of Windows (see Figure 5-5).

- Standard users can change their BitLocker personal identification number (PIN) or password for the operating system volume or the BitLocker password for fixed data volumes. This change makes it easier to manage BitLocker-enabled clients because it means that users can choose PINs and passwords that are easier for them to remember.

- A new feature called BitLocker Network Unlock allows a network-based key protector to be used for automatically unlocking BitLocker-protected operating system volumes on domain-joined computers when these computers are restarted. This can be useful when you need to perform maintenance on computers and the tasks that you need to perform require a restart to be applied.

- BitLocker supports a new kind of enhanced storage device called Encrypted Hard Drive, which offers the ability to encrypt each block on the physical drive and not just volumes on the drive.

- BitLocker can now be used for failover clusters and cluster shared volumes.

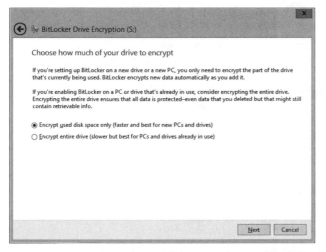

FIGURE 5-5 Encrypting only used disk space when enabling BitLocker on a volume.

Learn more

For more information about BitLocker in Windows Server 2012 and Windows 8, see the following topics in the TechNet Library:

- "What's New in BitLocker" at *http://technet.microsoft.com/en-us/library/hh831412.aspx*.

- "Encrypted Hard Drive" at *http://technet.microsoft.com/en-us/library/hh831627.aspx*.

Also see "Understand and Troubleshoot BitLocker in Windows Server '8' Beta," which can be downloaded from *http://www.microsoft.com/en-us/download/details.aspx?id=29032*.

DNSSEC

Domain Name System Security Extensions (DNSSEC) is a suite of extensions that adds security to the DNS protocol. DNSSEC enables all the records in a DNS zone to be cryptographically signed and provides origin authority, data integrity, and authenticated denial of existence. DNSSEC is important because it allows DNS servers and resolvers to trust DNS responses by using digital signatures for validation to ensure that the responses they return have not been modified or tampered with in any way.

DNSSEC functionality was first included in the DNS Server role of Windows Server 2008 R2 and has been significantly enhanced in Windows Server 2012. The following are a few of the enhancements included in DNSSEC on Windows Server 2012:

- Support for Active Directory–integrated DNS scenarios, including DNS dynamic updates in DNSSEC signed zones

- Support for updated DNSSEC standards, including NSEC3 and RSA/SHA-2 and validation of records signed with updated DNSSEC standards (NSEC3, RSA/SHA-2)

- Automated trust anchor distribution through Active Directory with easy extraction of the root trust anchor and automated trust anchor rollover support per RFC 5011

- An updated user interface with deployment and management wizards

- PowerShell support for configuring and managing DNSSEC

Configuring DNSSEC on your DNS servers can now be done with the DNS Manager console. Simply right-click a zone and select Sign The Zone under the DNSSEC menu option:

This opens the Zone Signing Wizard, and by following the prompts, you can select the Key Master for the zone, configure a Key Signing Key (KSK) used for signing other keys, configure a Zone Signing Key (ZSK) used for signing the zone data, configure Next Secure (NSEC) resource records to provide authenticated denial of existence, configure distribution of Trust Anchors (TAs) and rollover keys, and configure values for DNSSEC signing and polling:

Learn more

For more information about DNSSEC in Windows Server 2012, see the topic " Domain Name System (DNS) overview" in the TechNet Library at *http://technet.microsoft.com/en-us/library/hh831667.aspx*.

Also see "Understand and Troubleshoot DNS Security Extensions (DNSSEC) in Windows Server '8' Beta," which can be downloaded from *http://www.microsoft.com/en-us/download/details.aspx?id=29018*.

Up next: RTM!

We hope you've enjoyed this book, which has provided you with a technical "first look" at many of the exciting new features and enhancements coming in Windows Server 2012. Not every new feature of the platform has been covered here, and a few features may still change before RTM because much of the book was based on the beta release and post-beta builds of Windows Server 2012. But we've made every effort to make this book as accurate as possible so you can get a feel for the capabilities of the new platform.

The best way, however, of getting to know what Windows Server 2012 is really capable of is to try it out! So why not visit *http://www.microsoft.com/en-us/server-cloud/windows-server/v8-default.aspx* today and download the latest publicly available build of the product and put it through its paces. We're sure you'll be amazed!

—*Mitch Tulloch with the Windows Server Team*

Index

Symbols and Numbers

A

B

D

E

F

G

H

Q

R

S

About the Author

 **Mitch Tulloch** is a well-known expert on Windows administration, deployment, and virtualization. He has published hundreds of articles on a wide variety of technology sites and has written more than two dozen books, including the *Windows 7 Resource Kit* (Microsoft Press, 2009), for which he was lead author; and *Understanding Microsoft Virtualization Solutions: From the Desktop to the Datacenter* (Microsoft Press, 2010), a free ebook that has been downloaded over 140,000 times.

Mitch is also Senior Editor of *WServerNews*, the world's largest newsletter focused on system admin and security issues for Windows servers. Published weekly, *WServerNews* helps keep system administrators up to date on new server and security-related issues, third-party tools, updates, upgrades, Windows compatibility matters, and related issues. With more than 100,000 subscribers worldwide, *WServerNews* is the largest Windows Server–focused newsletter in the world.

Mitch has been repeatedly awarded Most Valuable Professional (MVP) status by Microsoft for his outstanding contributions to supporting the global IT community. He is an eight-time MVP in the technology area of Windows Server Setup/Deployment.

Mitch also runs an IT content development business based in Winnipeg, Canada, which produces white papers and other collateral for the business decision maker (BDM) and technical decision maker (TDM) audiences. His published content ranges from white papers about Microsoft cloud technologies to reviews of third-party products designed for the Windows Server platform. Before starting his own business in 1998, Mitch worked as a Microsoft Certified Trainer (MCT) for Productivity Point.

For more information about Mitch, visit his website (*http://www.mtit.com*).

You can also follow Mitch on Twitter at *http://twitter.com/mitchtulloch*.

What do you think of this book?

We want to hear from you!

To participate in a brief online survey, please visit:

microsoft.com/learning/booksurvey

Tell us how well this book meets your needs—what works effectively, and what we can do better. Your feedback will help us continually improve our books and learning resources for you.

Thank you in advance for your input!